THE SON OF GOD

SHARON LINDSAY

Prepare The Way

THE SON OF GOD

Series: Book 3

TATE PUBLISHING
AND ENTERPRISES, LLC

This novel is a work of fiction. However, several names, descriptions, entities, and incidents included in the story are based on the lives of real people.

The opinions expressed by the author are not necessarily those of Tate Publishing, LLC.

Published by Tate Publishing & Enterprises, LLC
127 E. Trade Center Terrace | Mustang, Oklahoma 73064 USA
1.888.361.9473 | www.tatepublishing.com

Tate Publishing is committed to excellence in the publishing industry. The company reflects the philosophy established by the founders, based on Psalm 68:11,
"The Lord gave the word and great was the company of those who published it."

Cover design by Nino Carlo Suico
Interior design by Jomel Pepito

Published in the United States of America

ISBN: 978-1-68028-127-9
Religion / General
15.03.24

To my son,
Donnie and his beautiful wife, Angela
They are the joy of my life.
They have great patience with me
and all my projects.

Contents

Introduction

Remember the former things, those of long ago; I am God, and there is no other; I am God, and there is none like me. I make known the end from the beginning, from ancient times, what is still to come. I say: My purpose will stand, and I will do all that I please. From the east I summon a bird of prey; from a far-off land, a man to fulfill my purpose. What I have said, that will I bring about; what I have planned, that will I do.

—Isaiah 46:9–11

Before creation, God the Father, Yeshua-Jesus, and the Holy Spirit had formulated a plan for dealing with sin. In the third book of the *Son of God Series*, that plan is now in full implementation. Yeshua has left heaven. He is the product of human and divine conception. He has experienced birth into a Jewish family. On the eighth day he was circumcised and named Jesus. He has grown *in wisdom and stature and in favor with God and men.*[1]

Jesus has grown up in a typical Jewish family in the town of Nazareth. He deals with the same web of relationships that all people deal with—family, friends, neighbors, and officials. He also has a web of heavenly relationships with his Eternal Father, the Holy Spirit, angels, Moses and Elijah. He is more than aware that he has enemies in the spiritual realm—Satan, fallen angels, and demons.

During his years of maturation when the Bible seems to be silent, Jesus learned about his divinity and made the choice to live on Earth within the limited ability of humanity. Now, every communication that heaven has ever had with humans is available to him. Every bit of authority that God had ever given to Adam belongs to Jesus. The power to do the miraculous is God working through him. For miracles, Jesus is dependant on Father God and the Holy Spirit.

Like all Jewish men, Jesus has learned a trade. He is a carpenter. Since childhood the books of Moses, the writings of the prophets as well as other scrolls of Jewish history and tradition have been available to him. Jesus has memorized large portions of the written word. He understands that the scriptures are about him. In regards to the laws of Judaism, Jesus is reverently observant. The opinions of men do not concern him. He lives totally directed by his Father God.

The Son of God: Prepare the Way is about heaven setting the stage for Jesus to move from the obscurity of Nazareth into the center of Jewish politics. Like pieces of a puzzle, God moves men into their appointed places. The young fishermen of Capernaum have become acquainted with Jesus. John the Baptist begins calling the people to repentance.

As John preaches and baptizes, there is a greater sense of expectation in the nation—the Messiah is coming. The Jews are looking for their Messiah, but they are expecting a military leader who will lead armies into battle and defeat Rome.

God brings a man from Rome, Pontius Pilate. Pilate engages Herod Antipas, the ruler of Galilee, in a power struggle that will last for years.

In the Temple, Caiaphas and Annas hold the power of the high priesthood. Men of the Sanhedrin: Nicodemus, Gamaliel, and Joseph of Arimathea make decisions for the land.

Satan is always the evil opportunist, working through family and neighbors while he waits for his chance to have a one-on-one confrontation with Jesus.

The Son of God: Prepare the Way is a fresh look at how all these characters touch each other and prepare for their parts in the most significant event in the history of the Earth.

Prologue

The Death of Adam

And Adam lived an hundred and thirty years, and begat a son in his own likeness, and after his image; and called his name Seth: And the days of Adam after he had begotten Seth were eight hundred years: and he begat sons and daughters.

—Genesis 5:3–4

From the throne room of the Eternal Rulers, Yeshua gazed into the limestone cave that had been the home of Adam and Eve since they had been expelled from their perfect garden home. Adam, his once beautiful creation, lay on a sheepskin-covered pallet.

"My son, I made you in my own image and I love you," Yeshua whispered.

The Eternal Father quietly commented, "It has been more than nine hundred Earth years since Adam ate from the Tree of Life. Now his body can no longer sustain the life we placed in him. It is time—"

"Look!" Yeshua was the first to speak what the Triune Rulers simultaneously knew. "Our enemy has entered the cave. He is hovering over Adam!"

The ever-burning Spirit of God flared. "Satan can only be there for one reason!"

"He is trying to steal my son!" Yeshua exclaimed.

"Such treachery cannot be allowed!" God thundered.

"I will go." The Spirit of God immediately poured his holy fire into the dimly lit stone chamber where Adam was sleeping.

Within the cave the Holy Spirit, like a glowing sword, sliced through the spiritual darkness. He separated Satan from the evil angels who supported him. Every fallen angel fled, and Satan, who refused to give ground, was forced back into the black recesses of the underground labyrinth.

"The Holy Spirit is here," Eve spoke to her son Seth. "I can feel his warmth."

"God is with us," Seth affirmed his mother's spiritual sense.

With a lamp in her hand, Eve moved close to her beloved husband. She held the little flame next to his face. "Seth, is your father still breathing?" she anxiously asked.

Seth, nearly the exact image of his father, leaned over his mother's shoulder and looked hard before responding. "Mother, the life the Creator breathed into my father is still with him, but I sense the Holy One who gave life to my father, Adam, will soon take that life back to himself."

"Adam's life belongs to me!" Satan angrily shouted past the wall of Holy Fire that held him in the dark recesses of the cave. "In the paradise that was his garden home, he chose to obey me!"

In the throne room of the Eternal Rulers, Satan's challenge rose like an accusing spirit. "The law of your universe states that all your created beings are free to give their allegiance. Adam gave his allegiance to me!"

"Adam repented of that choice," the Creator countered.

"And many, many times he restated that his allegiance was to the kingdom of the Omnipotent," Father God added.

"Too late!" Satan argued. "*The wages of sin is death!*"

"*But the gift of God is eternal life*,"[1] Yeshua countered.

"You cannot just give eternal life without first meeting the requirements of your own law!" Satan confidently argued. Then he added, "Death is mine. I have a spirit named Death. He holds the keys to the chamber where Abel and several sons of Cain wait in timeless oblivion. Soon, Adam will join them."

"I will meet the requirement of the law!" Yeshua declared with such finality the entire heavenly kingdom shook. Then Yeshua stood. With one finger he pointed toward Earth and with one word, "Sheol!" he created the Place of the Dead.

The earth beneath Satan's feet suddenly split into a deep gorge. Water rushed into the gorge. A dry rocky plain formed on one side of the river, while on the other side, beautiful vegetation covered the landscape. The entire river valley was then surrounded by impassable mountains and a double gate was set at the entrance.

"This is now the Place of the Dead," Yeshua announced. "It is temporary! It is a place of rest until I have met the requirements of my law. On the barren side, there are many underground passages. There, you may hold those whose allegiance to evil is unquestioned. But on the verdant side of the river gorge, all those who have whispered even one word of hope in the Holy Rulers of the Universe will wait in pleasant chambers and peaceful repose."

"Just what are they waiting for?" Satan sneered. "Every man and woman has turned their back on the laws of your kingdom. On both sides of the gorge, the sons and daughters of Adam belong to me."

Yeshua answered, "You may guard the gate, but my children wait for the sound of the shofar and the promised Deliverer."

In the cave, Adam stirred. Eve breathed a little sigh of relief and stepped back, moving the flame of the lamp away from his face. Seth remained standing near his father's bed. His eyes steadfastly studied the face of the man who had been formed by God himself. What was happening to his father? Never in the eight hundred years since he was born had he seen a human life just slip away. He knew about his brother Abel, who had been killed before his birth. He had seen animals killed for sacrifices, for clothing, but he had never seen a person die.

Adam stirred again. This time, he opened his eyes. First, he looked at Eve, and then he turned his eyes to look into the eyes of his son. "In the day the Lord put us out of our garden home he said to me, '*By the sweat of your brow you will eat your food until you return to the ground, since from it you were taken; for dust you are and to dust you will return.*'[2] I know my life is ready to depart from my body. Soon, only dust will remain. Call my children together so I may bless each one."

Kneeling at the foot of his bed, Eve began to sob quietly. In her heart, she cried, "It is my fault."

Her sob reached the Creator's ear, and immediately, he directed Gabriel and Michael to leave their guardian posts and fly to Eve with comfort and reassurance.

Solemnly, Seth led the eldest son of each generation into the cave. The rest of the extended family of Adam gathered and waited, sitting on the packed dirt immediately outside the cave and extending to the distant hills.

In the cave, Adam was sitting up, propped with pillows, Eve at his side. The angels from the throne room stood on either side of the couple, providing additional support. Gently, the Spirit of God offered his comforting embrace to each person who entered the room. Most humans remained unaware of the presence of heavenly beings, but Adam and Eve and their descendants who carried the promise of the seed, experienced the spiritual realm like a sixth sense. Each man bowed respectfully, first to Adam and Eve, and then to each angel. It was a reverent acknowledgement of God-given authority. As each man found a place on the cold cave floor, he pressed both hands to his lips before lifting them to the Spirit, giving devotion to the Eternal God even in the sadness of the moment.

Eve spoke first, "In the name of the Eternal Rulers, I welcome you into our home."

Then in a slow and weary voice, Adam said, "The Creator has spoken to me. My days on earth are about to end. I cannot argue this. He has been gracious to allow my life to continue until now. *To God belong wisdom and power; counsel and understanding. To him belong strength and insight; both the deceived and the deceiver are his.*[3] *My eyes have seen all this; my ears have heard and understood it.*[4]

"Seth." Adam called his son forward.

Seth knelt in front of his parents and each parent placed a hand on his head. "Your name means appointed. You were appointed by God to replace your brother Abel. You carry the seed of the promised Deliverer. That precious legacy has been passed to your eldest son, Enosh."

Seth motioned for Enosh to come forward and take his place.

Eve placed her hand on Enosh first and she said, "Your name means mortal. Because I was deceived by the serpent, you, like all of our descendants, were born to die. Because of this, *my face is red with weeping, deep shadows ring my eyes.*[5] *Even now my witness is in heaven; my advocate is on high. My intercessor is my friend as my eyes pour out tears to God; on behalf of all men he pleads with God as a man pleads for his friend.*[6] *My spirit is broken, my days are* also *cut short, the grave awaits me.*"[7] Eve laid her head on Adam's shoulder, and tears streamed down her face.

Weakly, Adam reached with his free hand and brushed the tears from his wife's cheek. Still caressing Eve's face with one hand and keeping his other hand on the head of his grandson, Adam continued, "*Mortals, born of woman, are of few days and full of trouble.*[8] You, my grandson, are like a tree. *Its roots may grow old in the ground and its stump die in the soil, yet at the scent of water it will bud and put forth shoots like a plant.*"[9] From the throne of

God, living water will flow, and from your offspring, there will grow a branch that will break the power of the Evil One.

"Kenan," Adam called his great grandson to kneel before him.

"Your name means sorrow. Just before you were born, your father, Enosh, visited the city Cane has built. He saw the sons and daughters of Cain. He witnessed their total disregard for the Creator. When Enosh offered them an opportunity to repent and return to the family, they threw stones at him. He returned to us, very sad. Your name commemorates that event."

Eve sat up and composed herself. For a moment, her mind slipped back to her firstborn son, Cain. Since their last contact with Cain, many generations had been born. Briefly, she wondered about those grandchildren, great-grandchildren, great-great…Then Eve put them out of her mind. Cain had given his allegiance to the Evil One. He had given his generations to the enemy of God. "Praise God," she declared, "The righteous will multiply and grow stronger!" Her declaration shook the newly placed gates of Sheol.

Eve looked directly at Mahalalel. Her eyes beckoned him.

He came forward to kneel before his great-great-grandparents. For a long moment, she looked into his face, then she closed her eyes, remembering. "When you were born, there was such a struggle to bring you into the world. I feared your mother would lose her life before you could be born. Finally, after days of labor, I saw the top of your head pushing into the world, and at that moment, I shouted, 'Blessed is the Lord!'" Eve opened her eyes and looked directly at Mahalalel. "From that time, your name has been Blessed is the Lord."

Adam then spoke, "God has heard your praises. He has seen your life and he is pleased.

"Jared," Adam beckoned Mahalalel's son.

Jared knelt beside his father. "You are a young man." Adam moved his slightly trembling hand from Mahalalel's head to Jared's head as he mused, "You're not even five hundred years old. I remember when I was young and strong like you. On the night of your birth, your father came to visit me. He wanted to give you a name that spoke of hope and future. Your name means to descend.

"The Holy One, the one who made my body from the elements in the dirt and breathed life into me, spoke to us that night. He repeated the promise he has made to me in many different ways. He said he would descend from the heavens to stand in my place and defeat Satan. That night, we named you Descend. Every time I see you, I remember God's promise."

Adam's eyes got a sad faraway look. "I remember when I first awoke into life. I had eternal life, and I was in the arms of Yeshua the Creator. I lost it"—Adam sighed—"I lost the right to see Yeshua's face." A tear ran down Adam's weathered face. "I long to feel the Creator's arms again."

Eve slipped her hand under Jared's chin and lifted his face. "Look, Adam! Look at Jared and remember God's promise. Hope and smile," she admonished.

At that moment, the Holy Spirit beckoned Enoch, Jared's eldest son.

Enoch stood in his place and began to speak. *"See, the Lord is coming with thousands upon thousands of his holy ones to judge everyone, and to convict all of them of all the ungodly acts they have committed."*[10]

Once more, Eve's mind wandered to Cain and his descendants. They lived beyond the river on a large flat plain. She had heard stories of Godless living and violence—it made her shudder. Once more, she turned her attention to the Spirit-initiated words Enoch was speaking.

"I hear the sound of a horn and a white horse stands in the sky. The horse has a rider who comes with judgment and vengeance. The rider carries a banner that bears his name, Faithful and True. His eyes are like fire and on his head are many crowns."

"Yeshua the Creator—that is the way he will come!" Adam exclaimed.

Alone in the bowels of the cave, Satan trembled.

Boldly, Enoch continued, "I see a large white throne. And from that throne, I hear a voice. *'Look! God's dwelling place is now among the people, and he will dwell with them. They will be his people, and God himself will be with them and be their God. He will wipe every tear from their eyes. There will be no more death or mourning or crying or pain, for the old order of things has passed away.'*"[11]

Enoch placed a hand on his son Methuselah.

Methuselah bowed his head, anticipating his father's anointed words. "You, my son, will live a long life. During your lifetime, you will see the evil that dwells with the descendants of Cain move into residence with the sons of Adam. As long as you live, God will allow both the children of Seth and the children of Cain to live unchallenged by heaven. But when life leaves your body and you join all these in this room who have gone before you into the unknown world of death, then your prophetic name, His Death Shall Bring, will see its fulfillment—God's judgment, a great deluge. Water will pour from the heavens and explode from the depths of the earth. God will wash the world and begin again, with the pure seed of Adam."

"Lamech," Adam called the son of Methuselah to his side. He patted the cushion next to him, so the young man would take a seat. "How many years have you lived?" Adam asked.

"Fifty-six," Lamech replied.

"There are many years in your future," Adam sadly responded. "Your name means despairing. During your lifetime, you will see great iniquity, and you will despair of finding any righteousness on the Earth."

Enoch then interjected, "The Creator says that you, Lamech, will have a son, a type of the Deliverer. He will be a comfort to you. He will make a way for man to escape the judgment of God. His name shall be Comfort. You will call him Noah."

"I am weary." Adam's voice suddenly became so weak that it was just a trembling whisper. "Return to your homes. I am going to the place the Creator has prepared for me."

Chapter 1

The Death of Joseph

Since the children have flesh and blood, he too shared in their humanity so that by his death he might destroy him who holds the power of death—that is, the devil—and free those who all their lives were held in slavery by their fear of death.

—Hebrews 2:14–15

"Adam, Adam, my son." Yeshua wept as the gates of Sheol opened. He watched as his angels carried Adam, the man who had been made in the image of God, to his resting place. "I will not leave you. I will not leave any of my children in this place." Yeshua vowed through his tears. "I am coming to take you back to my dwelling place. We will share our lives with each other eternally!"

Jesus suddenly woke up. His pillow was wet with tears. Briefly, he remembered the dream, an experience from his heavenly life, relived.

"Yeshua?"

It was the familiar voice of the Eternal One, his Father.

"Yes, Father," Jesus responded as he sat up on the bed that had once belonged to his grandfather, Heli. He opened his eyes, but there was no moonlight. The interior of what had been his grandfather's house was dark. Jesus strained his eyes, but he could not see the outlines of the room's simple furnishings. The house contained a darkness so deep that Jesus could not even see his own body parts.

Jesus spoke to his Father, "If I could not feel my hand, I would not know I had a hand."

"Does the darkness disturb you?" Father God asked.

"*Let him who walks in the dark, who has no light, trust in the name of the* L*ORD* *and rely on his God*,"[1] Jesus answered.

"You are about to walk through a darkness you will not understand," God informed. "It is a darkness I have declared. To you and to all who know me, it will seem inconsistent with my character, but you must trust me."

Immediately, Jesus heard hurried footsteps and then there was pounding on his door. Disregarding the darkness, Jesus quickly felt his way to the door and pulled on the latch. His younger brother Jose stood in the doorway holding a small lamp.

"Mother says to come, quick! Father has stopped breathing!"

Jesus was throwing his cloak over his shoulders and hurrying after his brother as Jose continued, "Mother woke up, and father was lying beside her, dead. She said to get you quickly and not to speak to anyone else."

"Father God?" Jesus silently petitioned heaven.

There seemed to be no response.

"Father?" Jesus cried audibly and more urgently. He sensed the presence of God's Spirit, but neither the Eternal One nor his Holy Spirit was speaking.

The little flame on Jose's lamp suddenly flickered and went out. Darkness enveloped both men. They immediately stopped in their tracks. Hurried travel was now impossible. Still, they continued. Walking slowly and cautiously, the sons of Mary made their way, trusting that their feet knew the well-trodden path.

"Why? Father God, you have directed me to bring others back from death." From the bottom of his heart, Jesus bombarded the throne room of the Eternal One. "Father, I have restricted myself to live as a man; therefore, I am as helpless as any other man except for your directive. What is your directive?" Tears were streaming down the face of Jesus.

God had not spoken, but the scriptures Jesus had memorized since boyhood answered, "*The righteous are taken away to be spared from evil. Those who walk uprightly enter into peace; and they find rest as they lie in death.*"[2]

"There is a light!" Jose was the first to spot the lamp that was burning in the window of their family home. Both men began to move more confidently, hurrying to meet the crisis.

Mary met them at the gate. "Stay here," she tersely directed Jose as she grabbed Jesus by the hand and forcefully pulled him into the room where his father lay. Mary pulled Jesus all the way to the bed. Then she stopped and looked up at her eldest son expectantly.

"Mother," Jesus cried as he wrapped his strong arms around her. "I can do nothing unless I am directed by my Father, God."

"Ask him," Mary demanded through her tears. "Ask him. Surely, he will hear. Surely, he cares."

"He cares," Jesus assured her. "*Precious in the sight of the LORD is the death of his faithful servants.*[3] He weeps with us. He feels our pain." Jesus's tears fell on Mary's uncovered head, and Mary's tears soaked his rough cloak. "Do not fear, Mother. Do not fear for Joseph. *Know that the LORD has set apart the Godly for himself.*[4] I have seen the place where the righteous dead repose. It is a paradise. The righteous dead are placed within the gates by the angels of God. You must trust the Eternal One. There will be a day when you will share your life with Joseph again."

"I know about the resurrection—" Mary choked on her words. "The Messiah will come. The gates of Sheol will open, and the dead will come up from their graves." She looked questioningly at Jesus. "I thought—but when?" Her voice sounded hollow and hopeless.

"Father God has set a time. He has not revealed that time to me, but I am certain of the event," Jesus answered as he comforted his mother. "And for yourself, do not fear." Jesus pulled back a little to look his mother in the face. "I will care for you. Your other sons will also see that you never want. Now call the mourners. James and I will prepare the bier. We will lay my father in the burial cave just before sunset."

Slowly, Jesus opened the door to his father's carpentry shop. His eyes scanned the room. Each tool was placed exactly as his father had left it. An unfinished job—an inlaid table for the estate of Salmon, the olive grower, waited in the middle of the shop. Jesus took a deep breath. Without the presence of his father Joseph, the shop seemed to possess an unnatural emptiness.

James stepped up behind him. "I can't believe father has passed on." James moved over to the corner where long timbers leaned against the wall. "Our father was not even completely gray-haired."

"We worked together, all day yesterday," Jesus responded as he took the smooth flat timbers James had selected. "Father seemed completely healthy. He had no complaints. He even worked a little longer than I did."

"Why would God allow such a thing to happen?" James turned to Jesus as he spoke. The question hung in the air between the two brothers. With his eyes, James seemed to shout, "You are the one who studies the scriptures. You are the one who converses with God. So give me an answer."

For a moment, Jesus dropped his head. He was waiting to hear the response of Father God, but he heard nothing. Sadly, he returned his gaze to meet his brother's eyes. "I have asked the same question, but I have received no answer."

"So now the judgment of God is on our family?" James bitterly rejoined. "For what? What have we done?"

"What have you done to displease the Almighty?" Satan joined the conversation and flung his accusation through the mouth of James.

Jesus did not reply immediately. Instead, he picked up the flat timbers and began to lay them side by side, all the while waiting for the familiar voice of the Holy Spirit to bring enlightenment.

Instead, all he heard were sneering accusations from Satan. "You have chosen to live as a man, and man cannot please God. God is not satisfied with you, and he is no longer speaking to you. Listen to me! Your father, Joseph, an ordinary man with ordinary flaws, has paid the price for you. God took him to teach you."

Satan then repeated his accusation, "The great and loving God has taken your father away from his family to the Place of the Dead so he can teach you something. And Joseph's last thought was extreme annoyance at you because you left the shop early to go study the scriptures. With anger in his heart, he passed into my arms, and I carried him into the barren regions beyond the gates of Sheol."

Jesus stopped lining up the timbers that were to be used for the bier. He caught his brother's eye and calmly said, "*Bear with me a little longer and I will show you that there is more to be said in God's behalf.*[5] *God is mighty, but he despises no one.*[6] *He does not take his eyes off the righteous; he enthrones them with kings and exalts them forever.*[7] I have not sinned. Neither has any misdeed of Joseph, our father, brought this grief to our family. God is righteous. He informs men if they have arrogantly sinned. He brings correction and opportunity for repentance into their lives.

"How can you be so certain?" James asked. "In the synagogue, the rabbi teaches that we suffer afflictions and death because of our sins."

"I have spoken to you the words of the Eternal One. He does not lie. Yes, there are consequences for wrong choices, and God does bring punishment on those who refuse to repent. But God's heart is always for repentance, so he gives many opportunities before he brings destruction. The righteous, and our father was a righteous man, can trust in God."

The path that led to the burial caves just south of the town wound up and around the rock-strewn hills that bordered Nazareth. The shrill wails of the town's mourners sent wildlife scurrying further into the uncultivated hill country. With sad and somber steps, Jesus, James, Jose, Simon, and Jude carried the bier, each son of Mary shouldering the weight of the flat wooden platform that held Joseph's shrouded body.

For Jesus, each step was a prayer, a plea for his Father in heaven to respond. "Father, why? There was so much life in my father, Joseph. He was not infirmed. God, why did you take him? Look at my mother; see how she grieves. Her heart is broken. She does not understand, and I do not have answers to comfort or satisfy her."

The procession of mourners arrived at the cave where the people of Nazareth laid their dead. Jesus and his brothers kept the wooden platform level as they lowered it to the ground. Ahaz and Harim, the sons of Moshe, hurried forward to put their shoulders to the large stone that covered the entrance. Slowly, the stone moved, and the black gaping entrance to the cave became visible.

Moshe stepped forward. He placed a hand on Jesus's shoulder. "I am so sad." His tears fell onto the hard-packed earth at Jesus's feet.

"You were a good friend to my father." Jesus reached out and embraced one of his father's lifelong friends.

"Last year, I laid my wife in this cave." Moshe sobbed on Jesus's shoulder as he spoke. "Her bones are to the right as you enter the cave. After the Feast of Weeks, I will come back and place them in a burial box. I don't want you to have to stumble around in there. So, let me tell you, I remember there is a place to the left as you enter the cave. You can leave your father's body there. It will not be disturbed until you and your brothers return to place his bones in a box."

Jesus nodded. He kept the weeping man firmly in his embrace as he assured, "We will not disturb the resting place of your wife."

Behind him, Jesus sensed that Ahaz and Harim held lit torches. With one more quick embrace, Jesus turned away from Moshe. Jose stepped forward, offering Jesus a piece of linen to wrap around his face. "The smell of death escaped when the cave was opened. I am sure the odor will be overpowering inside," Jose commented. "All the spices and ointments in the world cannot mask the smell of decaying flesh. Let's place father quickly."

Mary stepped up beside her sons. She was wrapping a piece of linen around her head, covering her nose and mouth.

"No, Mother." Jesus removed the cloth from her face. "You do not need to go in there. We will place your husband and our father. Say farewell out here."

With his arm around his mother's shoulders, Jesus gently propelled her to the head of the bier. Fresh mourning broke out as Mary knelt beside Joseph. Jesus also dropped to his knees beside his mother, supporting her with his own muscular body.

Carefully, Mary picked up the small cloth that covered her husband's face for one last look, a final good-bye. "You were a good man, Joseph. You were the gift of God to me." She choked on her words. "I can't believe you were with me yesterday, and now—you are gone." Mary's shoulders shook and her tears fell on the lifeless face of her husband. Tenderly, Mary touched her husband's face. Then she spoke to him again, "You gave me four strong sons and beautiful daughters. I have many special memories." Mary paused, and she turned her tear-filled eyes away from Joseph. She looked up into the eyes of her eldest son. "Has your Father—"

Jesus understood the unfinished question. Sadly, he shook his head as he replied, "On this matter, God is remaining silent. Only his scriptures speak to me. "*Man born of woman is of few days and full of trouble. He springs up like a flower and withers away; like a fleeting shadow, he does not endure.*[8] Man's days are determined; God has announced a decree, the number of months and years. It cannot be changed. The only word I have from God is trust! That word is for you too."

Mary responded with a resigned nod of her head. Jesus helped her to her feet, then he turned to his brothers. "It is time." He quickly tied the linen cloth over his mouth and nose. Then he bent with his brothers to lift Joseph's body.

At the mouth of the cave, Ahaz and Harim held the torches with one hand and covered their mouths and noses with their other hand. The sons of Mary quickly entered and laid their father's body, still on the bier, on the cold packed-earth of the cave. Jose, James, Simon, and Jude quickly turned and exited the cave. As the young men left the cave, Ahaz and Harim took their torches and moved away from the odor that drifted out of the darkness. But Jesus remained. In the spiritual, he saw Death gloating over the life that had passed from the land of the living into the realms of the dead.

"Speak to that spirit!" the Holy Spirit commanded.

Forcefully, Jesus ripped the linen cloth away from his mouth. His words penetrated the limestone walls and traveled all the way to the Gates of Sheol. "By the authority of the Eternal One, I declare the prophetic words of the Eternal Rulers of the Universe as they are recorded in the writings of the prophet Isaiah to be true and eternally binding. God *will destroy the shroud that enfolds all peoples, the sheet that covers all nations; he will swallow up death forever. The Sovereign Lord will wipe away the tears from all faces, he will remove the disgrace of his people from all the earth. The Lord has spoken. In that day they will say, 'Surely this is our God; we trusted in him, and he saved us.'*[9] This *weeping may remain for a night, but* the Mighty God, whose servant I am, has promised *rejoicing comes in the morning.*"[10]

Torchlight flickered on the cave walls. James called from the entrance, "Jesus, come out of there!"

Looking directly at the mute and now somber spirit of Death, Jesus prophetically added, "The wrath of the Creator is eternally upon you because you have taken his sons and daughters. Your power will soon be destroyed." A wave of weeping overtook Jesus as he abruptly turned and exited the cave.

Jesus sat with his family while their neighbors came to grieve, to share their meals and their memories of Joseph, the good carpenter of Nazareth. After seven days the traditional time of mourning and remembering came to an end. Jesus stepped out of his family home and entered the carpentry shop to complete the job he and his father had been working on.

In the shop, there was an aching emptiness that begged to be filled. Jesus picked up several of the small pieces of wood he had previously cut and began to fit them into the design he and Joseph had agreed upon. It seemed so natural to speak to his father Joseph to ask, "The lighter or the darker piece of wood?" Then with the question on the tip of his tongue, Jesus had to stop and remind himself that his father Joseph no longer had any part in the world of the living.

"I miss him," Jesus spoke to his Father God. "Part of my heart went to the grave with Joseph, my father."

God answered, "Every man and woman who has ever lived has suffered the loss of someone they love."

At that moment, the Holy Spirit joined the conversation. With one sweep of his fiery hand, the wall of the shop seemed to disappear and in its place scene after scene. Noah was buried in a cave. His three sons, Shem, Ham, and Japheth wept over his body. A multitude of mourners followed the body of Shem. Generation after generation, Jesus saw the dead bodies and the weeping families of his ancestors. The procession of Death seemed endless, and in the memory of Yeshua the Creator, Jesus knew every face and every name.

Overcome with grief, Jesus sank to the floor of his father's shop. "A part of my heart has gone to the grave with every person who has ever died," Jesus cried. "Oh, the price, oh, the price all men have paid because of Adam's disobedience," he moaned. The emotional pain seemed overwhelming. "*Sin entered the world through one man, and death through sin, and in this way death came to all men.*"[11]

"This death is just temporary," God spoke into the mourning heart of his son. "You are going to wrestle with Death and strip his power away. Just as one man who disobeyed my law brought death to all mankind, one man who refuses to disobey my law will break the power of Death and bring eternal life to all who will accept his gift. You have come to Earth to redeem all that Adam lost. Our enemy Satan is constantly petitioning me like he petitioned me for the life of faithful Job. He insists as my hedge of protection is removed from the things and the people you love, you, like most people, will question me and doubt my perfect plan for you."

At that moment, the fiery hand of the Holy Spirit pulled back another curtain, and Jesus saw a mighty angel standing in the counsel of heavenly beings. He was tall, possessing a magnificent wing-span, yet his body did not glow with the holiness of the other heavenly beings. Then, Jesus saw himself as Yeshua the Creator rise and challenge the approaching angel, "*Where have you come from?*"[12]

"My enemy is an ancient foe," Jesus commented.

"He is the one who is testing you," God responded. "Your experiences with him will not be unlike those of my servant, Job."

Jesus watched as the supernatural drama unfolded.

With a cocky sneer, the angel replied to the Creator, "I have come *from roaming through the earth and going back and forth in it.*"

Then, Yeshua *said to Satan, "Have you considered my servant Job? There is no one on earth like him; he is blameless and upright, a man who fears God and shuns evil."*

"Does Job fear God for nothing?" Satan replied. Have you not put a hedge around him and his household and everything he has?[13] *But stretch out your hand and strike everything he has, and he will surely curse you to your face."*

Then the LORD said to Satan, "Very well, then everything he has is in your hands, but on the man himself do not lay a finger."[14]

The scene faded away and only the instruction of the Holy Spirit remained. "As you approach the season of presenting yourself as the Deliverer your people have been looking for, Satan will be given greater and greater access to you. I have warned you, just as I warned Adam and Eve in the garden. 'Beware, he is a deceiver!'"

Chapter 2

Jesus, the Eldest Son

The Lord your God will raise up for you a prophet like me from among your own brothers. You must listen to him.

—Deuteronomy 18:15

So much evil and so much goodness together in one building, Jesus silently mused. He lifted his prayer shawl from his shoulders and settled it over his head before stepping into the synagogue of Nazareth for the evening service that welcomed the Sabbath. Taking his usual place on one of the wooden benches that had been placed on three sides of the room, he first noted the bench had a little unsteadiness to it. His carpenter's mind immediately assessed a weakness in the supports, and he made a mental note to take the bench to his shop after the Sabbath hours. Then, he took in the spiritual atmosphere of the place that was the center of worship for the growing town of Nazareth. The spirits named Religion and Tradition made this building their headquarters. The men of the town brought with them their own demons—Pride, Dishonesty, Lust, Bitterness, even Murder. Every evil attached to man had assembled to acknowledge that the Eternal God had created Earth in seven days. By his spoken word, he had created the universe and all its beings, and now he commanded their attention.

The Spirit of God was also present. He flowed around and throughout the room, slipping beneath the prayer shawls where he was welcome while ignoring those who had allowed their demons to build substantial barriers to his presence.

"My son," the Holy Spirit whispered a warm greeting that caressed the heart of Jesus in a way no other man in the synagogue was caressed.

Jesus responded to the heavenly touch. He closed his eyes and opened himself without reservation to all God had for him. His skin tingled with the electricity of heaven. Quiet tears slipped from his closed eyes as his most tender emotions were aroused.

"You are so open to me," the Spirit continued. "I would touch every man in this place as deeply as I touch you if they would allow themselves to be touched."

The service began. "Blessed are you, O Lord, our God and God of our fathers…" The men of Nazareth bowed and swayed as they chanted the traditional prayers of their people. Jesus chanted with them. His chanting was not the rote reciting of ancient words, but his own heartfelt adoration presented to God, his Father.

Chebar, the president of the synagogue, along with Lemuel, the teacher of the synagogue school, carefully placed the Torah scroll on a large covered table. They rolled it open to the portion for the week. Then both men paused and looked around the room, their eyes searching for someone to read, someone who could read without stumbling over the ancient Hebrew. Their choices were limited. Nazareth was a town of craftsmen and farmers, but one craftsman, the carpenter, read exceedingly well.

Lemuel looked at Jesus, then back at Chebar. Both men knew Jesus was very skilled in both reading and interpreting the scriptures. But sometimes, the way he read and the comments he made left the entire town in a state of agitation. Still, he was the best choice.

Chebar gave a little shrug with his shoulders as if to say, "What else can we do?"

Lemuel nodded in silent agreement.

So with a nod of his head and a beckoning gesture, Chebar intoned the traditional invitation to the bema, "Come forward to the Torah, Jesus son of Joseph."

"Go," the Holy Spirit confirmed the opportunity with one word.

Respectfully, Jesus moved to his place behind the table. With genuine reverence he chanted the reader's prayer, "Blessed is the Lord God, who has chosen us above all people, and given us his word in the Torah."

Lemuel pointed to the beginning of the passage, and Jesus took the fringes of his prayer shawl, touched the Hebrew characters, and then kissed the fringes. It was a traditional act for most men, but for Jesus, it was a public demonstration of his love for the laws and the words of God.

Jesus began to read from the fifth book of Moses. His voice was clear and commanding.

The demons trembled, but silently held their ground. Unless one demon was foolish enough to manifest and challenge the Holy Spirit authority within this man, they were confident they would be allowed to remain.

As Jesus continued reading the words Moses spoke to the Israelites as they were poised to cross the Jordan, he suddenly sensed the increased power of the Spirit within him. His voice rang out with commanding authority. *"I will raise up for them a prophet like you from among their fellow Israelites, and I will put my words in his mouth. He will tell them everything I command him. I myself will call to account anyone who does not listen to my words that the prophet speaks in my name."* [1]

Then Jesus stopped reading and looked piercingly into the hearts of his neighbors. There was a long uncomfortable silence. Every man seemed to be nailed to his seat by the penetrating dark eyes of the carpenter. "Moses said this prophet would be among you." Without hesitation, Jesus repeated the words that the Holy Spirit burned into his mind. "Are you looking for him? Do you know how to recognize him? He is not coming to lead an army against the Romans. He is coming to turn men's hearts back to God, the Father of us all. I speak this day to the fainthearted, to those who despair of ever seeing their Messiah. Fortify your hearts with hope. This prophet that Moses speaks of and the Messiah are the same person. He is among you, even now."

Jesus had not completed the portion that was to be read for that Sabbath day. But without even glancing at the two men who were responsible for the order of the service, he stepped back from the open scroll and confidently chanted the closing blessing over the reading, "Blessed is our God who has given us his truth and planted eternal life in our midst. May his word be sealed in our hearts. Amen"

Without acknowledging either the president of the synagogue or the local rabbi, Jesus abruptly left the bema and the building. His Father God, through the Holy Spirit, was calling him to go up into the rocky hills that surrounded Nazareth for a time of intimacy and instruction.

Night had fallen. From his seat on a small patch of grass on a rocky hillside, Jesus looked down on his hometown. Along the paths that led to the synagogue, little lamps that had been lit and placed before sunset flickered as they outlined the way to each home. The door of the synagogue opened. Jesus watched as the men began walking toward their homes. They moved slowly in groups of three or four, pausing here and there as their conversations became too intense to continue walking.

The Holy Spirit settled himself to converse with Jesus. "Chebar and Lemuel are very upset with you." As he spoke, the Spirit pulled the angry faces of the president of the synagogue and the local rabbi into close proximity so Jesus could see the evil expression on each face. "You disrupted the order of their service. You raised a politically dangerous topic. You did not ask their permission to shorten the reading, to leave the bema, or the building. Their pride has been insulted."

"Was it their service?" Jesus rhetorically queried. "I thought the point of gathering to worship was to please God. Wasn't it his service?"

"You and I understand the concept of laying yourself and all the works of your hand and your mind down. Chebar and Lemuel do not understand. Tradition, Intellectualism, Pride, and many more Satanic spirits have blinded them. They do not know how to forget themselves and just give glory to God."

"They are missing a beautiful experience," Jesus stated as he enjoyed the tingling radiant energy that transferred from the Holy Spirit to his body. "Chebar wants to find another carpenter to build the new addition onto the synagogue," the Spirit informed.

"He thinks he can punish me because I will not conform to his synagogue rituals? He does not understand. I only do the things my Father God tells me to do," Jesus responded.

"Your brothers are also very upset." As the Holy Spirit spoke, he showed Jesus that James and Jose were in heated discussion with Chebar. "James feels your actions always make life difficult for him."

"Well, James can build their addition," Jesus calmly suggested. "He can negotiate a price, obtain the materials, and do the work. His carpentry skills are good. I'll just step out of the way."

"I knew you would be the peacemaker," the Holy Spirit replied. "It pleases me that you have embraced peace and meekness. Spend the rest of the Sabbath on this hill, then on the first day of the week, return to your home and make preparations to go to Capernaum. Spend a few weeks repairing fishing boats, then travel to Jerusalem for Passover. Celebrate the feast in Bethany in the home of your friend Lazarus."

In his heart, Jesus agreed with the Holy Spirit as he wrapped himself in the heavy cloak that used to belong to his father,

Joseph. Peacefully, he stretched out on the ground to sleep through the night.

"Oh no!"

Jesus opened his eyes and looked around in the early morning grayness.

"You can't drop your lamb here!" a female voice groaned. "Come on, move! You are too close to the edge of the cliff."

Quickly, Jesus got up. It took only a moment to see that one of the town's shepherdesses was struggling to move a pregnant ewe away from where the hill dropped off. Jesus hurried to her assistance, manually lifting the animal and carrying it to the level grassy spot where he had spent the night.

"You're one of Baruch's granddaughters." Jesus turned the statement into a question. With keen spiritual sensitivity, he noticed the shepherd girl had many of the kind and caring qualities he had appreciated in her grandfather, the old man who had been the shepherd of Nazareth when Jesus was a boy.

"Yes, I'm Deborah." She knelt beside the ewe and placed a calming hand on the animal. "I stay with the flock from the beginning of the Sabbath until its end every week so no one needs to miss synagogue services." As she spoke, she moved her hands around the animal's abdomen, trying to determine the health and position of the baby within.

"Don't you ever observe the services from the women's section?" Jesus gently asked. His question was meant to draw her out. He already knew the answer. Anyone with eyes could see. Even though Deborah had a beautiful face and an equally beautiful spirit, her back was terribly hunched, a deformity from birth.

"No," she answered with sweet acceptance.

"This animal will give birth very soon," Jesus commented as he knelt beside the shepherd girl to observe that the translucent bag the lamb had lived in while inside the womb was beginning to protrude from the birth canal.

"I know," the shepherdess replied. "I suspected she was ready when she separated herself from the flock last night. I've been looking for her all night."

"You must be very tired," Jesus kindly commented. "Do you want to rest while I keep an eye on this animal for you?" he offered. "When I was a boy, I used to help your grandfather with the flock."

"I can't rest until I know this lamb has been safely birthed," Deborah answered while looking directly at what appeared to be not one but two translucent sacks bulging from the back end of the ewe.

"Twins!" Jesus exclaimed as he remembered the times when he, as a boy, had assisted Baruch with an occasional birth.

"I should be seeing at least one head," Deborah stated as she leaned in for a closer look.

"The newborns are stuck, side-by-side in the birth canal," Jesus offered the information the Holy Spirit had given him.

Immediately, the shepherdess reached for the horn of oil that was attached to her belt. She poured some on one hand and then carefully slipped that hand inside the animal. With the bulk of his muscular body, Jesus held the ewe in a resting position, on its side.

"You are right," Deborah said as she withdrew her hand. "I will have to push one of the lambs back into the womb so they can be delivered one at time."

"Are you strong enough?" Jesus asked while he silently petitioned his Father for assistance.

"I don't know," Deborah answered with transparent honesty. "I have never done this alone. I have watched my mother and my aunts handle many a difficult birth, but—"

"You are not alone now," Jesus encouraged.

"I am afraid I may be somewhat hampered by my deformity," Deborah softly admitted. "I may not be able to reach as far as I need to." She looked down at the village of Nazareth. "There is not enough time to go and get help. The lambs cannot stay in the birth canal very long."

A little smile played at the corners of Jesus's mouth. The Holy Spirit had instructed him for this moment. "I will hold the mother," Jesus suggested. "You slip your hand back inside the ewe and push the smaller baby back into the womb. Push as far and as hard as you can. When you have done all you are able to do, cry out, 'God, help your servant!' Then, continue trying."

"There is nothing else to do," Deborah resolutely responded as she poured oil over her hand one more time. Positioning her body as close to the ewe as possible, she gently inserted her hand. Her fingertips found the babies, still safe in their amniotic sacks. Pushing her arm farther into the mother, she was able to determine that both animals were correctly positioned except for being wedged side-by-side. Between contractions, she began to push the smaller baby back into the womb. It was hard work. The baby only moved back a little each time, and then she had to hold it in place during the next contraction that was meant to push the baby out in the opposite direction.

After much straining and reaching and pushing, Deborah cried, "I need to push farther than I can reach."

"Don't give up!" Jesus encouraged. "Call on God!"

"God of Abraham!" Deborah cried out while she struggled to keep the baby in place through a hard contraction. "Remember your servant girl as she tries to bring your creatures into this world!"

With one hand, Jesus reached over and lightly touched the hump on the shepherd girl's back. Immediately, there was an audible crackling as her rigid, deformed spine straightened. Deborah's eyes suddenly opened very wide and she gasped in total amazement.

"Push just a little further," Jesus urged her to forget about herself and continue moving the lambs into a safe birthing position.

"I-I…my back—" Deborah started to try to explain what had happened.

"Just take care of the lambs," Jesus restated.

Returning her attention to the lambs, Deborah gave a final push and felt the smaller baby slip back behind the one that was ready to be born. Within moments of withdrawing her hand, one after the other the babies slipped out onto the grass. Immediately, the mother responded by smelling and licking. Jesus used a handful of grass to wipe the membrane away from the first baby's face and to stimulate it into taking its first breath while Deborah attended to the other twin.

"We did it!" Deborah stood up and began cleaning her arm with an extra piece of cloth that she had pulled from her belt.

"Yes, we did!" Jesus affirmed.

Then, just to get her to use her back, Jesus asked, "Do you know how to use a sling?"

"Of course," she answered.

"Let me see how accurate you are." Jesus urged.

Quickly, she put a stone in the pouch of her leather sling and began to swing it easily around and around. As she turned her body for the release, her back moved with a fluidity she had never experienced in her life. The stone sailed away free of the pouch, but Deborah did not notice. Her hand was on her back, trying to feel her spine.

"My back! My back!" She started to scream excitedly and jump around.

"Your back looks beautiful and straight," Jesus stated as he burst into joyful laughter.

"But how?" Deborah stopped jumping and looked inquiringly at Jesus.

"You did all you could, and then you called on God," Jesus answered. "He saw your need, and he had compassion on you. So now, I will ask my mother to look for you in the women's section of the synagogue."

"I will be there," Deborah eagerly responded. "I want to hear you read. I have heard you read very well."

"What else have you heard?" Jesus asked.

"I've heard you make some of the men very angry. Your comments make them feel like they have fallen short of pleasing God," Deborah answered.

"What do you think?" Jesus continued to press.

"It is the Sabbath. The men of the village would have risked the lives of these lambs. They would have gone to get my mother or one of my sisters to help with this birth. Unless it was their own ewe or there was no other woman to do the work, they would not have willingly helped me. I think maybe God does smile on you more than others," Deborah stated. Then she turned her attention back to the mother ewe who was nursing both babies.

Midmorning on the first day of the week, Jesus strode into the carpenter shop that had once belonged to his father Joseph and now belonged to the sons of Mary and Joseph. He carried a freshly cut bundle of willow branches, which he propped upright, against the wall. His entrance disrupted both James and Jose who had been chiseling pieces of light weight timber into the shoulder pieces for yokes of oxen. "I cut some willows for the underpinnings," Jesus stated.

"After you cut the Torah reading short and walked out of the service, Chebar was ready to go to Sepphoris to find another master carpenter to build the addition to the synagogue," James angrily informed. "It is important to maintain good relationships in this town. It is good business, and our family needs the business!"

"Chebar will be satisfied if he doesn't see me at the construction site," Jesus calmly responded. "You can run the shop. Jose is a capable assistant. Even Simon has enough carpentry experience to be very helpful. I will go to Capernaum and repair fishing boats. Most of the fishermen are not so invested in themselves. My presence doesn't annoy them."

"Not so fast!" Mary stepped through the doorway that separated the carpentry shop from the rest of the house. "Jose needs a wife! The synagogue is going to pay us for building the addition. Part of that money can be used to negotiate a wife for your brother. Now that your father has passed away, it is your duty to arrange for each of your unmarried brothers to have a wife."

Responding calmly to his mother's directive, Jesus turned to his younger brother, "Do you have someone in mind?"

"No." Jose stopped working and fidgeted with the wood shavings on the work bench. "It's mother's idea."

"I understand," Jesus replied with a knowing inflection.

"Well, how else am I going to have grandchildren?" Mary verbally defended her request while she gave Jesus a sharp look that said, "You refuse to get married, but I should be able to expect you will help me find wives for your brothers!"

"James is married, and he has two children," Jesus pointed out.

"Room after room should be added to this house and I should have a courtyard filled with new daughters and grandchildren," Mary insisted.

"I have met the perfect girl for Jose," Jesus said.

Mary immediately stopped talking and waited for her eldest son to say more. James and Jose also gave their oldest brother their full attention.

"Deborah the granddaughter of Baruch," Jesus announced.

"Deborah?" Mary said the girl's name with a horrified gasp. "She has a hump on her back the size of an overgrown melon!"

"When was the last time you saw her?" Jesus responded.

"When she was a child her mother used to bring her to the well. I touched it! It was solid like a rock. How could you even suggest her name to me?" Mary was aghast.

"While I am in Capernaum, go visit her home. I'm sure you can come up with some legitimate reason to see her mother. See what Deborah looks like now that she has matured into a young lady," Jesus suggested. "When I return after Passover, we will speak further on this subject. And, Jose?" Jesus turned to his younger brother. "Deborah is often with the flock over the Sabbath hours. You might take a Sabbath's walk near the flock and see this young lady for yourself."

Jose responded with a little self-conscious laughter.

Jesus just smiled warmly at his younger brother, but James quickly cut the warmth out of the moment by making a verbal jab at both of his brothers. "Jose is like you, Jesus. He is afraid to take on the responsibilities of a wife and family. He would not even consider the idea if our mother did not push to extend our family."

"No," Jesus responded. "Jose has much to give to the right wife. Wisely, he is willing to wait until God reveals her."

After defending his brother, Jesus left the carpentry shop and went to what was once the home of his grandfather, Heli. This was the place he called home when he was in Nazareth. It was the place where he had access to his grandfather's extensive collection of scrolls.

The late afternoon sunlight fell across an open scroll that was spread across a low wooden table. The words, dictated by the Holy Spirit and originally penned by the prophet Isaiah, seemed to beckon Jesus to sit and read. Easily, he lowered himself to a comfortable position on the floor and began to read. "*I am God and there is none like me. I make known the end from the beginning, from ancient times what is still to come. I say: My purpose will stand, and I will do all that I please. From the east I summon a bird of prey; from a far-off land, a man to fulfill my purpose.*"[2]

Geber squinted at the Hebrew characters he had just penned. His lips moved as he read.

> *Listen to me, you stubborn-hearted, you who are far from righteousness. I am bringing my righteousness near, it is not far away; and my salvation will not be delayed.*[3]

Then he set his reed pen on the small table beside his pot of ink. The late afternoon sunshine poured through the wide mouth of the desert cave, illuminating the fresh script. "Righteousness is not far away," Geber softly repeated some of the words from the text as he waited, hoping to hear the Spirit of God comment on the scripture.

Unexpectedly, a shadow fell across his work. Instead of the quiet voice of the Holy Spirit that often explained the ancient prophetic words, Geber heard a familiar assertive voice announce, "It's time!"

Geber, the Essene teacher, looked up to see his friend, John the son of Zechariah, standing in the entrance to the cave. Curiously, Geber noted that John was no longer wearing the white robes of the Essene fellowship. Instead, he wore a short, roughly woven camel's hair tunic. It was tightly cinched at the waist with a wide leather belt. Other aspects of John's appearance were still typical—his long black hair was divided into seven twisted locks, and those long locks were pulled together at the back of his head with a thin strip of coarse fabric. John's dark facial hair, which had never been touched by a razor, extended down across the front of his rough clothing, past his waist.

"Don't remain bent over your copying tables!" John's black eyes blazed with a Spirit-inspired fire as he commanded the attention of every white-robed man in the Qumran scriptorium. "The Spirit of God has spoken to me. The Spirit said, 'Today, *you will go on before the Lord to prepare the way for him, to give his people the knowledge of salvation through the forgiveness of their sins.'"*[4] For a long moment, John's eyes held the eyes of every man in the cave where scrolls were painstakingly copied. "Come!" he repeated as he turned to walk out of the cave.

Immediately, Geber rose from the place where he had been working. Several others left their copying tables, and without a spoken word, they followed the rough-looking young man who had just called them away from their pens and scrolls and their monastic lifestyle.

"Where are we going?" Geber asked as he caught up with John and matched his long-legged stride.

"First, to Jerusalem." John's answer was short.

"I thought Jerusalem would be the place," Geber spoke with a measure of satisfaction. "It's time for those teachers who sit with their disciples on Solomon's Porch to hear what the Spirit of God has to say!"

"I will not be running to the Temple, begging them for an audience or a place to teach," John responded. "The Spirit of God has provided another arena where his message will be proclaimed. The people of Jerusalem will come out into the desert to hear what the Spirit has to say. Even the men who are considered pillars of the establishment will come."

John, followed by those men from the Essene community who had been sitting under his Spirit-filled instruction for years, paused by the cave that had been his home for the past twelve years. Momentarily, he stepped into the cool darkness of the cave. Almost immediately, he came back out shaking the dust from a worn brown mantel.

Could it be? Geber wondered. Then he shook off the thought. A piece of fabric could not survive so many years even in the dry climate of the desert. But as he watched John throw the tattered piece of woven camel's hair over his shoulders it was as if the present moment had moved back into that moment in Israel's history when Elisha had picked up Elijah's mantel and placed it over his own shoulders.

Chapter 3

Rome, Judea, and Galilee Converge

In the fifteenth year of the reign of Tiberius Caesar—when Pontius Pilate was governor of Judea, Herod tetrarch of Galilee, his brother Philip tetrarch of Iturea and Traconitis, and Lysanias tetrarch of Abilene—during the high priesthood of Annas and Caiaphas, the word of God came to John son of Zechariah in the desert. He went into all the country around the Jordan, preaching a baptism of repentance for the forgiveness of sins.

—Luke 3:1–3

Without respect for the dignity of the governorship, he had received from Sejanus, the regent for Tiberius Caesar, Pilate leaned over the wooden rail of a Roman galley. He heaved his dinner of stale bread sopped in fish sauce into the choppy waters of the Great Sea. Then with one hand clutching the amulet that hung around his neck, he chanted a brief prayer to Neptune, the Roman god of the sea. "If only Neptune would be merciful and calmly sleep," Pilate muttered as he held his stomach. Then, he slowly lowered his body to sit on a wooden bench and wait for his misery to pass.

"Sir?"

Pilate looked up to see Longinus, the centurion who had accompanied him from Rome.

"The harbor has been sighted," the centurion informed as he gestured toward the eastern horizon.

Once more, Pilate stood and moved to the rail. Gripping the wood with his massive cavalry man's hands, he steadied himself and willed his body to submit to his mind. As Pilate spoke, his eyes were fixed on the horizon. He could just make out the massively tall statues that marked the entrance to the harbor. "While I was in Rome, Herod Antipas spent an entire afternoon with me describing this harbor his father had built. The details were unbelievably boring. At the time, I did not know how much I would long to move this ship into its calm waters."

"I'm surprised Antipas had an entire afternoon to spend with you," Longinus remarked. "He is a very popular man, observed at all the official functions."

"With Herodias, the wife of his half-brother, Philip, on his arm," Pilate wryly finished the centurion's thought. "Antipas spent the afternoon with me because he needed to evaluate how much of a threat I would be to his established power in the region. I needed to evaluate him also." Pilate then added with his characteristic bluntness, "The man is a bore!"

"That's not what the ladies of Rome have been saying!" a feminine voice joined the conversation. "Antipas has been having quite an affair. All of Rome has been abuzz. And never forget, Emperor Tiberius enjoys his company."

Pilate looked up to see his wife Procila coming to the rail to get her first glimpse of the land that would become her home.

"Herodias has obtained permission from the emperor to divorce Philip and marry Antipas." Procila continued the conversation by adding the details she had gleaned from the ladies at the various social events that had been a regular part of her life in Rome. "She has made Antipas promise he will dispose of that dreadful Nabataean princess he has been married to for nearly twenty years. With my own ears, I heard Herodias state she would not share her palace with any woman from a backward nation."

"Hmph! Does Antipas with his Edomite ancestry meet her royal standards?" Pilate cynically asked.

"He is a wealthy man, and he has the ear of the emperor." Procila asserted.

"I have to admit; he is the most powerful of all the sons of Herod the Great," Pilate added. "He and I will struggle over that power, I have no doubt."

"Antipas is visiting Emperor Tiberius on Capri now," Longinus informed.

"I am not without important friends," Pilate countered. "I have the approval of Sejanus. He is the proxy ruler for Tiberius."

"I had a dream," Procila turned the conversation with a soft compelling voice.

Pilate immediately gave his wife his complete attention. "You dreamed Sejanus would give me this governorship, and the next day, I was summoned to meet with the man who is holding the empire together while Tiberius stays on the Island of Capri. You observed the flight of the wild geese and predicted this would be a difficult crossing. I have no doubt the gods speak to you. What have you been told?" Again, Pilate took one hand from the ship's railing and grasped the amulet that hung from his neck. The gods were speaking, and he had great respect.

Before speaking, Procila also grasped the amulet that hung from her neck. "Last night as I slept, I saw Herodias holding a silver platter and on that platter was a man's head. I did not recognize the man, but as I watched, the face of the man changed into the face of Antipas."

"He is bringing destruction into his own house," Pilate commented. Before returning to his conversation with Longinus, he muttered a brief supplicating prayer to Jupiter, the master of the gods.

"It is good to keep the gods of Rome on your side," Longinus commented. Then he added, "For now, you have several months while Antipas is still in the homeland of the empire. Before he returns, you can establish yourself as a power to be reckoned with in this Jewish land."

"The gods have revealed to me the weakness of my rival," Pilate stated. Then he turned to his wife who was leaning against the rail, intently studying the coastline of her new home. "Perhaps the wife of Antipas, ruler of Galilee, would like to visit our palace in Caesarea?" Pilate widened his eyes meaningfully as he spoke. "You, my dear wife, could host her along with her servants. I know you have brought several personal servants with you from Rome, and I'm sure they know how to entertain royalty."

"The servants will talk," Procila responded with a meaningful inflection.

"I'm sure your servants will share with her servants all the news regarding recent social events in Rome and on Capri," Pilate confirmed as his thin lips pursed into a slight shrewd smile. He turned back to conversing with the centurion who commanded his small contingent of personal troops.

"I hear the real power struggle will be with the Jews and their leaders," the centurion steered the conversation away from the social intrigue that was typical in elite Roman society. "The Jewish population has never accepted the fact that they are a conquered and occupied people. Jerusalem is as hostile as freshly invaded territory."

Pondering the statement of his military aide, Pilate turned and studied the small contingent of Roman soldiers he had been allowed to bring with him. "We need to show these people what it means to be occupied by Rome," Pilate asserted. "Prepare the standards for when we disembark!" he issued his first order as governor of Judea to his military aide. "From the first moment I step foot on this Judean soil, these people will know Rome has arrived! We'll make a show of it!"

"Procila?" Pilate pulled his wife back into his conversation with Longinus. "I need to know the most auspicious time to disembark from this vessel."

"As the sun sets, I will observe the seabirds," Procila responded, and then she returned to studying the horizon. Gradually, the coastline transformed from an indistinct strip of rocky land into hills covered with beautiful buildings. "Look! There's the temple to Roma and Augustus," Procila exclaimed as she pointed to a gleaming white building high on a hill overlooking the massive stone breakwater that created the famous harbor of Caesarea.

"After disembarking, we will go directly to that temple and sacrifice," Pilate responded. "I desire for the gods to smile on me."

"The soldiers will also go to the temple," Longinus confirmed Pilate's desire that the gods of Rome be satisfied.

"I want to visit Jerusalem soon after I arrive," Pilate continued making plans with his military aide. "I'll come into the city with at least a legion. The standards will go first, then the trumpeters."

"The standards never enter the city of Jerusalem," the centurion cautiously informed.

"What?" Pilate exclaimed. "No wonder these people consider themselves enemies of Rome! They have never submitted to the authority of Rome."

"The emperor has given the Jews the right to continue their allegiance to their one God. One of their God's laws is they are not to make an image or any type of likeness. They are not to bow or even look upon an image. The standards are embellished with likenesses of the emperor and the gods of Rome. These are an offense, especially to the religious leadership of the nation," Longinus explained.

"Who are these people that dare to offend the emperor and the gods of Rome?" Pilates asked incredulously.

"They are people who do not intermarry with other races, and they gather in Jerusalem several times a year for national celebrations. They are of one mind, and it only takes an unfortunate word or a mindless gesture to throw this nation into rebellion," the centurion warned. "Before each of these national celebrations, the troops from Caesarea are moved to the fortress in Jerusalem.

It is a show of Roman force, a promise of swift retaliation should their national celebration turn into a rebellion. Most of the governors have also attended each national celebration."

"This time, the troops will enter the city with the standards," Pilate stated.

Longinus looked Pilate in the eye, soldier to soldier. "A statement?"

"A careful statement," Pilate affirmed. "I am the new governor, and I represent the Roman Empire. The standards will enter by night. We will choose a time between their festivals. One ordinary morning, when the city is not overcrowded, Jerusalem will wake up, and the presence of Rome will be an accomplished fact. I will allow them a few weeks to get used to the standards flying from the Roman fortress, then I will enter the city."

Behind the governor and his military aide, the sails of the Roman galley were being lashed to the cross beams. Thirty-two oars simultaneously hit the water, and the steady beat of the rower's drum set the rhythm for the oarsmen. The ship was now approaching the entrance to the harbor, lurching and then gliding to the rhythm of the oars. As soon as they cleared the breakwater, Pilate felt his stomach settle. That was a good omen.

"Longinus? Tell the captain to bring some fresh food aboard. I want some fruit and some newly baked bread. Let's see what this land has to offer," Pilate directed. Then he turned to his wife, "Procila, you are a woman of great spiritual discernment. I want you to study this religion that is so important to these Jews. I need to understand its weaknesses, and the points where we hold commonality. Find out what they do in their Temple."

"Make way! Make way!" The Temple guard moved out through the ornate Eastern Gate away from the Temple grounds. "Clean! Clean!" One guard noticed Ichabod the beggar in his usual spot. With his foot, he shoved the beggar, nearly pushing him off the step. "This procession is clean!" he restated as he, along with his other guardsmen, continued to break a path through the normal crush of worshipers.

From his crumpled position at the far edge of the step, Ichabod watched as a young red heifer was led out through the Beautiful Gate by children whose feet had never walked on unsanctified ground. Well-known men, important in their Temple positions, followed. Ichabod could name each man. Near the end of the procession, three of the priests solemnly processed in front of the high priest. Each priest carried an armful of hyssop, scarlet cloth, or cedar branches. The procession, a rare and sacred one, exited the Temple Mount and continued across the bridge to the altar that had been constructed on the Mount of Olives directly opposite the gate. Caiaphas, the current high priest, was the last man in the procession. After a week of seclusion and frequent purification rituals, Ichabod observed the high priest seemed to walk with more humility than he normally possessed.

The people who had been streaming onto the Temple grounds now reversed directions and followed the procession. For a few moments, Ichabod found himself sitting alone. The entrance to the Temple known as the Beautiful Gate remained strangely deserted until Geber, the aging Essene teacher accompanied by a hairy, roughly dressed man, stepped onto the wide empty step.

"John, from this spot we can observe the burning of the red heifer, and you will not become unclean by the proximity of the dead animal," Geber commented.

The man is a Nazirite, Ichabod mused as he studied the stranger's obviously uncut hair and piercing black eyes.

Ichabod heard John respond. "I am here to receive instruction from the Lord regarding the truth of this sacrifice. But you may go on over." John gestured toward the bridge.

"No," Geber replied. "Please repeat for me the words the Holy Spirit speaks. I also desire to be instructed by the Spirit of God."

After his first assessment of the two men, Ichabod carefully turned his body away. His eyes were fixed on the rituals that were taking place on the other side of the bridge. But at the same time, he listened. The beggar was so used to living the life of the people and the Temple through the conversations he heard while sitting at the gate that he did not know how to wrap himself in the cloak of his own world and leave them out.

"The Spirit has come," John spoke softly and confidently.

Ichabod sensed a pressure on his shoulders, like someone had placed a very heavy woolen cloak on his back. He looked around and saw nothing but the two unusual men. Unobtrusively, he scooted his deformed body a little closer to their conversation.

John was speaking, "This is the only sacrifice of a female animal. The Spirit says this flawlessly red heifer is representative of the seed of the woman. All that is human and fleshly in the promised Deliverer will be burned up. Only that part which is divine will remain to come before God and represent mankind. But first there must be a cleansing."

Geber interrupted, "The high priest is removing his white garments and stepping into the pool that has been set up close to the altar. He is immersing himself totally. Is that the cleansing the Spirit is speaking about?"

"Immersion in water is merely symbolic of a deeper cleansing," John replied. "That man, Caiaphas, is still unclean. His motives are as contaminated as a dead animal and the deeds he will do in his lifetime are as black as ashes. It is prophetic that his hands will soon be covered with the blood of this sacrificial animal. Washing his hands, even completely washing his body cannot prevent uncleanness from the blood that will be on his hands."

From his sitting position on the step, Ichabod could just make out the form of the high priest ascending the steps to the altar that had been specially built for this one sacrifice. The animal was still alive but securely bound and laid upon the firewood. Facing the Temple, Caiaphas stood close to the animal. His voice carried across the valley as he asked, "Is this a red heifer?" Three times, the people shouted their affirmative response. Then Caiaphas slit the throat of the animal and caught its spurting blood in his other hand. With his free hand, he now dipped his fingers into the blood that pooled in the palm of one hand. Then he flicked the blood seven different times over the crowd in the direction of the Temple. Another priest then stepped forward to light the fire. For a long time, the crowd silently observed the burning of this special offering.

"Is the Spirit still speaking?" Geber quietly asked.

"God has come to earth encumbered by flesh. He is constrained and heavy with flesh like this heifer is heavy with muscle and bone. That animal"—John pointed across the bridge to where the sacrifice was burning—"was between three and four years old. For the same length of time, the Deliverer will allow us to examine him. To look at every hair on his body to see if there is any part that is not truly perfect. The animal that is now on the altar never felt the weight of a yoke or a burden. The Deliverer, when he comes, will never accept the burdens and constraints men would like to put on him. He will only respond to the directives of heaven. When the time of his sacrifice has come, the Deliverer who is the seed of the woman will be lead away from the city across this bridge to an established place of execution. His blood will be on the hands of the Temple priests; yet, it will be atonement for the people." Faithfully, John repeated the words of the Spirit but with very limited understanding.

"Is this scarlet?" the voice of the high priest could clearly be heard from the mountain directly across from the Temple gate.

The people replied, "That is scarlet!"

John repeated the words of the Spirit, "A royal robe for the King of kings."

"Is this cedar?"

Ichabod could see that the high priest was holding a fist full of branches high above his head.

"That is cedar!" the people shouted their response.

"*You must not leave his body on the tree overnight. Be sure to bury him that same day, because anyone who is hung on a tree is under God's curse,*"[1] Geber quoted from the last book of Moses. Then he looked quizzically at John.

"I know," John responded. "I, like you, do not understand what the Spirit is saying. Still, I speak it. And I wait to hear God's explanation."

"Is this hyssop?" Caiaphas shouted his question to the crowd that pressed around the burning heifer.

"Yes, that is hyssop." The response of the crowd was deafeningly loud.

"The blood of the Passover lamb was applied to the doorposts of our people with branches of hyssop," Geber commented.

"And hyssop will be used to sprinkle the waters of cleansing that will be made from the ashes of this red heifer. This animal died for the cleansing of those who have been contaminated by sin," John added the thoughts that the Holy Spirit had placed in his mind.

As both men continued looking across the valley to the site where the burning of the red heifer was almost complete, they saw the high priest wrap the hyssop and cedar in a piece of scarlet cloth. With a single thrust of his arm, he quickly placed the bundle in the middle of the burning animal.

The crowd broke into spontaneous cheers.

Suddenly, the directive of God exploded in an audible voice that both Geber and John clearly understood, "Go to the Crossing of Elijah at Bethany, east of the Jordan. There you must warn the Israelites about their impurity. They must keep themselves *separate from things that make them unclean, so they will not die in their uncleanness for defiling my dwelling place which is among them.*[2] As I warned Adam, warn my people, 'surely, death will be the result of disregarding and disobeying my directives.' Shout to every man and woman who passes over the Jordan, 'Repent!

Surely the day is coming; it will burn like a furnace. All the arrogant and every evildoer will be stubble.[3] *Remember the law of my servant Moses, the decrees I gave him at Horeb for all Israel.*[4] For those who revere the name of God there is my promise that brings healing and places their names in the books of remembrance that are always in the throne room of God.

Even as I speak these words to you, My Deliverer, the promised seed of the woman, the Passover Lamb is in the land. You will see my Spirit in the form of a dove and you will hear my voice again when I reveal him to you. Go now, in the spirit of Elijah. As a symbol of inner cleansing, immerse people in living water. Turn the hearts of the people back to the father of all mankind so the heart of God can return to them."

Both John and Geber immediately moved to leave the gate. For one moment, Geber paused to glance at the beggar who always sat at this spot. The man lay face down on the stone step, overcome by the heavenly presence of God's Spirit.

"May the Holy One bring healing to your body and to your soul," Geber pronounced a blessing as both men went straight away to carry out the command of God.

Studying the piles of scrolls that were stacked in floor-to-ceiling cubicles, Manaen slowly moved around the perimeter of the architectural library in the palace of Herod Antipas in the city of Tiberius on the shores of Galilee. He was looking for the plans for the queen's apartments. Phasaelis, the wife of Antipas, wanted her bathhouse enlarged. He pulled out several rolled parchments. Then he turned to the table in middle of the room and spread one open, but he could not concentrate on the lines and measurements. There were footsteps in the corridor, the steady measured footsteps of a man on palace business, accompanied by the quick tapping of childish feet.

Four-year-old Casper burst into the room before his father. Cuza strode through the curtained doorway after him. "Look! Uncle Manaen, look!" Casper waved a polished wooden sword in the air and then made several quick stabbing motions.

"I had a sword like that once." Manaen held his hand out so the boy would allow him to take the sword and examine it more closely. "Antipas and I used to spar with each other. I would always have to be a Parthian. And since I was only the son of the wet nurse, I would always have to surrender to the young son of the king." Manaen was speaking more to Cuza than to the boy. He returned the sword to Casper with a sweeping bow and then asked the boy's father, "Do you have a message from Antipas?"

Cuza tossed two rolled parchments on the table. "Antipas is en route from Rome to Caesarea. According to this message, he should have boarded a royal vessel a few days ago. Depending on the weather and the length of time they spend in various harbors, he could arrive within fifteen to thirty days."

Manaen picked up the parchment roll that had been sealed with the signet ring of the Herods. His eyes quickly scanned the message. "It says we are to be informed that his niece, Herodias, is traveling with him. We are to prepare a set of guest rooms for her and her attendants here at the palace in Tiberius."

"Isn't this Herodias the wife of his half-brother, Philip?" Cuza asked.

"You have to have grown up in Herod's family to know who is related to whom and how many different ways they are related," Manaen knowingly commented. "Herodias is the granddaughter of Herod the Great. She is married to her uncle who is the half brother of Antipas." Then, with a slightly suspicious inflection he added, "Her husband was in Rome. Why isn't he coming with her?"

"I do not know the answer to that question," Cuza replied.

"And this other message?" Manaen picked up the rolled parchment and briefly studied the broken seal.

"It's from Pontius Pilate, the new governor of Judea," Cuza informed. "Actually, it is from his wife. She has invited Phasaelis to spend a week with her at the royal residence in Caesarea."

"Is Antipas acquainted with Pontius Pilate?" Manaen asked. "What is the purpose of this invitation?"

"Always suspicious," Cuza commented.

"You must remember," Manaen responded, "I grew up with all the sons of Herod the Great. As a child, I played their games. As an adult, I have continued to observe their games. Some of their games have proven deadly."

"Well?" Cuza asked. "Shall we give this message to the queen and provide a royal escort, or do we politely decline for her?"

"Let's go to Caesarea," Manaen stated. "I want to size up this new ruler."

Cuza chuckled, "It's going to be an interesting month! Antipas might even arrive before it is over! I'll tell my wife, Joanna, to help the queen prepare."

Casper suddenly interjected himself into the conversation, "Am I going too?"

"No," Cuza replied. "You will stay with your grandmother in Capernaum."

Casper sighed. Then he turned away from the adults to continue thrusting the heavy draperies with his wooden sword.

Chapter 4

The Good Samaritan

But he waited to justify himself, so he asked Jesus, "Who is my neighbor?" In reply Jesus said: "A man was going down from Jerusalem to Jericho when he fell into the hands of robbers. They stripped him of his clothes, beat him and went away, leaving him half dead."

—Luke 10:29–31

"Yeshua, my son." Jesus opened his eyes as the familiar voice of his Father broke into his dreamless sleep. "Gather the fish and feed my fishermen." Jesus understood the command. Many times, as he slept on the beach not far from his Uncle Zebedee's boat landing, his heavenly Father had called him to feed the fishermen both physically and spiritually.

By the light of a nearly full moon, Jesus quickly threw off the heavy cloak that had been his covering for the night. Then he removed all his clothing down to his knotted loin cloth, the most basic of undergarments for all Jewish men. Moonlight highlighted the well-defined muscles of his back and chest as he casually bent to pick up one of the small circular nets that had been spread out on the rocks nearby.

In the predawn darkness, the surface of Galilee was only separated from the night sky by silver-tipped ridges of gently undulating wavelets. After securing the net to his waist with a long handwoven cord, Jesus confidently waded out into the cold water of the lake. With an easy circular motion, he tossed the net onto Galilee's surface. It hit the water with a soft smack and then sank beneath the gray wavelets.

"Fish!" Jesus spoke one word, a command that momentarily turned the area where the net had sunk beneath the lake's surface into a churning mass of tails and fins. Immediately, Jesus began pulling on the rope attached to his waist, closing the net and at the same time bringing it closer to shore.

The first rays of the morning sun were just skimming the tops of the mountains and hills that bordered the Sea of Galilee when Jesus struck a flint sending sparks into a little pile of dry grass. He guarded the little flame, carefully adding twigs and finally larger sticks until he could squat by the fire and dry himself while he cleaned and prepared the fish for roasting.

Suddenly, like a ball of red fire, the sun burst over the eastern mountains and threw a scarlet cloak of reflected light across the lake's surface. Standing, stretching out his cramped leg muscles, Jesus looked across the lake to see Zebedee's fishing boats approaching their landing. He could tell, by the way his uncle's vessels rode on the water, their catch had been moderate.

"It has been a difficult night for these men," the Holy Spirit added information to the observations Jesus had made. "During the night, the wind whipped up the waves and pushed these boats away from their fishing spots. They spent the night dragging their anchors and trying not to lose their nets. Still, toward morning, they caught some fish."

"Did I sleep through those winds and rough waves?" Jesus asked.

"Yes," the Spirit responded. "You have so completely placed your well-being in my hands that your sleep is rarely disturbed by any earthly turmoil."

The fire was now a bed of glowing coals. Holding each fish by the tail, Jesus laid them one by one on the coals. Watching them carefully, he turned each fish once then moved it to a basket that belonged to his Aunt Salome.

The boats were tied to their moorings, and the catch was sorted. Then the fresh fish were turned over to the women who efficiently hung each one on a rack to dry. Matthew, the tax collector, busily moved from rack to rack counting the fish. Jesus pulled the last of his cooked fish off the coals. The morning meal was ready for the fishermen.

James, the oldest son of Zebedee, was the first to spot the bed of burning coals and the basket of freshly roasted fish. "Jesus is back!" he shouted.

James's announcement was greeted with smiles and a few cheers. The men all knew Jesus. He came to their wharf area regularly, to greet them with roasted fish and then to set up his carpentry bench. As he worked on boats and the various implements of the fishing trade, he spoke to anyone who cared to listen. Mostly, he explained the scriptures, and the men loved to hear what he had to say.

"I have a boat that needs a few patches," Uncle Zebedee was the first to approach the carpenter.

Jesus held the basket so his uncle could pick up several of the crisp flat fish. "As soon as the men have eaten, ask some of them to haul your boat out of the water," Jesus responded.

Zebedee squatted on his heels and began to eat. More men arrived. Jesus served each one. There was always enough fish in the basket—never too few, never too many.

Jesus watched the men as they ate. Most were simple men. Six days each week they fished and one day they rested and went to the synagogue. Only taxes and bad weather complicated their lives. Prompted by the Spirit, Jesus studied each man, looking briefly into each pair of eyes to see if any demonic spirits stared back. The eyes of his cousins, James and John, were clear and untroubled. Jesus then looked at Zebedee's new fishing partner, Jona. He could see nothing unusual. Jona's two sons Simon Peter and Andrew were nearby. Jesus looked at them and smiled to himself. He could see those two were hungry for more than a meal of fish. Their souls craved spiritual food. Finally, his eyes rested on his Uncle Zebedee. The man was shifting his weight and keeping his eyes on the ground.

"What's on your mind this morning," Jesus probed his uncle's thoughts.

Zebedee looked up and Jesus saw the spirit of Guilt looking out through his uncle's eyes.

"Tell me, Jesus," Zebedee responded with a question. "If I come across a Samaritan fishing out on the lake and I see his boat has been damaged, is it my duty to rescue him? Zebedee hesitated and cleared his throat before adding, "I mean…should I risk my boat and my crew not to mention subjecting myself to all the inconvenience of ceremonial cleansing?"

"You seem to have given this situation a lot of thought," Jesus replied. "Did such an incident ever occur?"

"Well…," Zebedee hesitated again.

During that pregnant pause, the Holy Spirit like lightning flashed a scene across the mind of Jesus—two fishing boats struggling with the waves and the wind. One boat had lost its mast. White capped waves were washing over its sides. The fishermen were crying for help while they bailed water as fast as they could.

"There was a storm last night," Jesus stated what the Spirit of God had revealed to him.

Zebedee responded to the opening Jesus had offered, "We were fighting not to lose our anchors or break a mast. I saw another boat. I knew it belonged to Gerizem." There was another pause, and then Zebedee burst into a small tirade, "That Samaritan dog is always trying to fish in my territory. He knows each family has designated sections of the lake!"

"His mast had broken and his boat was taking on water. We could not help him without swamping our own boat," James broke into his father's outburst.

"You could not have gotten a boat to him," Zebedee snapped back at his son, "but I am more experienced. Maybe if I had cut the nets, lightened our boat...," Zebedee let his words trail off into an uncomfortable sigh.

"What happened to Gerizem?" Jesus gently asked.

"I don't know," Zebedee answered.

"Your heart is troubled because you expect if the situation had been reversed, he would come to your rescue," Jesus stated.

"He is a Samaritan dog!" Zebedee angrily protested. "He is not my neighbor. Surely, God does not expect me to risk my life, my fishing boat, and my crew for a Samaritan dog!"

"Are we not all the children of Adam?" Jesus asked. "*Have we not all one Father? Did not one God create us? Why do we profane the covenant of our fathers by breaking faith with one another?*"[1]

"So?" Zebedee angrily retorted. "Are you saying that he and I are equal in the eyes of God, and that I neglected my duty to love my neighbor when I did not risk everything to help him?"

"All heaven stops to honor the man who risks his own life to come to the aid of another man." Jesus repeated the words the Holy Spirit placed in his mind for that moment.

"I could sail out and look for him," Zebedee resentfully muttered.

"Maybe you could just sail out far enough to throw him a rope and tow him to shore," Jesus suggested as he pointed toward a badly battered fishing boat slowly drifting close to the horizon.

Immediately, Zebedee jumped up calling, "James! John! Come help me."

"Please, someone? Help me," Toma groaned. The pain in his side and the throbbing in his head made it impossible to move his body. Joseph's cousin, a favorite and close relative to Jesus and his family, lay beaten and robbed on the Jericho Road. Opening his swollen eyelids a bit, he found the glare of the noonday sun nearly blinding. Someone should be coming along this road. He comforted himself with hope that help was on the way. Toma drifted into temporary unconsciousness.

When he woke his throat was parched. His fingers felt sticky. Carefully, he lifted one arm and brought his hand up to where he could view it through the slits of his swollen eyelids. Blood, his hand was covered with blood. The successful trader groaned again as he let his hand fall back into the dust of the road. Toma could do nothing to help himself.

He could do nothing but lay on the hard dirt road and remember the faces of the men who had suddenly leaped upon him from the boulder-strewn hillside. There was one face that tugged at his memory. Toma thought he had seen that face before. It was a younger, more frightened face that he remembered.

Slowly, a foggy scene from the past crystallized in Toma's mind. It was the blacksmith's shop in the town of Nazareth. Toma forced his mind to focus on the memory. Joseph was with him. Young Jesus was there, along with many of the men from the town. And there was a young man, an escaped slave, who was accused of stealing a lamb.

That was the face! Toma's memory honed in on the event. Most of the men from Nazareth were sympathetic. Who would not want to help a young Jewish man who had just escaped from Roman slavery?

Toma lost the scene. For a while his mind drifted, then it seemed to wake into the dreamlike moment when a man sent by the Galilean arrived at the blacksmith's shop to purchase swords. The men of Nazareth allowed him to free the slave so the young man could make an uncontested escape. With a sigh, Toma let his memories slide away again.

After a brief rest, he tried once more to move his body, but his limbs would not respond to his mental commands. Instead, nauseating pain rolled through Toma's rib cage, pushing his thoughts into black nothingness.

After a time, Toma again became aware of his situation. He also sensed a shadow had fallen across his body. He opened his eyes just a fraction, just enough to see a Levite standing over him. A Temple musician, Toma thought as he caught a glimpse of the flute the man was carrying. "Help me?" Toma's voice was a hoarse whisper. He had not finished his strangled request before the shadow and the Levite quickly slipped away. Toma understood. The man was moving away from a situation that could possibly compromise his ability to serve in the Temple during the Passover services.

Deeply disappointed, Toma managed to softly cry, "God, remember your servant. I have a wife and two children. Hear and act on my behalf."

As if his prayer had been answered, Toma instantly heard another set of approaching footsteps. This time, he managed to raise his bloody hand as he weakly cried out, "Help me?"

"Unclean!" an alarmed voice responded.

Through his nearly closed eyes, Toma watched a Temple priest as he scurried to the opposite side of the road to avoid being contaminated.

"Is there no one in Israel who will come to the aid of a man who has been beaten and robbed?" Toma moaned as he slipped back into parched unconsciousness.

The sun was dropping behind the barren hills where robbers squabbled over the purse they had lifted from a Jewish merchant earlier in the day. The cooling air and the unmistakable clip-clop of a donkey's hooves seemed to call Toma out of his traumatized sleep. With his tongue, he tried to moisten his roughly cracked lips, but his tongue was as dry as the dust on the Jericho Road. Concentrating on commanding his muscles to respond, he tried once more to open his eyes. He wanted to see the face of this traveler. He wanted to look him in the eye, but his eyes would not open.

The rhythmic clip clop of the donkey's hooves slowed and then stopped. Toma sensed additional coolness as a shadow fell across his face. He smelled the musty smell of the donkey and knew the animal had stopped very close to his head.

Was it hopeless? Toma wondered. Would this man dismount to take a close look, but then, like the others, hurry away without touching the body of a dying man?

A man's hand slipped under his head, and Toma felt a wine skin pressed to his lips. The wine was so sweet, so wet, so wonderfully satisfying.

"Who did this to you?" a man asked as he began to clean the worst of the blood from Toma's face and hands.

"Robbers," Toma muttered. "Barabbas," Toma whispered the name of the one desperate renegade he had remembered from the days when the Galilean had staged a revolt against Rome. Barabbas was the man who had stepped forward after his thugs had beaten Toma's body beyond resistance. With one swipe of his knife, he had lifted the bag of coins Toma was carrying from Jerusalem to Jericho. Their eyes had met. Recognition had briefly passed between the two men as Barabbas had spoken to Toma, "Times are difficult, friend."

In Bethany for the Passover season, Jesus worked with the servants from the household of Lazarus to gather scraps of wood from the building site. "We'll need more wood than this," Jesus commented as he tossed an armload into the roasting pit behind the main house. With the ease of a man who was comfortable with the physical requirements of his profession, Jesus picked up his two-man saw and pointed to a dead tree beyond the barn. "We'll take that tree down." The servants followed him.

It was evening when Lazarus, along with his younger brother, Nodab, and Martha's husband, Jessie, returned from the Temple with their prepared Passover lamb. Jesus looked up from stoking the fire. With a grimy hand he wiped the sweat from his forehead. "Better let the fire burn down a bit before you start cooking," he advised. "I think you want more coals than flames so the outer meat does not get charred."

The men set their lamb on the flat stones that made a patio near the fire pit. The skin that had been removed from the animal was now loosely wrapped around the carcass. It fell away from the dead animal, exposing a whole lamb, completely skinned and drained of blood. The animal was elongated on a pole of pomegranate wood. Both ends of the wooden pole protruded from the raw meat.

For a long moment, the Holy Spirit drew the attention of Jesus away from the fire to that uncovered Passover lamb. Every year of his life since before the age of twelve, Jesus had seen a Passover lamb, but never before had he been drawn to contemplate the dead animal. *He was oppressed and afflicted, yet he did not open his mouth; he was led like a lamb to the slaughter.*[2] Jesus considered the scripture from the prophet Isaiah. He had always understood it referred to the Messiah, but as he stared at the slaughtered lamb, an animal that had been reduced to raw flesh stretched out on a pole, his soul identified with that lamb, and his physical body began to shake.

Jesus's physical reaction only lasted a few moments. No one even noticed when he stepped away and went to the pool to wash and to be alone with Father God and the Holy Spirit.

Martha moved efficiently around the table where the men of her family along with their favorite guest, Jesus of Nazareth, stretched out comfortably on the sets of cushions that surrounded the Passover table. Experienced at serving, Martha quickly refilled each cup with wine, and then she looked over the table for empty platters and dishes that could be removed. For a brief moment when her hands were filled, she wondered where her sister Mary was. But there was much to be done and she could not waste time on that thought.

"The last cup!" Lazarus announced. "The cup of praise!"

"*I will take you as my own people, and I will be your God*,"[3] Jesus quoted from the second book of Moses. Then every person in the large banquet room emptied their cups.

Lazarus set his cup on the low table and turned to his guest. "Explain the words of Moses for us," he requested.

Jesus paused a moment before replying. He was listening for the voice of God that directed his every word and his every action.

The Holy Spirit responded to the moment by lightly tickling Jesus's toes.

Curiously, Jesus looked at his feet. They were resting comfortably on a plush cushion. On the floor beside the cushion sat Mary, the youngest sister of Lazarus. Her head was resting on the same cushion where Jesus rested his feet. Her black hair fell like a beautiful dark mantel around her face. She was asleep. Then Jesus noticed the band of silver coins the girl was wearing across her forehead, her dowry.

At that moment, Mary woke up. Her light brown eyes met the warm dark eyes of Jesus.

"Mary," Jesus spoke her name as if she was the only person in the room and as if he had completely forgotten the question her brother had asked. "You are going to be someone's wife! Who are you promised to?"

"Jonathan, the younger brother of Simon, the vineyard owner and wine merchant," Mary answered. Then she offered a little more information. "Jonathan is a perfumer. He has a shop in Jerusalem and he is building a room behind his shop. That will be our home."

Jesus gave Mary one more warm congratulatory smile, and then he turned back to Lazarus. "Every time we drink the four cups of Passover wine, we affirm our marriage covenant with God. He has made a contract with us, not unlike the contract you negotiated with Simon so Mary could become the wife of Jonathan. Every year, we reenact and recommit to our betrothal. God is the bridegroom and Israel is the bride."

"Jonathan plans to come and take Mary to his home in Jerusalem." Nodab, the younger brother of Lazarus asserted his thoughts. "How is God going to take us into his home in heaven?"

"Haven't you heard that Enoch, the seventh from Adam, prophesied, '*See, the Lord is coming with thousands upon thousands of his holy ones?*'"[4]

"Tell me, Mary." Jesus turned his attention back to the nineteen-year-old girl who sat at his feet. "How do you know Jonathan is going to keep his word? Will he really come?"

"He gave me these silver coins." Mary pointed to the silver coins that were securely woven into the band that held her hair in place beneath her mantel. "And"—she lifted a beautiful oval alabaster vile that hung from a cord around her neck—"Jonathan made a special costly perfume, just for me."

Jesus turned back to Lazarus and Nodab. "God has secured his contract by his own word in the Torah and through the prophets. More than that, he is securing his promise to come for his people by presenting himself as a man."

"Are you speaking of the Messiah?" Martha's husband, Jessie, inquired.

"Those teachers who rightly interpret the writings of Moses and the prophets teach the Messiah will be God in the flesh, the Son of God. In the Book of Enoch, he is called the Word who spoke earth into existence."

Lazarus asserted, "The Essene teachers say he will be coming soon with his angels to conquer the Romans."

"You must remember the protocol of the wedding," Jesus responded. "First, the prospective bridegroom presents himself to the family and proves himself worthy of their daughter by fulfilling the obligations of the marriage contract. Before he can actually come for her, the bridegroom must leave and return to his home where he prepares a place for her to live. Only after that is accomplished does he come with a procession of attendants to make her his wife."

Jessie stared intently at Lazarus's friend from Nazareth. "So, you are saying that the Messiah has to come twice?" he asked.

"Yes," Jesus answered. "First in humility, asking to be heard, offering everything he is and everything he owns. But when he has fulfilled the terms of the contract, he will come again, this time proudly leading a procession, ready to take possession of his bride."

The men stared at Jesus in puzzled silence. The confusion on their faces was easy to read. As Jesus looked around the room, reading each reaction to his teaching, his eyes fell on Mary. She was smiling broadly.

"I can see it," she said. "I remember when Jonathan came to speak to Lazarus. He held nothing back. He offered everything he owned for me. I think he would have given his life if he could have."

"Mary? How did you know?" Lazarus interrupted his youngest sister.

"I was peeking through the window," Mary giggled.

Jesus laughed with Mary and everyone else in the room as they imagined Mary sneaking and peeking in on her betrothal arrangements.

"I think Jonathan had heard you had turned down many before him," Nodab commented.

"A girl from a poor family could not afford to wait until she is almost too old to get married," Martha asserted with a little huff.

"Mary has chosen to follow her heart." Jesus affirmed the girl with another smile. "She does not let the demands of society dictate her life."

"Well, there are certain things that are expected of women." As she spoke, Martha pointed to the table scattered with crumbs and used dishes.

Mary quietly responded to her sister's admonition by removing the empty plate in front of Jesus and then continuing to clear the table.

A loud knock on the courtyard gate suddenly disrupted the after dinner conversation. A servant hurried into the room, speaking to Nodab. "A message has come from Toma's wife. Toma has not returned from his trip to Jericho. She expected him home before the Passover celebration."

Nodab responded, "Tell Elisheva that I will travel the Jericho Road in the morning, and I will inquire after her husband. Then I will come to her with the news."

"Shall I travel with you?" Jesus asked.

"No," Nodab replied. "Toma was making some arrangements with the Jericho merchants so their goods would be ready when our caravan arrived in Jericho. I know the merchants. I will speak to each of them."

"Jesus, the addition you are building for me will be completed in just a couple of days, but please, spend the entire week of Unleavened Bread in my home. Stay even longer," Lazarus invited. "Then after the holiday—"

"Jonathan is coming to take me to his home in Jerusalem during the second week after Passover," Mary inserted her thoughts into the male conversation as she continued to clear the table.

Jesus smiled at her again. "That occasion would be worth staying for," he responded.

"Mary!" Martha inserted herself into the conversation. "How do you know Jonathan is coming then?"

"He sent me a message. He told me to be ready. He said he would be coming during the second week of counting the Omer," Mary replied with certainty.

"He is sending you messages! He should be communicating with Lazarus. This kind of behavior demonstrates why it is best for girls to marry before they turn thirteen," Martha asserted.

"As they get older, they begin to take charge of their own destiny instead of waiting patiently and relying on the judgment of those who are older and wiser. You know so much about this wedding, I wonder if you did not arrange for Jonathan to come ask your brother for your hand in marriage!"

Mary's eyes twinkled mischievously. She did not reply to her older sister's little tirade. Instead, she quickly smothered a little giggle and quickly exited the room.

"Do not trouble yourself, Martha," Jesus advised. "Mary will always follow her heart. She will not be bound by the archaic rules of society."

"Jesus," Martha responded, "you do not understand. The women of Bethany talk about Mary. They talk about each man she has turned down. They talk about how old she is—getting married when she is past her best childbearing years. She is frivolous. She dresses like every day is a feast day. She laughs at the wrong times and plays with the children when she should be working with the women."

"Be happy for your sister," Jesus continued his kind advice, "and allow yourself some time to be frivolous. Play with your children and leave the spinning and washing for another day."

Slowly, Toma opened his eyes. The room was dark and cool. His mind groped to orient itself to this unfamiliar place. He sensed he was resting on a straw-filled mattress. Carefully, Toma shifted his weight. Immediately, his senses were overwhelmed with pain, and he fell back into unconsciousness.

Another day passed, and Toma regained consciousness again. This time, he was not alone. A strange man was washing his body with cool water.

"Who…? Where…?" Toma tried to speak.

"I'm the owner of this inn."

Toma looked into the face of a Samaritan man.

"Normally, Jews do not stop at my inn, but a traveling Samaritan found you. He brought you here. For a few days, he cared for you himself. Then he had to continue his journey."

"How…?"

Toma did not have to complete his question. The innkeeper continued, "You were lying at the edge of the road. At first, it appeared you had been beaten to death. But the man who found you saw that breath was still in you, and he intervened to save your life. Were you carrying money?"

"Yes," Toma responded as he began to remember. "I am a caravan merchant. I was traveling to some of the local vendors to arrange for their merchandise…," Toma's voice trailed off.

"You have been seriously injured, my friend." The innkeeper placed a cool wet cloth on Toma's forehead. "I believe several of your ribs are broken. There may be other internal injuries. Did you try to fight the robbers?"

"If I had had a sword with me," Toma muttered.

"If you had had a sword, those bandits would have taken it from you and used it to end your life!" the innkeeper emphatically stated. "The bandits along this stretch of the Jericho Road have no mercy, and they no longer make a distinction between Romans, Samaritans, and Jews. They are looking for anyone who might be carrying a purse, and they will take that purse with whatever amount of force is necessary."

"Several times a year, I give a large sum of money to a man who passes it on to a man who passes it on to the bandits in this area. It is for safe passage. I thought—"

"You need nourishment," the innkeeper said as he propped Toma's head and then pressed a cup of warm lamb broth to Toma's lips. While Toma carefully sipped and swallowed, the innkeeper continued his commentary, "The Roman soldiers are closing in on the desperate men who hide in the hills and rob the rich. It is just a matter of time. For now, we must all remember that a cornered animal is the most dangerous."

Toma finished the cup of broth, and then he closed his eyes as he sank weakly and painfully back into restorative sleep. When he woke again, a small lamp was burning beside his bed and once more the innkeeper was in his room.

"Friend," Toma got the innkeeper's attention. "I have the means to pay for all your services. I am very grateful. I just need to send a message to my wife in Bethlehem. She will contact my trading partners."

"Do not trouble yourself," the innkeeper replied. "I have been paid. The man who brought you here left me two week's wages. Like you, he is a traveling merchant. He has frequented my inn many times. He told me when he returns, he will pay any additional expenses."

For a moment, Toma was speechless. "Who is this man? Do you know his name and his town?"

"No. He did not leave that information with me, but I will see him again," the innkeeper replied.

"Still," Toma continued, "tomorrow, I must send a message. My wife will be concerned."

Chapter 5

The Politics of Rome

That day Herod and Pilate became friends—before that they had been enemies.

—Luke 23:12

Cuza and Manaen stopped side by side. Each man remained on his horse, taking in the magnificent view of the Great Sea and the palace gardens. Manaen broke their contemplative silence. "When Antipas and I were boys, we were inseparable companions. He and I used to hide and chase each other all through those gardens." Manaen pointed toward a lower level of the governor's residence where lush vegetation and massive columns surrounded a large rectangular pool of water. "I remember when his father, Herod the Great, was building this palace. Antipas and I climbed all over those rocks, and we would wade into the sea from that little bit of sand."

"This palace is breathtaking," Cuza responded as he dismounted onto the paved courtyard in the reception area of the palace complex. He paused and slowly turned, taking in the full panorama of the palace grounds. "Water on three sides, from a military perspective this place is a natural fortress."

Both men quickly turned away from the magnificent view and returned their attention to their responsibilities. Standing as the official representatives of Herod Antipas, they watched as the curtained chair that carried Phasaelis, the royal wife of the ruler of Galilee and Perea, was carefully leveled and then lowed to rest on supporting blocks. The chairs that carried her two court attendants were also lowered, and the ladies-in-waiting emerged from behind their curtains.

Cuza exchanged glances with his wife, Joanna, one of the ladies-in-waiting.

Manaen commented, "It was wise of you to recommend Joanna for one of the royal traveling assistants. She can easily make you aware of any difficulties."

Cuza nodded his response as he spoke under his breath. "The new governor approaches."

Manaen quickly glanced up and saw Pontius Pilate standing in the arched doorway. With equal subtlety, Manaen observed, "He's military. See the knee-length tunic, the purple stripe along the hem of his toga and those military sandals." There was no time to say more.

Servants scurried to take the reins of their horses.

As Pilate came within speaking distance, both men formally bowed and exchanged proper greetings. Without further conversation, Cuza and Manaen followed the new governor of Judea into the heated area of the palace where guests were entertained.

"Welcome!" Procila hurried forward to greet Phasaelis. Joanna pulled the curtains aside and assisted the royal wife of Antipas as she stepped down onto the pavement. "Our home in Caesarea is modest." Procila understated the magnificence of the palace that Herod the Great had constructed. Insincerely apologetic, Pilate's wife continued, "This is not Rome, but every comfort we have is at your disposal."

"Do you have a bath?" Phasaelis asked. "Three days of dusty travel—well, you understand."

"I will tell the servants to build a fire and heat the rooms. Let me show you to your quarters," Procila led the way while Joanna and Lila gave quick directions to the servants who had traveled with them. Then both ladies hurried to catch up and walk respectfully behind the wives of the two most powerful men in the region.

"Do you like this room?" Pilate asked as he sipped his warmed wine.

Cuza briefly glanced at the mosaic floor, the cleanly plastered walls and the arched ceiling before responding, "The view is everything. What can match reclining after a delicious meal and sipping warmed wine while the sun is dipping into the western sea?"

"I have been here many times." Manaen subtly asserted his lengthy association with the family of Herod.

"Ah, yes, you and Antipas have been together since birth," Pilate repeated the information he had been given prior to this visit.

"My mother nursed both of us," Manaen replied.

"Almost," Pilate emphasized the word before adding, "like brothers." He took a few more sips of wine and then asked Cuza, "Have you heard from Antipas? Has he communicated from Rome or Capri?"

"His ship could enter this harbor any day," Cuza answered.

Pilate shifted a little uncomfortably and Manaen caught the movement.

"Antipas knows during a time of transition he needs to be present to oversee the interests of the emperor." With one sentence, Manaen softly pushed his point. The Herods always had direct access to the emperor.

In the changing room of the royal bathhouse, Joanna assisted Phasaelis as she removed the long piece of fabric that draped beautifully from her shoulder and looped gracefully around her slim body. Lila then lifted the full-length sleeveless gown that covered her mistress's short linen tunic, and then her short tunic. Joanna turned and offered Phasaelis a lightweight cloak made of Egyptian linen. "Will this be enough covering for a little exercise?"

Phasaelis nodded as she allowed Joanna to place the cloak over her shoulders and to secure it with several jeweled pins.

Lila began to undo the braiding in her mistress's hair while Joanna removed her own clothing until she was wearing only a simple tunic. The three women began to walk briskly around the colonnaded chamber, pausing now and again to stretch. "Traveling in those curtained chairs was very confining," Phasaelis commented.

"Stretching every limb as far as possible feels delicious," Lila added. Their exercise was cut short when Procila arrived with servants carrying towels, containers of oils and perfumes, combs, and sponges.

"Come." Procila led the way into a heated room where long benches were draped with smooth sheets of crisp fabric. "My servants have just the right touch. They will oil your body and scrape away the dirt from this journey. Just lay down on one of the benches."

Without any shyness, Procila unfastened and then dropped her own cloak. Naked, she walked over to one of the benches. "In Rome, the ladies often get together at a bath. We have the most delicious times. We don't even bother with cloaks." She stretched out and her servant began to massage her skin with oil.

"This is Judea," Phasaelis softly stated, "and I am Nabataean not Roman. I will be more comfortable with a little covering as we move from room to room in the bath. And I prefer that my own attendants see to the bathing process." As she spoke, she moved to one of the benches. Joanna stepped forward to remove her mistress's cloak and strategically drape her exposed body with a towel. Then Joanna stepped back while Lila began to oil Phasaelis's skin and to scrape away the dirt with a thin curved piece of metal. After Lila had completed oiling and scraping away the dead skin and dirt, Joanna held the cloak like a curtain, in front of Phasaelis while Lila poured warm water over her mistress from head to toe. Then she slipped a clean short tunic over her head.

"The next room is quite hot," Procila warned as she led the way into a very steamy room.

Joanna could feel the heat from the fires that burned beneath the floor stones not far from this room. If it had not been for the thickness of the double-soled sandals each woman wore, it would have been impossible to walk on that floor. She held Phasaelis's hand as her mistress stepped down into the hot water in the pool. Then she stepped away, allowing Procila, who had also entered the pool, to hold a conversation with Phasaelis.

Sitting on a bench near the wall, sweat beaded on Joanna's forehead and trickled down her face. One of Procila's assistants came over and sat beside her. "When our mistresses move back into the warm room for a final massage and a light supper, we can soak in the baths.

"If I get permission, I will welcome that refreshment," Joanna replied.

"Permission?" Procila's servant laughed lightly.

"Permission is given for many things these days. Did you know the emperor has given Herod Antipas permission to marry his brother's wife?"

"Where did you hear such a tale?" Joanna incredulously asked.

Before she could get more information, Joanna saw Phasaelis moving to leave the pool of hot water. Immediately, she hurried to her side with a helping hand and a dry towel.

"Come," Procila motioned as she spoke. "A dip in the cool water will revive us." Without any covering, the wife of the governor of Judea hurried ahead into the chamber where both the water and the air were cool and stimulating after the heat of the previous chamber.

Joanna wrapped Phasaelis in a dry towel while whispering to her mistress, "Is the visit going well?"

"Procila is telling me about the party life in Rome. Evidently, Antipas was at every party she attended."

"It is important to see and meet the people who are in power," Joanna commented. "I'm sure that is the reason your husband attended so many social functions. Let's hurry into the cool room before the steam in here overpowers us." Both Joanna and Lila propelled their mistress into the next chamber.

Procila was already stretched out in the shallow pool of cool water. Phasaelis, still properly covered by her short wet tunic, stepped into the pool and sank into the water beside her hostess. Joanna overheard her ask, "Tell me Procila, what have you heard about events on the Isle of Capri?"

Carefully, Joanna stepped back and leaned against the cool stones of the chamber. She could see that Lila was deep in conversation with another of Procila's servants.

"This is not good. This is not good," Joanna whispered to herself. "I wish I could speak to Cuza right now."

The centurion Longinus first viewed the sacred city of the Jews by the light of a half-moon. The limestone walls picked up the luminescence of the night so they seemed to glow with a light that was supernaturally their own. As the centurion led his troops on their silent march toward the city, an unnatural chill went through his body, like a premonition that supernatural experiences were waiting for him in this city.

Pragmatically, he shook off those nonsensical thoughts. He dug his heels into the flanks of his horse and rode ahead to signal the guard to open the gate of the Roman fortress attached to the Temple complex and overlooking the northern entrance to the city.

"Who approaches?" a sentry challenged.

"Longinus of the Italian Regiment. I bring fresh troops and orders from your new governor, Pontius Pilate."

Longinus could hear the massive wooden gates opening. Torch light suddenly illuminated the darkness. Longinus moved his horse to the side as he watched the one hundred men under his command. With typical Roman discipline, they marched four abreast up the stone ramp. At the entrance, the standards briefly dipped and the posted guards saluted, fist to chest.

Longinus, militarily erect on his horse, followed his men. In the vast courtyard of the fortress, his men remained in formation, waiting for orders. "Place the standards!" Longinus ordered.

There was a sudden scurrying as soldiers, their heads covered with animal skins, marched double quick to post the long poles topped with Roman eagles and images of Emperor Tiberius on the upper ramparts of the fortress.

From the corner of his eye, Longinus saw one of the soldiers, a regular at this post, slip away from the courtyard. Moments later, the commanding officer was hurrying into the courtyard, still rubbing sleep from his eyes.

Longinus remained on his horse. He was not meeting this man as an equal. Without a word of greeting or acknowledgement, he pulled a parchment scroll from a pouch attached to his belt. Imperiously, he handed Pilate's handwritten orders to the commander of the fortress.

Briefly, the commander read the orders, then he looked up at Longinus. "The ceremony to turn command of this fortress over to you will take place now. I do not want to be the Roman in charge when the light of dawn hits those standards." He turned to give a few orders to his men, and then he turned back to Longinus, who had dismounted and now stood at his eye-level. "Fresh from Rome, I hope the new governor knows what he is doing."

A trumpet sounded. It echoed through the long stone corridors of the military barracks. With oaths and a little confusion, six hundred soldiers, mostly Syrians, jumped out of their beds and quickly dressed in military garb. Muffled drums called the men into formation. In less time than it takes to bake a flat cake in a hot oven, seven hundred men stood in precise rows in the courtyard of the fortress.

From opposite sides of the paved area that was the staging arena for all operations, Longinus and the commander of the Fortress of Antonia faced each other. To the beat of the drums, they approached each other with uniform strides. When they met, eye-to-eye and face-to-face, the commander thrust into Longinus's outstretched arm a bundle of silver arrows. "The command of this fortress is yours. You are responsible for these men and for the peace of Jerusalem. May the gods be kind to you."

Longinus yawned. It had been a long march. His own men were sleeping. He had posted fresh troops from the fortress, a double guard prepared to respond to any uprising. Now he waited for dawn.

Torches burned in the courtyards of the Jewish Temple. Standing beside one of the standard bearers on the rampart overlooking the Temple, Longinus could just make out the magnificence of the columns, the white floor stones, and the golden altar where coals glowed like the gold-plated crown on the small rectangular building where the Jews conducted their secret ceremonies. Speaking to the soldier beside him, Longinus remarked, "I read when General Pompey took the city he went into the most sacred and secret chamber of this Temple. He went into the place where their God is said to reside. There was nothing there. It was an empty room."

The soldier responded, "I hope you are not thinking about going into their sacred building. The emperor has given them the right to kill anyone, even a Roman, who places one foot in their sacred areas. Signs are posted throughout the Temple complex."

Longinus did not respond to the soldier, but he stored the information in his mind as he turned to study the eastern horizon. Pale grayness softly radiated from behind the dark hills. From the highest point on the Temple, a solitary silver trumpet announced the beginning of a new day. Longinus turned his attention back to the Temple courts. He could see teams of white-clad Levites working together to open the massive Temple gates. Near a pool of water, the lamb for the morning sacrifice was being examined and then washed. It was a calm, efficient scene. Briefly, Longinus considered delegating responsibility to a junior officer and getting some sleep.

"Sacrilege!" An alarmed voice suddenly pierced the early morning quiet.

The new commander of the Roman fortress stared down to see a man looking up at the freshly placed standards. Quickly, the man covered his eyes while he screamed, "The law of our God has been defiled!"

There were more angry voices. White robed men began rushing into the courtyard that faced the northern wall. Longinus did not understand everything the men said, but their body language spoke volumes. Every priest and every Levite abruptly stopped their morning routine. Some fell to their knees and ripped their clothing. Others ran to notify higher Jewish officials.

"These people are not a military threat," Longinus sarcastically commented to the standard bearer who stood beside him. "Look at them, running around like ants when their nest is disturbed!"

A soldier from the gate hurried forward and handed the commander a rolled parchment. "The images must be removed from the city immediately!" Longinus read the message that had been sent to him by the highest ranking Jewish priest, a man named Caiaphas.

"Bring me a parchment," Longinus responded. "I'll send him an answer, 'The standards remain by order of Pontius Pilate, the new governor of Judea.' Then I am going to sleep. Wake me if there are any violent protests."

As the messenger hurried away, Longinus took one last look at the chaos in the Temple courts. His eye caught the eye of one white-robed priest. The priest was looking up at the offending images. The man was shouting in Hebrew, the language of their scriptures. "*You shall have no other gods before me. You shall not make for yourself an idol in the form of anything in heaven above or on the earth beneath or in the waters below. You shall not bow down to them or worship them; for I, the LORD your God, am a jealous God.*"[1]

"What is that man saying?" Longinus asked the standard bearer who stood beside him.

"It is the law of their God," the experienced foot soldier answered. "Their God is a god who cannot be seen, and they believe his name is too holy to be spoken. I have been at this post for several years. I have seen their feasts and their passion for their God. It is a greater passion than any religious passion I have ever witnessed."

"Look," Longinus pointed. "See, they are closing the Temple gates. They will not be worshiping today. Their passion is not as great as you think."

Just after the time of the morning sacrifice, the beggar, Ichabod, was carried to his usual spot by the Beautiful Gate. Strangely, the ornate gate was closed. The beggar was puzzled and wondered if there was wisdom in allowing himself to be left for the whole day. He noticed there were people on the street. A few were climbing the steps, equally puzzled by the closed gates. Ichabod decided to remain for the morning. He sent his father's servants home and settled himself into the well-worn leather chair that was both his vehicle of transportation and his seat. Strategically, he placed his beggar's pot where it would be noticed by anyone who ventured up the steps for a closer look at the closed gate. Then he waited.

Normally, at this hour the famous rabbis began their leisurely strolls to the Temple to meet and instruct their disciples. He could expect groups of two or three to stop on the steps and converse, then to pause and drop a coin in his beggar's pot as they passed through the gate. But this morning, everyone on the street seemed to be in a hurry. Two members of the Sanhedrin stopped at the foot of the steps. Ichabod could not hear their conversation, but their body language revealed they were both anxious and agitated.

A few men stopped and joined their conversation. Their voices grew louder, and the beggar could now pick up snatches of their angry exchanges.

"We'll send a delegation to the emperor."

"Tiberius promised we could worship our God with no interference from Rome."

"*You shall not make for yourself an idol in the form of anything in the heaven above or on the earth beneath or in the waters below*!"[2] The well-known teacher, Nicodemus, had moved up the steps above the distressed gathering. He raised his voice to be heard above every other voice as his first finger jabbed the air in the direction of the Roman fortress attached to the Temple complex. "The eagle of Rome! The face of Tiberius! They are on the fortress wall! They are overlooking the courts of our God!"

Young Gamaliel, who came from the most prominent family of rabbis, stepped up beside Nicodemus. He also spoke to the swelling crowd, "Those images can be seen from nearly every part of the Temple!"

Elders, priests, Levites, and rabbis along with their disciples continued to fill the street below the steps that led to the Beautiful Gate.

"We're going to the governor's palace!"

"We will appeal to Pontus Pilate!"

Nicodemus and Gamaliel urged the incensed and determined men to be unwavering.

"We will be there in three days, and we will stay until we get an audience with the governor."

The last comment Ichabod heard was, "Pilate will have to listen to us!"

The street emptied, and the beggar found himself sitting alone by the Beautiful Gate. "If I had legs like other men," Ichabod mused, "I would go with those men. I would confront the new governor with the rights the emperor has given the Jewish nation. I would defend the law of Jehovah." Then, he let out a long discouraged sigh. "I am a cripple and a beggar. That is the will of Jehovah for me." Alone on the now empty steps, Ichabod looked at the sun. He knew the gates would remain closed, and no one would be admitted to the Temple courts while such desecration was on display. He also knew he would not be carried home until the sun reached its zenith.

"Phasaelis, I do not know how much truth we have heard over the past few days," Joanna held her mistress's hand while Lila dabbed her tear stained face with a cool cloth. "Sometimes, stories are told just to cause distress."

"Why would Procila make up such a story?" Phasaelis cried.

"My husband of twenty years wants to put me away so he can marry his half-brother's wife! I was twelve when I was given in marriage. Antipas made a written agreement with my father. It includes a statement that says I can never be put away. Antipas can have concubines. He can even have other wives, but I am always the royal wife."

Joanna heard a knock at the door. She answered it.

Cuza motioned for his wife to step into the corridor. "We have news. Antipas's ship is in Cyprus taking on supplies," he informed. "It is a slow, heavy galley so it will be at least a week before he arrives."

"From Procila's servants, we have heard the most distressing news...," Joanna relayed the information.

"It is most likely true," Cuza responded as he recalled the last directive he had received from the ruler of Galilee.

"Phasaelis wants to leave at dawn. She does not want to return to the palace at Tiberius. She wants to go to the fortress that borders her homeland. She is hurt, and she wants to stand on its walls and see the desert lands of her people."

"She should go," Cuza said. "It would not be good for her to confront Antipas or meet Herodias in this palace. The servants will travel with you. Manaen and I will stay to escort Antipas back to Tiberius."

Joanna nodded, and then she returned to prepare her mistress for the trip.

Manaen and Cuza stood at an upper window in the palace that belonged to the governor of Judea. "It's been nearly a week," Manaen pointed out the window as he spoke to Cuza. "Those protestors are not going away."

Cuza sucked in his breath as he gazed down on more than two hundred Jewish men, important men. The entire leadership of the Jewish nation was sitting in silent protest. The courtyard was packed. "Let's see how the new governor handles this situation," Cuza commented.

"I think the new governor caused the situation," Manaen responded. "I understand he foolishly sent the Roman standards into Jerusalem."

"I can see our new governor has given a great deal of attention to studying the people he intends to govern," Cuza asserted with undisguised cynicism. "Has he come out to address this crowd?" Cuza asked.

"No, he is ignoring them." Manaen answered.

"Ignoring them?" Cuza gasped. "Does he know this is not a protest of workers? These men are the rabbis and leaders of the nation! I recognize some of them. That man"—Cuza pointed—"is the high priest Caiaphas, and next to him is his father-in-law, Annas. There is Simon the son of Hillel. He's the new president of the Sanhedrin. Pilate needs to listen to these men if he is going to govern this country!"

"Look!" Manaen pointed to the edge of the crowd, to men in ill-fitting robes with swords beneath their clothing. "Those men are not Jews!"

"Pilate is infiltrating the crowd with his soldiers. They've put robes over their uniforms, but it's not much of a disguise," Cuza added.

"There's going to be a bloodbath," Manaen muttered under his breath.

"Can we stop it?" Cuza asked.

Quickly, Manaen turned to a servant and said, "Take a message to the governor. Tell him I expect Antipas will arrive today."

Before the servant could relay the message, Manaen and Cuza saw the new governor of Judea step onto the balcony that overlooked the crowded courtyard. His judgment seat was put into place, and Pilate sat to rule on the matter at hand.

In response, the men in the courtyard stood.

"How long will you camp at the entrance to my palace?" the new governor imperialistically demanded.

"Until the standards are removed from our holy city," the president of the Sanhedrin stepped forward as he responded.

"You are a conquered nation," Pilate replied. "The standards will remain in Jerusalem."

"Oh no!" Cuza gasped.

The Roman soldiers who were around and throughout the crowd threw off their robes and raised their swords. Instantly, each Jewish protestor dropped to his knees, bent his head to the ground, and bared his neck.

One lone voice spoke. It was Rabbi Nicodemus. "We would rather die than desecrate the law of Jehovah."

At that moment, Manaen saw a servant whisper in Pilate's ear. "My message has been received," he said with obvious satisfaction. Never taking his eyes from the governor, Manaen continued, "Pilate cannot afford for Antipas to arrive on this scene. He cannot afford for the man who is a favorite of the emperor to report a slaughter of this magnitude. His governorship would end before it began. Manaen saw Pilate jerk his thumb upward, the sign that was used in the sporting arena to indicate a brave gladiator should live. It was an obviously irritated gesture.

The soldiers sheathed their swords, and Pilate gruffly announced, "The standards will be removed." Then, he quickly rose from his seat of judgment, turned his back on the crowd, and reentered his palace.

"That was a bold and shrewd move," Cuza complimented Manaen as he watched the slowly dispersing crowd.

"Never forget," Manaen responded, "I grew up with the Herods."

Chapter 6

A Wedding and a Divorce

At that time the kingdom of heaven will be like ten virgins who took their lamps and went out to meet the bridegroom. Five of them were foolish and five were wise.

—Matthew 25:1–2

"Mary?" Lazarus stepped into the kitchen where his sisters were preparing a meal for the men who were helping Jesus put a new roof on the donkey barn. "I have received a message from Jonathan."

Immediately, Mary squealed and jumped to her feet. The wooden bowl that had been in her lap tipped over and the dough she had been kneading flopped onto the floor tiles.

"Mary!" Martha protested her sister's impulsive carelessness.

"Jonathan is coming for you tonight." Lazarus grinned as he delivered the news. "Prepare your bridesmaids. Pack your clothes."

Mary squealed again as she impulsively hugged her older brother and then turned to hug her sister Martha. One look at Martha's no-nonsense face and the fresh dough resting on the dusty floor quelled the squeals in Mary's throat. Mary's arms dropped into a helpless apologetic pose. "I'm sorry about the dough. I won't eat. There will be enough for Jesus and the workmen," Mary said as she looked at the dough that remained in her sister's wooden bowl.

Martha's heart softened. Her heart always softened when Mary was repentant. "Go, prepare for your wedding procession. I can get a servant to quickly make another batch of dough."

"Jesus is checking the wagon wheels now," Lazarus added. "We will pull the wagon up next to the house so you and the servants can load all your belongings."

"I need a messenger!" Mary breathlessly announced. "I have ten bridesmaids, and they have to dress and bring their lamps. And they need to gather in the courtyard to wait until Jonathan arrives with his party."

"Toma's son, Seth, has been helping the men all morning. I'm sure he can deliver your messages," Lazarus suggested.

Mary squealed excitedly again as she ran out of the kitchen.

Still smiling, enjoying his youngest sister's excitement, Lazarus turned to Martha. "Just make a light meal for the men. I will send the workers home early so we will be ready to go to Jerusalem with the wedding procession."

With the help of one of the workmen, Jesus pulled the heavy wagon close to the main house. Servants were already piling everything Mary owned on the mosaic courtyard stones.

"Yeshua?"

Jesus heard Father God call his name. Straightening up from moving the wagon, he paused and listened.

"Come away and sit with me," God invited.

Jesus noticed a shaded bench close to the gate. Waving his helper back to the roofing job, Jesus settled himself to converse with his Father.

"I want to speak to you about your wedding," God initiated the conversation. "I am arranging your marriage. Your bride, like Mary, will have turned down many offers of marriage. She will be willing to wait beyond all reason for her perfect bridegroom.

She will endure mocking and slander for the joy of sharing her future with you."

"How will I recognize my bride?" Jesus asked.

"She will bring you everything she owns. Nothing will be held back."

Jesus looked at the growing piles of items Mary was bringing to her new home. He wondered if the wagon could carry so many things. At that moment, Mary popped her head out the door and spoke to the servants who were helping her, "Be careful with the drinking cups. Jonathan cannot drink from chipped cups, and shake the dust out of those blue draperies. They are for Jonathan's house."

"Everything Mary owns is for Jonathan. She would even give her life because his love is so precious to her. She keeps his promise with her, the price he paid—ten pieces of silver. She has sewn those coins into the headpiece she always wears. See the alabaster bottle of fragrance around her neck? It reminds her that her betrothed is a sweet fragrance. Before you return to your position in heaven, your betrothal will be complete. Pieces of silver will be paid. You will drink the cup, and you will leave with your bride my fragrant Spirit of comfort and power."

Comfort, comfort my people, says your God. Speak tenderly to Jerusalem and proclaim to her that her hard service has been completed...[1] The words of the prophet Isaiah rolled through the mind of Jesus. *For your Maker is your husband—the LORD Almighty is his name—the Holy One of Israel is your Redeemer.*[2]

"Sons and daughters of Abraham, you are my bride," Jesus spoke tenderly as if all the descendants of Abraham were embodied in one beautiful young woman, and that young woman was sitting beside him. "*With everlasting kindness I will have compassion on you.*[3] *As a bridegroom rejoices over his bride, so will your God rejoice over you.*[4] I am your kinsman redeemer."

The Holy Spirit responded by enveloping Jesus in prophetic vision. Glorious scenes of heaven displaced the reality of Earth and flesh. High and lifted up, Jesus shared the throne with his Father the Eternal One. Trumpets sounded, choirs sang, he saw twenty-four royal attendants and four magnificently unusual creatures fall on their faces worshiping the Triune God on his throne. And filling an infinite space before the glorious throne stood a multitude dressed in pure white linen. In his glorified body, Yeshua-Jesus rose and stepped away from the sapphire throne. His arms were stretched out and welcoming. There were scars on the palms of his hands.

"Hallelujah!" the response from the multitude was like loud peals of thunder and cascading water. With blazing scared feet, he stepped forward again. "My bride!" His warm words caressed each individual. "You have made yourself ready. Come, share the wedding banquet with me. Share the wedding week and the intimacies of the bridal chamber with me. You are mine and I am yours. We will always be together."

As the vision ended and Jesus came back into the dullness of the courtyard, the Spirit of God spoke, "You have seen those who I am inviting to your wedding feast—the Wedding Supper of the Lamb." Jesus was surprised to find that evening had fallen. The courtyard was filling with young girls wearing garlands of flowers and carrying little flickering lamps. From across the courtyard, Lazarus called, "Jesus, are you coming with us? I have a wedding garment for you. I don't know when Jonathan will arrive, but we will be ready."

"Yeshua?"

Jesus woke immediately and sat up on the cushions that had become his makeshift bed while waiting for Mary's bridegroom to arrive.

"The bridegroom has been delayed," God informed. "Go out and speak to Mary. Tell her to believe every promise Jonathan has made."

Quietly, Jesus stepped out of the formal banquet room where he had been sleeping and began to stroll through the courtyard of the estate. The bridesmaids all lay on pallets near the water jars. Their lamps had gone out and they were sleeping in their wedding garments. Lazarus was in his own bed. Jesus could hear his snores through the open window. Near the gate, a slight movement caught Jesus's eyes. His keen ears picked up a few tiny sobs.

"Mary?" By the light of the moon, Jesus could see Mary sitting on a bench near the gate. She was not sleeping. He moved to her side and extended his hand. "Mary, why are you weeping?" He took her young hand in his large work-hardened hand.

"Jonathan has not come." More sobs shook her body. "I don't know what has happened to him."

"He has been delayed." Jesus spoke with such certainty that Mary stopped crying and looked into his face.

"How do you know?" Mary asked.

"God woke me and said, 'Go tell Mary that Jonathan has been delayed.'" Jesus smiled broadly as he continued, "God saw your tears. He knows how deeply you care for Jonathan. He has ordained this marriage for you." Reaching past Mary, Jesus pulled the latch string, and the gate swung open. "Look down the road."

"I see torches!"

"The wedding party is coming. Go wake your family and your bridesmaids," Jesus directed.

"The bridegroom is coming!"

Jesus heard the faintly heralded announcement, and then he repeated it at the top of his voice, "The bridegroom is coming! Wake up! Prepare!"

Immediately, the courtyard came alive, but Jesus was not part of the activity. The Holy Spirit had called him away from the preparations.

"Your own bride will wait until the night is nearly past. She will weep and despair. Doubt will assail her. I, the Comforter, will come to her just as you came to Mary tonight."

"We need more oil!" Five of Mary's bridesmaids suddenly rushed past Jesus and out the gate.

"Not everyone who waits for the bridegroom will have sufficiently prepared to endure," the Holy Spirit continued his commentary. "When the bridegroom is at the gate, those who are not prepared will not be able to join the bridal party. A day of joy for some will be a day of great disappointment for others."

The courtyard on the estate of Lazarus was suddenly filled with boisterous young men. A beautifully decorated sedan chair was lowered to the ground, and Mary, so radiant that she glowed through the veil that covered her face, stepped forward to meet her bridegroom.

For a hushed moment, Mary and Jonathan faced each other. Only Mary's veil separated the two.

"Don't be a Jacob!" a rowdy voice broke the silence.

"Lift the veil, Jonathan!" another voice concurred.

"Make sure you have the bride you paid for!" Everyone laughed.

Smiling, enjoying the excitement and joy of the moment, Jesus watched as Jonathan reached forward to lift the veil.

"Only the bridegroom can lift the veil." The Holy Spirit spoke into the mind of Jesus. "For now, and until the day of your wedding, humanity will only see you obscurely. But on that day when you return to Earth for your bride, the veil will be removed, and she will see you clearly."

One of Jonathan's groomsmen moved the torch closer so Jonathan could see the face of his bride. Mary smiled. Jonathan smiled back. Their eyes held each other until someone called out, "It is already past midnight!"

Jonathan drew back the curtain on the sedan chair, and Mary seated herself for the journey back to Jerusalem. Strong young men shouldered the chair. The five remaining bridesmaids carefully held their lamps while they began precise and practiced dance steps. Exuberantly the procession exited the courtyard.

Jesus followed, walking with Lazarus and some of the men who had come from Jerusalem.

"Jonathan loves Mary, and Mary loves him," Jesus commented to no one in particular, yet he received a response.

"They are children. They think their feelings are important. Jonathan needs to establish his business. Mary needs to have babies," a well-dressed man critically pointed out. "Neither one has a solid, practical head!"

Immediately, Jesus sensed a harsh coolness and knew those critical words were inspired by spirits called Jealousy and Bitterness.

Before Jesus could respond to the man, Lazarus jumped into the conversation, "Jesus, have you met Simon the wine merchant? He is Jonathan's older brother. Simon, this is Jesus the carpenter from Nazareth. Jesus put an addition on the main house, and now, he is directing my servants as they reroof the old donkey barn. He has promised me, no more leaks!"

Jesus acknowledged the introduction, and then he asked Simon, "How is your wine business doing?"

"At the end of the last growing season, I had an excellent crop. I produced enough wine to satisfy the Jerusalem merchants, and I managed to export a lot of the wine that has been aging in the caves on my estate," Simon responded with obvious satisfaction.

"Toma took it off his hands," Lazarus inserted a little information into the conversation. "I witnessed the bargaining. Two gladiators in a Roman theater could not have dueled more intensely!"

Intent on responding to Simon's initial comments, Jesus said, "Simon, you are looking at Mary and Jonathan the same way you look at your ledger sheets. Jonathan is just starting his business, and he has little to show. His assets would probably fill less than a page. But tonight, he is the wealthiest man in this wedding procession. He has hope and plans for the future. He has faith in his new wife that she will do him good and not bring evil into their home. And above all, he has love. The challenges of life are guaranteed to everyone. Only love will see them through the difficulties that lie ahead. Love *always protects, always trusts, always hopes, always perseveres.*[5] God has blessed Mary and Jonathan with love for each other."

"Jonathan has also been blessed with a wealthy older brother. He wants me to help him build a secure storage room on his shop." Simon steered the conversation back into his own self-interest. "Carpenter, how much would you charge to do the job?"

I would need standard wages for two laborers and a professional carpenter, in addition to materials. The job would probably take four days," Jesus answered.

"There are men who work for less than standard wages," Simon challenged.

"Yes, but usually they are inexperienced. Sometimes, they make up the difference by using flawed materials," Jesus responded. "Good men should be paid standard wages for quality work and quality materials."

"I would be a poor man if I paid all the men who work for me a standard day's wage." Simon chuckled to himself as he pointed to his younger brother at the head of the bridal procession. "That young man will find out he can't buy and sell with dreams and impractical emotions," Simon gruffly stated.

"It all depends on where he builds his home," Jesus responded. "Each kingdom has its own currency. To be great in the Kingdom of God, one does not need to buy and sell merchandise. One only needs to trade in faith, hope, and love."

"Your thoughts are too abstract for me," Simon replied dismissively.

"Here is something not so abstract," Jesus continued the conversation with a revelation from the Holy Spirit. "On your left arm, there is a worrisome lesion. Since before the Feast of Esther, it has not healed."

Simon gasped and by the light of the torches, Jesus observed the color had drained from the man's face.

"How do you know that?" he fearfully demanded.

Without answering his question, Jesus continued, "You fear you have somehow contracted leprosy. Since money cannot bring about a cure and hope is worthless to you, the outcome will be as you fear."

"No!" Simon deigned the words Jesus spoke as he turned and hurried ahead to walk with someone less disturbing.

"Jesus?" With one word, Lazarus questioned the exchange that had just taken place.

"The Eternal One knows every man's thoughts and secrets. At times, he reveals them to me," Jesus answered his friend's unspoken question.

Repeated shofar blasts interrupted all conversation. Someone shouted, "Open the gate and let the bridegroom enter!"

The door in the city wall beside the massive wooden and brass gates was opened and the bridal party squeezed through to continue on to the house Jonathan had built behind his perfumer's shop.

"It is done!" Antipas pushed his signet ring into the soft wax that held the rolled parchment closed.

"Don't you want a lawyer to read over this decree?" Cuza cautiously asked.

"I have permission, personal permission, from the mouth of the emperor. As of this moment, Phasaelis is no longer my wife," Antipas declared.

"Exactly what is her status?" Manaen asked.

"Ummm," Antipas considered his answer. Then he said, "Royal concubine."

"And," Manaen pressed, "what are the rights and privileges—"

Cuza injected, "As well as the duties of the royal concubine? We have not had such a titled person. I am the one who oversees protocol and disbursements from the royal treasury. Just what is Phasaelis now entitled to?"

"Get our marriage agreement from the room of documents. She can have whatever her father and I agreed to," Antipas stated with a little exasperation.

"Cuza and I have carefully read the document," Manaen responded. "We read it after we received your first communication regarding Herodias."

"So, why are you asking me all these questions?" Antipas demanded.

"The marriage contract clearly states that Phasaelis can never be divorced. She must always have the title of royal wife," Manaen carefully explained.

"She can live in any palace that belongs to the Herods. She can have servants and some access to the treasury, but Herodias will not take second place to anyone! And Tiberius has made a decree that nullifies this old contract! Are there any more questions?" Antipas demanded. Then looking directly at Manaen he added, "If Phasaelis objects, remind her. My father would not have given her a decree of divorce or a palace to live in. He would have had her head cut off."

"I remember your father well," Manaen responded, "and I can explain to her in great detail. Historically, in the family of Herod, both wives and sons who have outlived their usefulness have been killed to make way for their replacements."

"The woman should be grateful," Antipas puffed up a little as he spoke. "Tell her I am a magnanimous ruler. Emphasize my generosity. Also, let her know that over the years, her services have been more than satisfactory. I may come to her again in the future."

With carefully set, non-expressive faces both Cuza and Manaen nodded their understanding. Formally, they bowed and exited the room. In the corridor Herodias, a picture of high Roman fashion passed the two officials. Glances were exchanged, but nothing was said.

As Cuza and Manaen continued to walk toward their offices her shrill and demanding voice followed them, "Well, Antipas have you ended your marriage to that Nabataean woman?"

Manaen winced, but he did not comment until they were well away from the royal chambers.

Cuza was the first to make a remark, "I don't think Herod's half-brother Philip is going to make a fuss over this arrangement."

"The wives of the Great Herod would never have dared to speak to him in such a demanding tone," Manaen stated. "I am surprised Antipas allows it."

Then both men turned to the task of penning a message that would accompany the divorce decree.

Kheti walked with Nodab near the front of the camel caravan as it made its way along the Roman road that ran east from Sepphoris. "This will be my last trading journey," Kheti informed his young partner. "Toma will soon recover from his encounter with the bandits, and I will then leave the traveling to both of you. As for myself, I have my eye on a little shop in Jerusalem. I can sell our caravan wares there. I also expect a percentage of the profits from each journey."

"Discuss the financial arrangements with Toma." Nodab diverted the conversation by pointing to several sedan chairs stopped by the side of the road. "Even royalty must stop and deal with the demands of their bodies," he commented.

"It looks like the caravan of an important person," Kheti observed. "Three sedan chairs, mounted soldiers, wagons of relief bearers. I see several women."

Before Kheti's trading caravan actually reached the point where the royal caravan had stopped, a mounted soldier rode out and blocked the road. Looking down from his horse he declared, "Your caravan will have to wait until Phasaelis, the royal wife of Herod Antipas, has resumed her journey and has moved well beyond the stench of your camels."

"Will the wait be long?" Kheit asked.

"She has just received a messenger from her husband, the king. She is reading the parchments now." The soldier then asked, "Where are you taking your goods?"

"First to Jericho, then we will travel south to Petra," Kheti responded.

"Wait!" the soldier restated his order, and then he galloped over to another officer. Curiously, Kheti and Nodab watched as information was passed from person to person. After a little time, a small rolled parchment was passed from hand-to-hand. The soldier on horseback returned to Kheti and Nodab. "When you arrive in Petra, deliver this parchment to the guard at the palace gate. Do not read it. Do not fail to deliver it."

"This is important?" Kheti inquired.

"It is a personal message from Phasaelis to her father King Aretas."

"I will be honored to deliver her message," Kheti responded.

"Phasaelis said not to delay you so your caravan may now continue on its journey." The soldier pulled on the reins of his horse and moved his animal to the side of the road.

Kheti tucked the parchment into the folds of his belt, and Nodab signaled for the caravan to move forward.

"We are resting at the Jericho palace," Joanna penned a message to Cuza. "The journey has been long and exhausting. After receiving your message, Phasaelis wept for the remainder of the journey. Traveling seemed nearly impossible. Anger has now replaced her tears. She has been very vocal about this breech in her marriage contract. She has threatened to have her father defend her honor with his army. Keep Antipas and his new wife in Tiberius until we are able to move on to the desert palace at Machaerus. Phasaelis is anxious to continue, but the bearers need to regain their strength. I am sending this message by currier. There will be time for you to send a reply before we resume our journey." Joanna signed her name and rolled the parchment before sealing it with the seal of her mistress.

Chapter 7

John the Baptist

There came a man who was sent from God; his name was John. He came as a witness to testify concerning that light so that through him all men might believe. He himself was not the light; he came only as a witness to the light.

—John 1:6–8

Near the river crossing, Longinus dismounted and tied his horse to the twisted trunk of a wild olive tree. With the experienced eye of a soldier, he scanned the crowd gathered there.

Where the road dipped into the murky water of the Jordan River, the men who made their living ferrying travelers from one side to the other had tied their long flat boats to stout posts that marked each anchorage. Higher on the bank, some Jewish priests and scribes from the Temple huddled in worried conversation. Closer to the river, a few soldiers loitered. Longinus could tell by their uniforms that they were Syrians in the service of King Herod Antipas. The rest of the milling crowd seemed to be comprised of common Jewish folks, standing in small groups, conversing, and waiting.

Waiting? Longinus rolled the word around in his military mind. What are all these people waiting for? With his back to the river, he continued to study the steadily expanding crowd. Why has such a mixed group of people gathered at this isolated river crossing?

Unexpectedly, the conversations ceased. Longinus looked around. He could sense the anticipation of the people, and he could also feel eyes on his back. With his hand ready on the hilt of his sword, he quickly turned and came face-to-face with a strangely hairy, dark-eyed man. Only two paces separated Longinus from what appeared to be a desert wild-man. The man's black beard, heavy with particles of desert sand, was the longest the clean shaven centurion had ever seen, and the rest of the man's hair seemed to have never been touched by either a razor or a comb.

Without blinking, the strange man stared at Longinus, and without flinching, the centurion returned the stare. "What is your name?" the centurion gruffly demanded.

Unintimidated by the Roman uniform, the man who wore a simple camel-skin garment cinched at the waist by a wide leather belt, returned the centurion's steady gaze. Unnerved, the commander of the Antonia Fortress had to briefly glance away. At that moment, the roughly dressed man answered, "I am John son of Zechariah." Then in the same breath, John turned his own question on the Roman officer, "Why have you come to this river crossing?"

Longinus was startled by the question. Ordinary Jews did not question Roman officers. But this unusual man exuded such power and confidence! Longinus shivered involuntarily. Many times he had looked deeply into the eyes of other men. In battles, he had seen Fear. In Roman society, he had seen Arrogance and Dishonesty. But he had never before seen eyes like the eyes of this man. There was no Fear. There was no Pomposity. Powerful authority and directness seemed to radiate through this man's eyes.

Longinus answered carefully. "I heard large crowds were gathering here, and I came to see if Rome needs to be concerned."

"Rome needs to be concerned. Jerusalem needs to be concerned. All of Israel needs to be concerned." As he spoke, John the son of Zechariah stepped into an open space at the river's edge. He raised his voice so everyone could hear, "The Eternal God sits on his heavenly throne. From there he observes the Earth. His eyes examine all of humanity. He sees those who love violence." John looked pointedly at the sword that hung from the centurion's belt.

"I don't know this god you are talking about," Longinus responded.

"He knows you," John replied. "He sees every action and hears every thought as if it were spoken. One day the just and the upright will see his face and rejoice. The wicked will be tormented with fiery coals and burning sulfur."

Turning his attention away from Longinus, John pointed to the representatives from the Temple in Jerusalem. "You are poisonous snakes, serpents cursed for deceiving men and women who are created in the image of God!"

Startled, the priests and scribes ceased conversing among themselves. One brave priest responded, "Are you pointing at us?"

Longinus quickly stepped to the side where he had a panoramic view.

"That troublemaker has no respect for you, the representative of Rome," a Lying spirit shot the thought into the centurion's startled mind.

"He targets your enemies." The Holy Spirit correctly focused Longinus on the huddled Temple representatives.

And Longinus vividly recalled recent tedious and sometimes heated meetings with various delegates from the Temple establishment.

John was still speaking directly to those men from the Temple, "Sons of Levi, who have inherited the Temple and its ceremonies, who stirred your heart to come to this river crossing? Do you recognize the contamination of sin in your life? Do you fear the Day of Judgment? It is a day when evildoers will burn. Priests and teachers will fall under a curse from the Almighty because they have misled the nation."

This crazy man is not the enemy of Rome. He is the enemy of my enemies, Longinus surmised. Settling down on an old timber, the centurion made himself comfortable as he continued to observe the various groups that had gathered to hear this fascinating individual.

"Are you the Messiah?" one of the men from the Temple asked.

"Why do you ask me such a question?" John challenged. "Are the blind receiving their sight? Are the lame walking? I am a voice calling out, "Clear a road in the desert for God! Level a highway for our God!" Before the new governor travels from Caesarea to Jerusalem for the next festival to the Lord, work crews will fill in every pot hole and level all the bumps in the road he will travel. Consider me the foreman of the work crew that is preparing for the arrival of God on earth."

"We are already God's chosen people. Isn't that enough?" an inquiring voice shouted.

"It is not enough that you are from the bloodline of Abraham. The inheritance God promised to Abraham's descendants will not be yours unless you turn your lives around," John answered.

"We are Abraham's seed!" one of the Temple representatives objected, while another hurled a stone in John's direction.

The prophet dodged the stone and then verbally hurled back, "Are you the only people capable of keeping the laws of Moses and bringing pleasure to the heart of God? From the stones that cover this hillside, God can create a new generation of sons for Abraham! Like fruit trees that do not produce, you will be cut down and thrown into the fire!"

The Temple representatives began lobbing stones in John's direction.

Laughingly, John dodged a few more. The crowd also began to laugh and mock the well-dressed men from the Temple who couldn't throw a stone well enough to hit a barge tied to its anchorage. The verbal exchanges between the people and the Temple representatives became more heated.

Longinus responded by standing and making his presence obvious.

The men who represented the Temple clearly understood the centurion's body language. They dropped the stones in their hands and resorted to shooting malevolent looks at the desert preacher.

"Stop living for yourselves," John turned from the Temple representatives to a group of tax collectors. "Collect only the taxes Rome requires plus a fair wage for each day you work. Don't you know every shekel you collect is recorded in the ledgers of heaven?"

Longinus noted the men appeared alarmed at the thought of heavenly documentation.

"What can we do?" one of the tax collectors shouted his question.

"We have not kept accurate records so we are unable to repay those we have overcharged," another tax collector added.

"Repent and from this moment, turn away from your former corruption," John answered. "Follow me into the river. We will wash away your old way of life. Each of you can go under the water, a dishonest man. The current will carry your dishonesty away and you will come up from beneath the water, a new man, reborn into good deeds."

Longinus watched as the prophet waded out into the river. The tax collectors followed him. One by one, each man stood in front of the wild-looking man, ducking completely under the murky waters of the slowly moving river. As each man broke the surface of the water, John placed both hands on either side of the individual's head and looked him directly in the eyes. "You are clean! Go from this place and live a holy life. Then our holy God will want to come and dwell with us."

"Can we be people that the God of Abraham wants to live with?"

Longinus turned to see the Syrian soldiers from Herod's regiment were asking the question. Interested in the Jewish preacher's response, the centurion turned his attention back to the fascinatingly strange man who stood knee-deep in the river.

"Don't threaten the people, don't make false accusations, and be satisfied with your wages," John replied.

"How should we live?" the crowd asked.

John answered, "Share your food with those who are hungry, and if you have two coats, give one to someone who does not have a coat. Come"—John gestured to the crowd as he stepped into deeper water—"be immersed in water. Act out your commitment to a new and changed life."

Longinus watched as the people surged toward the river. Other men, students of the Jewish prophet, stepped into the water. They also began speaking new life into each person as they came up from beneath the water.

Longinus heard hoof beats on the dry dirt road. Turning his head away from the amazing scene in the river, he saw a royal caravan approaching—several sedan chairs, horses, wagons filled with relief bearers, all accompanied by a military escort. Immediately, the centurion stood. Hurrying to his horse, he quickly mounted and rode back to meet the caravan. As Longinus approached, the caravan came to a halt. The sedan chairs were lowered and one woman stepped out of each curtained chair. Immediately, Longinus knew these women must be from the court of Herod Antipas.

The Roman centurion approached the ranking soldier at the front of the caravan and introduced himself, "I am Longinus, of the Italian Regiment and commander of the Antonia Fortress. May I assist you at this crossing?"

"Is the crowd hostile?" the ranking officer in charge of the escort asked.

"No," Longinus replied. "These people have gathered to hear an unusual preacher, and they are washing in the river."

Longinus noticed that the three royal women had walked down the road. They now stood close to his own horse watching the curious spectacle that was taking place in the river. He overheard one of the women say, "I would like to hear this unusual man. It is late afternoon. Tell the captain of the guard we will camp here for the night. In the morning, we will cross the river and continue on our journey."

Overhearing the women, Longinus said to the captain, "I would be honored to escort the royal women to the riverbank. This desert preacher is most interesting."

A campfire burned in front of the tent that had been erected for the ladies of the royal court of Herod Antipas. Joanna and Lila sat with Phasaelis. "I want to speak to that desert teacher," Phasaelis stated. "He seems to know what is right for each person. I want to know is my husband, Antipas, right?"

Joanna responded, "I see a small fire close to the river. That might be the prophet's fire. I could send some of the soldiers. They could bring him to you."

"Do that," Phasaelis directed.

John looked up. His hand, filled with dried desert locust, stopped in midair between his mouth and the burlap sack where he stored this high-protein staple. Four soldiers had stepped into the light of his campfire. He looked directly at the soldier whose helmet indicated he was the captain of the detail. "How can I help you?" John calmly asked.

"The royal wife of Antipas has camped nearby," the captain replied. "She has requested that we escort you to her campfire. She wishes to speak with you privately."

For a moment, John did not respond.

"Go," the Holy Spirit affirmed the request.

Tossing the handful of crunchy insects into his mouth, John rose. He shook the sand from his rough garment and from his long beard. Then by torch light, he followed the soldiers down the dark road to the royal campsite.

Curiously, John stepped into the firelight, while the soldiers who had escorted him stepped back into the dark perimeter of the camp. Three women sat on a heavy carpet in front of a tent. Respectfully, John bowed.

One of the women indicated he should be seated.

John squatted on his heels and waited.

"I am Phasaelis, the wife of Herod Antipas." The dark-skinned woman in the middle spoke first. "I listened to you this afternoon. You gave good advice to many different people in many different circumstances. How do you know what to say to all these people?" she asked.

"God, the God of the Jews, speaks to me through his Holy Spirit," John answered.

"I am not Jewish," Phasaelis continued. "Would your God speak to you regarding my situation?"

"Yes," John replied. "God is the God of the Jews and the God of the nations."

"Do you read?" the royal wife asked.

John answered, "I read Hebrew, Aramaic, and Greek"

"My husband, the king of this region, recently sent me a message." Phasaelis picked up a rolled parchment with a broken royal seal and handed it to John. "According to your Jewish laws, according to your God, can the king do this to me, and how should I respond?"

There was a long silence. The fire crackled. The women waited. John read the parchment. Then he stood and paced beside the fire. Finally, he stopped and turned to Phasaelis. "In Jewish culture, if a man puts his first wife away, she returns to the home of her father. According to the law that was spoken by the mouth of God Almighty and recorded in the third book of Moses, *If a man marries his brother's wife, it is an act of impurity; he has dishonored his brother. They will be childless.*[1] The Lord further commands,

'Keep all of my decrees and laws and follow them, so that the land... may not vomit you out.'"[2]

"What does that mean?" Phasaelis asked.

John began pacing again, and as he paced he spoke the words the Holy Spirit pressed into his mind, "Your husband the king has transgressed the law of God, and the law of God is greater than any word of permission that Antipas has received from the emperor of Rome. Your husband is in danger of losing the land God has allowed him to receive through the graciousness of the emperor. *Do not be deceived: God cannot be mocked. A man reaps what he sows. The one who sows to please his sinful nature, from that nature will reap destruction.*[3] Every man and every woman, even kings and their royal wives, must stand before the righteous God of the universe and be accountable for the way they have lived their lives. Those who repent of their misdeeds will be welcomed into the Kingdom of God, but those who live for themselves, disregarding the laws of God, can only expect torment. They will never know the pleasures of living with God."

"I have been very angry with Antipas," Phasaelis stated. "I have not seen him, but I have considered having poison put in his food. I have considered paying some servants to strangle him in the night. But you are saying your God will torment and destroy him for me?"

"*In your anger do not sin: Do not let the sun go down while you are still angry*[4]," John admonished. "Also, do not act on your desire for revenge. Leave room for God's wrath. Study the history of our kings. You will see that the Lord holds them responsible to set an example for the nation. Our God is an avenger for the abused and the innocent."

"I repent of my anger," Phasaelis whispered. "I will be satisfied with God's wrath."

"And possibly the wrath of your father," Lila added.

"Yes," Phasaelis agreed. "When my father, the king, receives my message he will send troops to avenge my honor. Antipas does not understand the code of honor the Nabataean people live by."

John spoke again, "The God of the Jews is also a God of honor. He speaks through his servants and honors the words his servants speak in his name. So, *This day I call heaven and earth as witnesses against you,* Herod Antipas, *that God has set before you life and death, blessings and curses. Now choose life, so that you and your children may live* [5] in this land. If your husband Antipas does the honorable thing, if he repents and sends Herodias back to her husband, and if he returns you to your position as royal wife, then blessings will rest on the house of Herod. But if he refuses to acknowledge the word of the Lord for him that I will publicly speak, then he will be expelled from the land, and he will die among foreigners. He will be a cursed man."

Turning back to Phasaelis, John added. "I will be at the river at dawn. Come down to the water and be immersed for the repentance of your sins. Then you can proceed and live a righteous life before the Lord. The sin of your husband will not be attached to you."

Phasaelis nodded her agreement and then dismissed the compelling desert preacher with a regal hand gesture.

John moved away from the royal campsite. Walking confidently down the dark road, he returned to the coals of his own fire. Geber was squatting by the glowing coals.

As John walked into the camp, the old Essene teacher looked up and stated, "I was concerned. Recently, a crowd gathered on the steps of the Beautiful Gate to hear two of our Essene friends. The commander of the Roman fortress saw that gathering as a threat to Rome. Both men are in prison now."

"That same commander was here today," John responded as he squatted so he could speak eye-to-eye with the man who had been his mentor since childhood. "I do not fear Rome and its soldiers. Neither do I fear our King Herod Antipas, but I would tremble not to speak the words the King of the Universe puts in my mouth. Tonight, I heard the word of the Lord for Antipas, the son of Herod the Great, and tomorrow, I will speak it publicly. Every person who comes to this river crossing is drawn here by the Spirit of God. I give a warning. I give a choice. I expose sin, so it can be dealt with. The words I speak are not my own. If the words were my own, then I would be terrified."

Geber softly responded, "Jeremiah spoke the uncompromising word of God. The king tormented him. Isaiah fearlessly rebuked King Manassah—"

"Our historians record that Isaiah was placed in a hollow tree and sawed in half," John finished Geber's warning. Then he added, "But remember, Ahab tried to kill Elijah. He could not find the prophet, yet at the command of the Lord, the prophet could find him. Elijah never died. He flew to heaven in a chariot of fire to be with the Lord forever." John stood and picked up his thread-bare cloak. He wrapped it around his shoulders. "I can sleep. My life is in the hands of God." He lay down on the sandy bank of the Jordan close to his smoldering campfire. Geber also lay down, and both men slept through the remainder of the night.

The early morning sun bounced off the ancient wind-carved cliffs of Petra. Kheti and Nodab led their camel caravan down the paved and colonnaded street that led away from the palace of King Aretas IV to the upper marketplace of the Nabataean capitol. Arriving at the market, the two merchants quickly negotiated a place to display their goods, and with the help of their drovers began to unload and lay out merchandise that desert dwellers rarely saw.

Kheti opened a basket of dried sardines, and housewives immediately gathered. He had just made his first sale when a detail of six palace guards burst into the market. "Where are the merchants who were just at the palace?" their captain loudly demanded. "We are looking for an old Egyptian and a young Jew with a camel caravan." The soldiers ran through the market, and with the help of willing informants quickly converged on the spot where Kheti and Nodab were deep into the bargaining process.

"Come with us!" The soldiers surrounded Kheti.

The points of their spears pricked the fabric of his desert robes. Still, Kheti responded with the unshakable poise of an experienced trader, "Does the king wish to see our merchandise?"

"His general demands that you answer a few questions," the soldier in charge responded.

"I will come," Kheti raised a calming hand.

The royal guards responded to the gray-haired Egyptian by lowering their spears.

"Allow me to bring a gift." Kheti stepped over to a large basket and lifted the lid. He brought out a bolt of fine Egyptian linen.

Nodab stepped over to his trading partner ostensibly to hand him a skin filled with aged wine.

Kheti took the opportunity to whisper, "If I don't return by morning, come to the palace and bring the silver coins."

Nodab nodded as he glanced warily at the soldiers and then at the high desert rocks that surrounded the city of Petra—escape was out of the question. Setting his face to mirror the mask of serenity that he saw on his partner's face, Nodab backed away. Without protest, he watched Kheti step forward. The palace guards formed an escort completely surrounding the aging trader. With military swiftness, the soldiers efficiently moved Kheti down the road and out of sight.

At the palace, Kheti found himself taken without delay into the presence of the head of the Nabataean army. With typical eastern manners, Kheti bowed low at the same time offering the bolt of Egyptian linen and the skin of fine wine as gifts for the general. The general curtly nodded, and one of his soldiers stepped forward to receive the gifts. The general responded with a quick perfunctory bow, and Kheti stood up, facing one of the most powerful men in the region.

"Are you the man who delivered this message from the royal wife of Herod Antipas?" the general abruptly asked as he held the opened parchment so Kheti could see the item he was referring to.

"Yes," Kheti answered. "Our caravans met on the road, and one of her guards gave me the parchment. He asked that I deliver it to her father's palace."

"Did you read it?" the general asked.

"The seal was not broken when I delivered it to the guard at the palace gate," Kheit responded.

"Then you do not know that the favorite daughter of our king has been dishonored and mistreated by her husband?" the general questioned.

"I was not aware." Kheti bowed again as he spoke, allowing his gesture to demonstrate his sympathy for the Nabataean princess.

"Phasaelis wants to return to her own country, to her own people and her family. She does not wish to remain, disgraced and abandoned in a foreign land." As he spoke, the general dropped the parchment on the table and paced a little as he pondered the problem. "Herod Antipas will not just allow her to leave, and I cannot just cross the border with troops at this time."

Kheti bowed again as he asked, "How can I be of service?"

"I want you to return to Israel immediately. Some of my soldiers will be your drovers. Your caravan will carry gifts from King Aretas to the royal wife of Antipas who by now is confined to the palace-fortress at Machaerus not far from our border. Once your caravan is within the palace walls, ask for Lila. She is a Nabataean attendant to the wife of Herod Antipas. My soldiers will hide Phasaelis and her attendant in the large baskets that your camels carry. You will bring both women back across the border. Before you enter the winding canyon that leads to this city, I will meet you with proper transportation for the daughter of the king." The general looked hard and direct at Kheti. "Are you willing?"

"I have just begun to sell my merchandise," Kheti cautiously informed.

"What is your merchandise worth?" the general responded. "I will purchase everything, but you will not be paid until you return with Phasaelis, the daughter of our king."

"My drovers? My partner?" Kheti cautiously asked.

"They will remain in Petra, well treated and provided for," the general replied.

"I need my drovers and my partner," Kheti negotiated. "I need men who are experienced with the camels and donkeys. I need men who know how to load and unload properly."

"Your partner is Jewish," the general raised his objection.

"That does not make him a friend of Herod Antipas," Kheti replied. "My partner is loyal to his God. He is only disgusted by a king who brings the morals of Rome into the land God gave his people."

"Go with your drovers and your partner, but I will keep half of your caravan until you return," the general countered.

"Agreed," Kheti responded with another short bow.

Chapter 8

The Feast of Weeks

Do not think that I have come to abolish the Law or the Prophets; I have not come to abolish them but to fulfill them.

—Matthew 5:17

"Jesus?" Larazus stuck his head in the door of the carpentry shed that was next to his donkey barn. "Are your ready to leave for the Temple? I want to arrive before the loaves go into the ovens, and I want to give my first fruits to the priests before the crowds become overwhelming."

"Almost, just two more nails." Jesus continued attaching a sturdy piece of leather to an unusual chair frame.

"What is this?" Lazarus stepped closer and ran his hand over the smooth wooden poles that protruded from the chair's frame.

"A gift for the beggar who sits at the Beautiful Gate," Jesus answered as he stepped back to study his work. With experienced hands, he quickly tested every joint. "It is his transportation and a comfortable way to sit above the hard stone steps."

"The beggar's name is Ichabod," Lazarus informed. "He's been sitting at that same spot for as long as I can remember, well, over twenty years."

"Yes, I've been making or repairing a chair like this for him every three or four years since I was about fifteen," Jesus responded.

"You know that beggar is from a wealthy Temple family," Lazarus informed. "That is the reason a place is reserved for him at the Beautiful Gate. His father and his brothers are the perfumers for the Temple. They could pay you."

"This is not about money," Jesus casually responded. "This is about God's compassion for a man who was robbed at birth. I know about his family. To them, Ichabod is an obligation and an embarrassment. As a cripple, he can never enter the Temple. He can never participate in the family business." Jesus picked up the chair, easily hoisting it over his shoulder. "Let's go!"

The two men strode toward a waiting wagon as Lazarus continued their conversation, "And there is always that nagging question. Everyone wants to know the answer, but they are afraid to ask: Who sinned? The parents? The child in the womb?"

Lazarus climbed into the wagon and moved the two sheaves of wheat that he was taking to the Temple for a wave offering. Jesus handed him the chair, which he wedged between sacks of produce. Pausing as he worked, Lazarus looked directly at his friend and asked, "So, who sinned?"

"Adam," Jesus answered with total confidence.

Lazarus carefully placed a sack filled with wrapped loaves of bread on the seat of the chair before jumping down next to Jesus. He signaled to his servants who prodded the oxen into rambling movement.

"Explain?" Lazarus asked as the two men fell into step, easily passing the slow-moving oxen.

"All curses were attached to the seed of Adam when he sinned. Some curses are activated by man's choices. Others are initiated by the deceiver who was in the serpent," Jesus answered.

"This curse?" Lazarus inquired.

"I blame Satan, the deceiver," Jesus answered.

For awhile, the two friends walked in silence. Then Lazarus spoke, "The rock wall of the old barn collapsed and fell on me. My bones were crushed, and I was dying. You touched me, and you spoke the words of God over me. Suddenly, my body was whole. Why is this chair the only thing that you do for the beggar? Can't you touch his bones and make them straight? Can't you do for him what you did for me?"

"I did nothing for you. I only obeyed the commands of God. I moved my hands as God instructed. His healing power flowed through them. I spoke the words God gave me. It is the word of God that breaks the curse. I can do nothing except the things God through his Spirit speaks to me." Jesus smiled at his puzzled friend. "And now that it is the Feast of Weeks you show your gratitude to God by bringing a double offering to his Temple."

"It is nothing more than the requirement of the law," Lazarus protested.

Jesus quickly replied, "When you obey the laws of Moses, which are the words of God, God works through you to break the curse. I noticed you left a generous amount of wheat in your fields for the poor. Is not food both healing and life-sustaining? So you are also a worker of miracles and a giver of life."

"We count seven weeks plus one day from Passover and then God commands us to gather in Jerusalem for the Feast of Weeks." Lazarus thought aloud. "We thank God for the wheat harvest. We bless the poor. We remember the giving of the law."

Jesus added, "Fifty days after Israel left Egypt they received the law. They heard the voice of God like thunder from the top of the mountain. He spoke each law...," Jesus continued to speak. He continued to walk.

But the Holy Spirit had taken him back to that time when his own voice as Yeshua the Creator had announced "*I am the LORD your God, who brought you out of Egypt, out of the land of slavery.*"[1] From the burning summit, Yeshua surveyed all the descendants of Jacob, nomads—fresh out of slavery. They were the hope of his kingdom, but they had no awareness of kingdom living.

"*You shall have no other gods before me.*[2]" Kingdom instruction began.

The earth shook and the people trembled. Satan, with his evil court, fled to a distant mountain refuge while every demon that had found a dwelling place in the camp escaped to hide in nearby caves.

"*You shall not make for yourself an idol in the form of anything in heaven above or on the earth beneath or in the waters below.*"[3] Yeshua spoke in the language of the Israelites and at the same time in every language that would ever exist. These laws were for all mankind. His plans were for all the descendants of Adam. This ragtag group at the base of the mountain—it was a starting point.

"*You shall not bow down to them or worship them; for I, the LORD your God, am a jealous God, punishing the children for the sin of the fathers to the third and fourth generation of those who hate me, but showing love to a thousand {generations} of those who love me and keep my commandments.*"[4]

Lazarus listened as Jesus quoted the familiar laws and then explained. "The law is like a barrier between God's people and the Evil One. The people fortify the barrier when they keep God's laws. They tear down the barrier when they break God's laws. The wise man has written, '*Whoever digs a pit may fall into it; whoever breaks through a wall may be bitten by a snake.*'"[5]

"Bitten by a snake?" Lazarus questioned.

Jesus answered, "A snake bite—a curse. First a choice is made. As Moses said to the children of Israel in the wilderness, '*This day I call heaven and earth as witnesses against you that I have set before you life and death, blessings and curses. Now choose life, so that you and your children may live.*'"[6]

"Ichabod could not make a choice in the womb," Lazarus brought the conversation back to their previous topic.

"And neither of his parents had the opportunity to make a choice," Jesus added. "The choice was made many generations before."

"Where is the fairness of God?" Lazarus questioned.

Jesus answered, "It is not unusual for God through his Holy Spirit to lead his people into physically challenging situations. Remember, God himself led Israel through the Red Sea and into the desert. Within a few days, they had only poisonous water to drink. The people were distraught and suffering. God showed Moses a tree that he cut down and threw into the water. Then the water became good to drink, and the people lived. The tree demonstrated the fairness of God."

"Now your words have really confused me," Lazarus threw his hands in the air as he spoke.

"Ichabod is like Israel in the desert. He is thirsty and waiting for life-giving water. He is waiting for the tree that will turn his bitter water into sweet water. Until that time comes, I will make him as comfortable as possible."

Lazarus shook his head again. "My heart agrees with every word you have said, but my mind does not understand any of it."

"Just believe whether you understand or not," Jesus replied.

Both men stepped off the road and sat under a shade tree until the wagon caught up with them. Then together, they went through the city gate and on to the pools to immerse themselves so they could enter the Temple.

"I smell baking bread, roasting meat, burning fat—"

"And the body odors of hordes of people," Pilate added his comment to the observations of his wife, Procila. Full of curiosity mixed with caution the royal couple walked along the fortress wall that overlooked the Temple courts. This was their first trip to Jerusalem, their first national feast. Pilate and Procila paused for a better look. "I do not believe I have ever seen so many people in one place," Pilate observed.

Longinus joined them.

"What is your report? How is the city?" Pilate asked.

"The city is full, but the people keep coming. Every road that comes into the city is packed with men, women, children, animals, and wagons full of produce. Should we close the gates?"

"No." Pilate shook his head. "If we close the gates, the people will panic. They will trample each other. Even with the extra troops, I do not believe I could maintain order without bloodshed. Then word would get back to Rome that the new governor could not maintain the peace."

"Look," Procila countered. "The people are peaceful. They are happy. Friends are greeting each other. Look at that mountain of produce. The people keep bringing baskets and baskets of food! The priests lift each basket above their heads and wave it before adding it to the pile. There is no threat."

"Money is coming in too!" Pilate pointed. "The treasury boxes are in those alcoves. Bags and boxes of coins are steadily coming in."

"Three times a year the people bring in the offerings they have been saving," Longinus informed.

"Animals are even coming in!" Procila exclaimed. "Those priests are taking the lambs two at a time and waving them over their heads before putting them in pens."

"I want to see that priest lift those oxen that are coming in," Longinus jested.

"Do you see who is behind that magnificent pair of oxen?" Pilate asked.

"Herod Antipas," Longinus responded. Then he snidely added, "He is carrying his own basket of produce. I didn't know he was a farmer."

Procila with a woman's eye for detail asserted, "His basket is overlaid with gold, and Herodias is with him."

"I see Manaen and Cuza as well as servants following with more gold and silver baskets, all heaped with produce," Pilate noted. "With gifts like that, the Temple establishment will overlook his marital indiscretion."

"He is united with the Jewish leaders in ways we can never be," Longinus commented.

"Antipas is a son of Herod the Great, and he is a man worth watching," Pilate agreed. "I need to keep him close. He has the ear of Rome, and at the same time, he is lining the pockets of the Jewish leadership. See if you can get a message to him. Invite him to eat in the fortress with me tonight."

"There are Jewish women in the party," Procila noted. "Could your messenger ask if one is willing to spend the evening with me?" Procila asked. "I have many questions about the Jews and their rituals. I want to speak with someone who can explain these things."

Pilate turned to Longinus. "Ask which woman in Herod's party is well versed in the rituals of the Jews, and invite her to dine with my wife."

"I will send a trusted Jewish servant," Longinus replied before saluting and turning to carry out his orders.

Holding Ichabod's new chair high above his head, Jesus worked his way through the masses of people pushing toward the Beautiful Gate. He could see the beggar squatting beside his old chair. The crowds were so great there was little room on the wide top step for the beggar to sit. It looked like he could easily be pushed off and trampled.

"Shalom, my friend." Jesus used his muscular body to create a barricade between the ever-moving crowd and the beggar. "I brought you a new chair. You can use the old one for firewood."

Ichabod's face broke into a snaggle-toothed smile. "I was wondering how I would manage when the leather seat completely separated from the frame," he commented. "Then you came, like an angel from God."

"God does not miss any man's need, even in a crowd of this size." Jesus squatted down next to the beggar. "Have the worshippers been generous today?" Jesus asked.

"There are too many, too eager to enter the courts with their offerings. They do not even see my little bowl," Ichabod responded

Staccato trumpet blasts followed by the sweet clear lilting of flutes filled the air. Those people who were still on the steps surged forward, hoping to find a place in the Temple courts where they could hear the reading of the laws God had spoken from the mountain.

Responding to the Holy Spirit insight that Ichabod's heart was moving with the people, longing to see the rituals for this holy convocation, Jesus began to describe what was now taking place at the altar. "Two large square loaves of yeast bread have been taken from the oven. Still warm, they are placed in the arms of the officiating priest, who leads a procession up the ramp to the platform beside the altar of burnt offering. There, he lifts those two large loaves and waves them before the Lord. Their aroma ascends with the smoke of the offerings that are still burning on the altar. The loaves are then carried back down the ramp and taken into the Chamber of the Hearth, where they will be eaten by the priests with the peace offerings. Next, the officiating priest lifts two lambs above his head, waving them before the Lord. The lambs are then slaughtered, the blood drained and taken to the altar. After the lambs are skinned, cut, and each part salted, they are carried up the ramp to the platform by the altar. Once again, they are waved before the Lord. Those two lambs are a peace offering, so they are also taken to the Chamber of the Hearth where they are prepared for the priests to eat."

"I am a Levite," Ichabod stated. "My father and my brothers, because they are the caretakers of the incense, will eat the bread and the meat from these offerings." The beggar sighed. "I have always wondered what it would be like."

In his mind, Jesus saw the throne room of his Father in heaven. He saw the books that were always open, and he saw the angels who faithfully record the deeds and thoughts of men. He saw the angel who stood by the Book of Life where the names of all the righteous were recorded. Jesus then responded to the beggar, "Thousands of men and women have walked through the Temple gates today, but that does not mean their names are recorded in the books of heaven. *The LORD does not look at the things man looks at. Man looks at the outward appearance, but the LORD looks at the heart.*[7] God has seen your heart"—Jesus looked directly into Ichabod's eyes—"and God is satisfied."

Giving the beggar a warm pat on the back, Jesus then stood and moved back down the steps. Pushing through the crowded streets, he made his way to the bridge that crossed the valley and led to the Mount of Olives. Somewhere over there, he expected to find his brothers and his mother, camping like thousands of other families who had come to the Feast of Weeks.

Dusk had fallen. Small campfires dotted the rock-strewn mountainside. Jesus moved carefully from one campsite to another, looking for the faces of his brothers. At one campsite, he looked into the face of a man who seemed so familiar that he paused.

"Simon, your childhood friend," the Holy Spirit informed.

"Simon? Simon son of Jethro?" Jesus approached the man who quickly jumped to his feet.

"Jesus? Son of Joseph the carpenter?"

Each man grabbed the other by the shoulders and studied how the years had changed their faces. There were so many memories, both good and bad.

"Are you still living in Nazareth?" Simon asked. "Are you a carpenter like your father?"

"Sometimes Nazareth, sometimes Capernaum or Bethany," Jesus answered. "James maintains the shop. I'm more of an itinerant craftsman."

"Your father?" Simon asked.

"We buried him in the cave near the village," Jesus answered.

Then both men paused. There was a moment of silence as each recalled the fathers they had buried. One man had been taken down from a cross. The other had died in his sleep. Both men shared an unspoken understanding.

Simon broke the silence, "We need a carpenter in Cana. I'm a blacksmith who has to double as a carpenter."

Jesus shook his head and laughed. "I'm not your man, but my younger brother Jose—he may want to have his own shop. I'll mention it to him."

A bright light suddenly flared above the Temple courts.

"They have lit the huge cauldrons of oil that will burn all night in the Court of the Women," Simon commented. "Are you going back to the Temple to hear the scriptures read throughout the night?"

"Yes," Jesus answered, "as soon as I see that my family is settled at their campsite."

"I'll see you there." Simon sat back down by his fire.

Jesus noticed a sword lay on the ground beside his childhood friend. "Did you father make that sword?" he asked.

Simon picked up his sword. "No, I did. My heart still burns for the Messiah, for the freedom of our nation. I keep it with me in case I should find the opportunity to fight for our people, to help run the Romans out of this land."

"You always were a zealot like your father," Jesus replied. "I heard that Rabbi Nicodemus and his disciples will be reading from the books of Moses tonight. If you are looking for me, I will be there all night."

Procila led Susanna, lady-in waiting for Herodias, up the narrow stone steps that led to the tower on the wall that the Antonia Fortress shared with the Temple. When they reached the highest level, a guard saluted and stepped aside for the wife of the governor. Both Procila and Susanna stood in quiet amazement.

The scene was breathtaking. Sitting on tall columns, four massive cauldrons of burning oil illuminated the entire Temple complex. The golden light from the burning oil danced around the white limestone walls and columns. The courts were not nearly as filled with worshipers as they had been in the morning. In the Court of the Israelites, a group of men sat on the stone floor. Their heads were respectfully covered with their prayer shawls. One voice could be heard reading from the Hebrew scrolls. From time-to–time, the men responded by swaying back and forth as they chanted prayers in unison.

After observing for a few moments, Susanna whispered, "I fear I may be breaking a law."

"How are you breaking a law?" Procila inquired.

"I can see into the Court of the Israelites as well as into the Court of the Priests. Women are not allowed to enter either," Susanna answered.

"What are they doing?" Procila inquired. "What are they reading? I cannot understand the language. What are they saying?"

"This feast commemorates the time that God spoke the law for his people at Mt. Sinai. The rabbi is reading from the laws of our God," Susanna replied. "The language is Hebrew. It is the ancient language of our people. Only the very educated can read it and understand it well. Most people do not really speak it any more."

"Do you understand what is being read?" Procila asked.

"Yes, this is a very common passage, something that every Israelite memorizes as a child." Susanna began to recite, "*Honor your father and your mother, so that you may live long in the land the LORD your God is giving you. You shall not murder. You shall not commit adultery. You shall not steal. You shall not give false testimony against your neighbor. You shall not covet your neighbor's house. You shall not covet your neighbor's wife, or his manservant or maidservant, his ox or donkey, or anything that belongs to your neighbor.*"[8]

"The laws of your God are broken every day in the Roman Empire," Procila commented. "In the city of Rome, especially among those closest to the emperor, there is no fidelity between husbands and wives. Many lies are told to facilitate gaining favor and power. Even murder is plotted and carried out. Everyone covets power and wealth, but above all, the powerful covet the ear of Tiberius."

"Sad to say, that is sometimes the case among our ruling class also," Susanna said. "But our rulers know better. They know the laws of God, and God will bring judgment on everyone who breaks his laws."

"I wonder what will happen to your mistress and Herod Antipas," Procila challenged.

Both women exchanged meaningful glances as they silently acknowledged how shamefully Antipas had divorced his wife and taken his brother's wife.

"Wait and see," Susanna answered. "My father who has managed property for the Herods for many years has seen much take place that is contrary to our holy laws. Often he has quoted to me the words of God from the fifth book of Moses, *'It is mine to avenge; I will repay. In due time their foot will slip; their day of disaster is near and their doom rushes upon them.'*"[9]

"Do you really believe that?" Procila asked.

"The history of our people and its rulers has proven that the words of God written in the books of Moses and the prophets are true," Susanna answered. Then with a slight challenge in her voice she added, "I suspect the words of God are also true for your society. Our God is not just the God of the Jews. He created the entire world. He also rules the nations, even the Roman empire."

"Can I read these books of Moses?" Procila inquired.

"They have been translated into Greek," Susanna informed. "Tell your husband you want a copy of the Septuagint. Those are the official Hebrew Scriptures in the Greek language. I know you can purchase them in Alexandria, Egypt, probably also in Caesarea."

A silver trumpet sounded to announce the second day of the feast. Those who had spent the entire night reading and listening to the law slowly made their way back to their homes or campsites. Jesus gave Simon a parting embrace and turned toward the triple Temple gate. From that gate he could see across the city walls. The red glow of the rising sun was moving across the valley.

As he had done many times before, the Holy Spirit allowed Jesus to see the warrior angels and the fiery chariots that always patrolled the walls of Jerusalem. Michael raised his sword in silent salute and the glorious host bowed to their Creator.

"The choice is always yours," the Holy Spirit whispered. "Ruler of the Universe or Son of Man."

As always Jesus responded, "I have chosen to live in the heritage of my mother, Mary. I am the Son of Man, a descendant of Adam. At the same time, I know both my divinity and my mission. As the Creator, I spoke the world into existence. I formed the first man and woman, pressing my lips to theirs as I breathed life into their bodies. I could not just let everything fall into the hands of Satan and then be eternally destroyed, so I have come to this world, understanding the weakness of fallen man and determined to restore him to eternal companionship with heaven."

The Holy Spirit continued the conversation, "For many years, you have been teaching informally, explaining the scriptures to whomever would listen. Now it is time for you gain the respect of the teachers in the Temple. Go to Solomon's Porch and sit in the place where the rabbis teach and argue the merits of their teaching. At first, children will gather and sit at your feet. Then I will call the learned men of the Temple to challenge you. Tell them the story of Ruth that is often told at this season."

Unquestioningly obedient, Jesus made his way to the colonnaded portico where groups regularly gathered to hear various teachers. He sat down in the shade of a tall column. A few boys were playing a homemade game with pebbles. "Are you a rabbi?" one of them asked.

Their game paused as all the boys waited for an answer.

"I have not been the disciple of any rabbi, but I have studied the scriptures, and I can tell you one of the stories for this holiday season," Jesus answered.

The boys put their pebbles in the folds of their garments and sat down to listen.

Jesus began. "In the days of our nation before kings ruled and while judges still directed the people, there was a terrible famine in the land. It was more than just a famine of food. It was also a spiritual famine. The word of God was seldom heard. *In those days Israel had no king; every man did that which was right in his own eyes.*"[10]

The compelling voice of a storyteller caught the ears of those close by, and both men and women found places to sit where they could hear a well-told story from their past.

"Elimelech, a father of the royal line of Bethlehem, along with his pleasant wife Naomi and their two sons Mahlon and Kilion were suffering during this famine."

"How do you know that the family was suffering?" someone suddenly challenged.

Jesus looked up to see one of the disciples of Nicodemus waiting for his reply.

"Do not the names Mahlon and Kilion mean weak and sickly?" Jesus countered. "Their parents feared that without proper nourishment both boys would die." Jesus continued his story. "Elimelech left his property in Bethlehem and took his family to the land of the Moabites, who were the descendants of Lot. While the boys grew to manhood, the family lived comfortably. Then Elimelech died. Naomi, in her sorrow, did not return to her family and friends. Instead, she found wives for her sons—Moabite women who had been raised to worship gods that demanded child sacrifices." As he continued the story, Jesus noted that more than twenty people had moved within hearing distance. Also, the well-known rabbi, Nicodemus, along with some of his disciples, had seated himself to critically listen.

"Continue," the Holy Spirit directed.

"Through her sons, the widow from Bethlehem held on to her comfortable life in that heathen land. After ten years had passed, she buried both of her sons, and she had no grandsons to hold her husband's property or to carry on his name. Brokenhearted and bitter, without property or wealth, Naomi began the humbling walk back to the home of her ancestors. Her two daughters-in-law accompanied her."

Reciting word for word from the ancient text, Jesus moved the story along, "*Then Naomi said to her two daughters-in-law, 'Go back, each of you, to your mother's home. May the LORD show kindness to you, as you have shown to your dead and to me. May the LORD grant that each of you will find rest in the home of another husband.' Then she kissed them and they wept aloud and said to her, 'We will go back with you to your people.'*

But Naomi said, 'Return home, my daughters. Why would you come with me?...No, my daughters. It is more bitter for me than for you, because the LORD's hand has gone out against me!'"[11]

In his heart, Jesus felt the emotional pain of the women. From the eternal mind of Yeshua the Creator, the Holy Spirit showed Jesus the first little procession of Jews returning with Ezra from their Babylonian captivity. Then he knew that Naomi was a type of Israel.

The people saw Jesus's eyes were full of tears and they said, "This man is a great storyteller. He feels with his characters."

With his calloused hands, Jesus brushed the tears from the corners of his eyes before continuing the story. "*Then Orpah kissed her mother-in-law good-bye, but Ruth clung to her...and replied,*

'Don't urge me to leave you or to turn back from you. Where you go I will go, and where you stay I will stay. Your people will be my people and your God my God. Where you die I will die, and there I will be buried. May the LORD deal with me, be it ever so severely, if anything but death separates you and me.'[12] When Naomi realized that Ruth had spoken a vow in the name of the God of Israel, she said no more."

"Is there a deeper meaning?" Nicodemus interrupted the story to probe the depth of this man's understanding.

"Naomi is a symbol of Israel in years past, removed from her land by the hand of God. Ruth is a non-Jew, representative of those in the nations who have come alongside to bring about our restoration in the land of Abraham," Jesus answered.

"The story, let's hear the story." A few voices protested the interruption.

Jesus turned his attention back to the people, "*So Naomi, full of bitterness and feeling the weight of God's judgment, returned from Moab accompanied by Ruth the Moabitess, her daughter-in-law.*[13] They arrived in Bethlehem as the barley harvest was beginning.

How fortunate that they arrived when the harvest was plentiful. Ruth, understanding that the workers in the field had to leave anything they dropped for the poor, went into the fields to gather grain. *As it turned out, she found herself working in a field belonging to Boaz, who was from the clan of Elimelech.*[14]

Immediately, Boaz, the owner of the field, took notice of the girl. Her kindness toward Naomi had been talked about throughout the town, and Boaz determined to reward the young woman with extraordinary kindness. *So Ruth stayed close to the servant girls of Boaz to glean until the barley and wheat harvests were finished. And she lived with her mother-in-law.*"[15]

Jesus could see that Nicodemus was listening intently. So he was not surprised when the well-known rabbi interrupted him again.

"If Ruth is symbolic of the righteous gentiles who have befriended Israel and Naomi is a symbol of Israel, who or what does Boaz symbolize?"

"Boaz is a symbol of the Anointed One, the only true kinsman-redeemer for Israel," Jesus answered. Without pausing for more commentary, Jesus continued. "One day, Naomi said to her daughter-in-law, 'Boaz is a kinsman-redeemer for our family. According to the laws of Moses, he can take you as his wife and together you can make an heir for my husband and his property.'"

"What must I do?" Ruth submissively asked.

That night at the threshing floor, Ruth followed Naomi's instructions. After Boaz had fallen asleep, she uncovered his feet and lay down.

In the night, Boaz awoke. *"Who are you?" he asked.*

"I am your servant Ruth," she said. "Spread the corner of your garment over me, since you are a kinsman-redeemer."[16]

Jesus smiled as he lifted the fringed prayer shawl that lay across his own shoulders. He held it out with one arm and covered a child who was sitting beside him.

Everyone understood that this was the garment Ruth desired to be covered with, the one that was symbolic of the protection and provision of God.

"Oh my daughter," Boaz said, "you have pleased me. There is another who is a closer relative. It is his right to take you and produce an heir before it is my right. I will go to him immediately. If I have his permission, I will certainly redeem you."

Everyone, even the rabbi and his disciples, was now listening intently.

Jesus smiled as he described the meeting between Boaz and the closer relative. "The closer relative did not want to produce a child with a Moabite woman Without hesitation he gave Boaz the right to be the kinsman-redeemer. *So Boaz took Ruth and she became his wife. Then he went to her, and the LORD enabled her to conceive, and she gave birth to a son.*[17] The son was named Obed, and Naomi was considered to be his legal mother. Obed had a son named Jessie and Jessie became the father of our great King David."

Knowingly, Jesus looked at Nicodemus. "You have a question for me?"

"Our oral history says that Boaz died immediately after his wedding night. How could he be a symbol of the Anointed One?"

Jesus answered, "It is not a mystery. Boaz died, but his seed lived and inherited the land. The land of Elimolech in Bethlehem has been passed down through the family of King David, waiting for the time when the prophecy of Micah became a reality. *Bethlehem...though you are small among the clans of Judah, out of you will come for me one who will be ruler over Israel, whose origins are from of old, from ancient times.*[18] It has already happened."

Immediately, the Holy Spirit broke into the thoughts of Jesus. "Go to your ancestral town, Bethlehem."

Without further conversation or explanation, Jesus stood and walked away from the people who were asking for another story. With only the slightest glance, he also walked away from Nicodemus and his disciples who were commenting and speculating among themselves as to the identity of this new teacher.

"Shalom!" Jesus called out the typical Hebrew greeting as he approached the home of Toma and Elisheva.

A moment later, the courtyard gate opened and a woman with part of her arm missing shaded her eyes and looked down the road to see who was approaching.

"It is Jesus of Nazareth," Jesus again announced his approach.

The gate closed. A few moments later, it opened again, and Joseph's favorite cousin, Toma, walked painfully out to greet Jesus. He leaned heavily on a crutch and winced with each step.

"Father?" Jesus looked toward heaven. "This man's caravan provided shelter for my family as we traveled to and from Egypt. He lost his own son, his wife, and his mother when the babies were killed in Bethlehem. Where is your compassion? Where is your healing?"

"Everywhere your hand shall touch," God responded, "I have given it to you."

Jesus felt the palms of both hands begin to burn. Eagerly, he moved forward to embrace Toma. "My friend, I heard about your encounter with the bandits." As he spoke, Jesus ran his broad hand along the man's spine, touching as much of his back as possible.

"I feel my health returning at the sight of you." Toma stood a little straighter.

But Jesus could see Toma continued to support his weight with the crutch.

"It has been more than fifty days," Jesus commented. "I thought you would be preparing for your next trading trip."

"When I was a younger man, I could take a beating and heal quickly." Toma shook his head despairingly. "I did not want to give up my hard-earned money. It took a hard blow to my head, and once I was down, they kicked me over and over in the ribs."

Jesus reached out and lightly touched the area that Toma was pointing to. He felt a surge of healing power as it flowed out through his hand.

Toma felt the energy also. His eyes widened, and he looked at Jesus. Old questions and old memories surfaced to form new questions about this new experience with the extraordinary son of Joseph and Mary. Toma straightened up. His crutch fell to the ground, and he turned to ask.

Before Toma could find the words, Jesus asked, "Is your pain gone?"

"Yes!" Toma began walking around, stretching and testing his new body.

"You? You did this?" Toma was stammering for the right words.

"I prayed to God for you," Jesus replied.

And Toma remembered, "Your father Joseph once told me you were a special child, and that your real Father was God."

Jesus nodded. "My Father God healed you."

"Come in! Come in!" Toma continued to test his body as he said, "I must tell Elisheva."

"No," Jesus responded. "I came to see the field of Boaz."

Toma stopped stretching and became the steady businessman. "Your father sold the field to Uncle Shaul. When he died, I inherited the land."

"When the trumpet blows to close the Day of Atonement, the land can be redeemed," Jesus said.

"You are the kinsman-redeemer. The land will be yours," Toma responded with humble gratitude for the health he was now experiencing. "We can sign the agreement today."

"No," Jesus answered. "I only came to walk on the land and to sign the papers that will leave the land with you."

Together, the two men walked toward the center of the town and then down the wide dirt path that led away from town. Toma led the way, stopping at a wheat field that was still being harvested. "My son, Seth, is overseeing the harvest," Toma said.

"That is a big responsibility for a young man," Jesus answered.

"He has taken over many of my responsibilities since my encounter with the bandits." Toma smiled. "I am proud of him." Toma pointed to a young man supervising the workers as they tossed the sheaves onto the wagon. Then Toma turned back to Jesus, "Do you want to see the house your father built? He built it on the foundation that Boaz had laid."

Jesus nodded.

The men continued walking. Toma spoke again, "Did your parents tell you story of the foreign dignitaries who came to see them when you were a baby?"

"Yes," Jesus replied.

"They camped in this field—tents, camels, servants. It was amazing!" Toma recalled. "My wife Sarah used to bring our little son Avrahm. They would walk this very path to your house."

"I know." Jesus put a comforting arm across the shoulders of his older relative. "The angel warned my parents. We escaped. I lived. But your family died." Jesus stopped walking and looked into Toma's eyes. "My mother still grieves for your wife and child."

"The kindness of God has eased my pain," Toma responded.

At the house, Jesus ran his trained hands over the exposed beams that supported the rock walls. "My father Joseph was an excellent carpenter," Jesus remarked.

"The house is rented," Toma informed. "I have all the records."

Jesus just brushed it aside with a wave of his hand. I came to take possession of my spiritual and historical heritage. I do not want the physical property."

Just as they walked to the back of the house, Jesus suddenly stopped.

Puzzled, Toma waited.

"This is the place where the prophet Samuel anointed David to be King of Israel," Jesus spoke what the Holy Spirit had shown him. Then he knelt on that spot and bowed his head.

"In the heavenly realms, the Spirit responded, pouring the golden oil of anointing on his head."

Jesus felt the oil hit his head and roll down his beard, but Toma was not aware that anything had taken place.

Allowing Jesus time to pray, Toma walked around, picking up several small smooth stones. When Jesus stood, Toma offered him the stones. "Who knows, maybe David used these very stones to practice with his sling."

Jesus answered with the prophetic words that the Spirit gave him, "Like David, I will soon face my enemy. I will come to him in the name of the Lord without armor, without the conventional weapons of war. There will be many stones in the place where I will meet him."

Toma did not know how to respond, but Jesus quickly put him at ease. "Come, let us get two witnesses and sign the deed so this land will pass on to Seth."

Chapter 9

The Road from Bethany to Nazareth

"I baptize with water," John replied, "but among you stands one you do not know. He is the one who comes after me, the thongs of whose sandals I am not worthy to untie." This all happened at Bethany on the other side of the Jordan, where John was baptizing.

—John 1:26–28

Squatting by the side of the dusty Jericho Road, Barabbas watched the barren hillside for the signal that a solitary traveler approached. It had been a long day. Many travelers had safely passed by the master robber. They had traveled in groups, some of them obviously armed. So far, there had not been a good opportunity to lift a purse or two.

Shifting his weight, Barabbas glanced at the sun. It was gradually dipping toward the western horizon. He sighed and thought of the desperate men who were expecting he would return with money that would purchase food and other necessities. Those men who looked to him for leadership were short-tempered fugitives, angry men capable of desperate behavior. Only his ruthless resourcefulness allowed him to maintain leadership status among the many thieves and cutthroats who lived in the rugged hills nearby.

From the corner of his eye, Barabbas saw a white cloth waving from a rocky ledge. Immediately, he moved to the wagon and the resting donkey he had strategically placed by the side of the road. With one swift kick, he separated the previously loosened wheel from the axel. Now he appeared to be a traveler delayed by an unfortunate malfunction. Replacing a wagon wheel was a two-man job.

Love your neighbor as yourself.[1] A memory from his childhood, a verse he had learned in the synagogue school, suddenly ran through Barabbas's mind. Every Jewish child learned that verse. It was part of the code of life for the nation. That was the reason he could expect a traveler to come to the side of the road and offer assistance.

Barabbas looked down the road. A man was approaching, a craftsman with a satchel of tools slung over his shoulder.

The sun moved ever so slightly until it was resting on the western hilltops. Barabbas squatted as if studying the severed connection between the wooden axel and the wooden wheel. With a slight turn of his head, he saw the lone traveler was now within a few paces of the wagon.

"Friend," Jesus called as he stepped to the side of the road. "I can help you with that wheel."

Barabbas felt a sudden unexplainable urge to run from the man who confidently approached. But he steadied his unusually jumpy nerves and gestured for the traveler to come to his assistance.

"Do you see the spirits that live with this man?" the Spirit of God spoke to Jesus.

In his mind, Jesus answered, "Yes, I see spirits that turn good men into criminals, and I see the rebellious angels they have called to stand by as reinforcements."

Jesus then remembered the words of Moses. "*Give generously to him and do so without a grudging heart…There will always be poor people in the land. Therefore I command you to be openhanded toward your brothers and toward the poor and needy in your land.*"[2]

"The God of our fathers has smiled on you today," Jesus said as he stepped up to the disabled wagon and pulled a small mallet from his tool satchel. "I am a carpenter, and this is a simple repair."

Dumbfounded, Barabbas could not respond. His feet seemed to have turned into blocks of stone and his hands refused to move. Within the strongholds of his mind, the demonic spirits who usually ran this robber's life found themselves bound by the proximity of holiness.

Jesus spoke again, giving Barabbas directions, "Pick up the axel and hold it level."

Unable to initiate his own actions, Barabbas moved only as he was directed and the wagon was quickly repaired.

Stepping back from the wagon, Jesus took a final look at his work. He gave the wheel a sturdy testing shake and then pronounced, "This is good."

His words sent a shiver through the fallen angels who cowered nearby. Each evil angel remembered when Yeshua the Creator had critically looked at the work of his divine hands at the end of each of the six days of Earth's creation. *And* Jesus, in his Godly creative role, *saw that it was good.*[3] Those words, pronounced at the close of each creation day, now put the divine stamp of approval on the carpenter's repair work.

Jesus then turned to the man whose plans had been revealed by the Holy Spirit. "Friend, I must advise you. Night will soon overtake those who are traveling on this road. There is danger in the darkness; bandits live in these hills."

"Several bandits are watching you now," the Holy Spirit informed.

"Take this purse." Jesus held out the pay Lazarus had given him for the jobs he had just completed on his estate. "Spend the night safely in the inn just up the road."

"No!" Jesus could hear the evil angels scream in protest. He could see the confusion of the demons on the would-be robber's face.

"You will not control this moment!" Jesus directed his nonverbal command to the representatives of Satan's kingdom. With openness and genuine concern for the man who had intended to rob and possibly injure him, Jesus stepped closer to Barabbas. He looked deeply into the man's eyes. "You have taken nothing from me. I am giving this to you." He pressed the bag of coins into the trembling hands of a murderer and a thief.

Then Jesus turned and continued his journey. He would be at Bethany beyond the Jordan before dawn. A few days after that, he would be back in Nazareth.

At the crest of the hill before the road descended through scattered clumps of people to end at the river crossing, Cuza and Manaen reined their horses to a stop. "Why are all these people at this isolated river crossing?" Cuza questioned the scene.

"Look!" Manaen pointed. "There are representatives from the Sanhedrin."

"And there are members of our king's palace guard." Cuza pointed to a group of soldiers. "Local tax collectors are standing close to the river," Cuza observed.

"Wealthy women with their servants," Manaen continued to make a mental list for the report he would give to King Antipas.

"Craftsmen, caravan merchants." Cuza continued scanning and evaluating the crowd. "Let's stay and see for ourselves what or who is the main attraction here."

"The Herods have always been suspicious of gatherings within their territories," Manaen commented. "Antipas will want a full report."

"Rome is equally suspicious," Cuza added as both men dismounted and led their horses to a patch of grass near the top of the hill. Spreading their heavy cloaks on the ground, the officials from the court of Herod Antipas settled down to share a wineskin and observe.

Removing his leather belt, John tossed it over a low-hanging branch before he waded into the quiet pool of water next to the ferry boat crossing. Following his lifelong practice of ceremonial washing, John dipped completely under the water three times. He remembered the story of Naaman the leper who had been healed during the time of Elisha. "Wash and be clean!" John announced as he came up out of the water for the last time.

"It is time for this nation to wash and be clean," the Holy Spirit broke into John's thoughts.

John waded to a rock near the river's edge. With his feet in the water and his back to the people, he sat down to focus on the words that the Holy Spirit had for him. At least a hand's length of both his beard and his hair floated on the water's surface. Every person on the hillside as well as those close to the crossing was aware of John's presence. But no one approached the solitary figure. There was something ruggedly awesome about the man.

"John," the Holy Spirit said his name with lifelong familiarity. "Consider Israel in the days of my servant Ezra. The people had corrupted the nation by taking heathen wives."

In his mind, John opened the scroll and remembered the words he had often copied while living with the Essenes. "*While Ezra was praying and confessing, weeping and throwing himself down before the house of God, a large crowd of Israelites—men, women, and children—gathered around him. They too wept bitterly.*"… "*We have been unfaithful to our God by marrying foreign women from the peoples around us. But in spite of this, there is still hope for Israel. Now let us make a covenant before our God to send away all these women and their children, in accordance with the counsel of my Lord and of those who fear the commands of our God. Let it be done according to the Law.*"

"John," once more the Holy Spirit said his name. "Herod Antipas, the ruler of this region, is insulting me. He is making my name a stench in the court of Aretas, king of the Nabataeans. *Rise up; this matter is in your hands…take courage and do it.*"[4]

With a determined gleam in his eye, John rose from the rock and waded to the shore. Conversations ceased and every eye followed his every movement. Like the ancient prophet Elijah who had ascended to heaven not far from this spot, John fastened his wide leather belt about his waist. Then he threw his tattered camel's wool cloak over his wet tunic. Purposefully, he stepped into the center of the road in front of the boat landing. For a long silent moment, he scanned the groups of people who had gathered hoping to hear him speak the words of God for this time.

Abruptly, he pointed to a group of rabbis, loudly demanding, "Are the words of Moses the words of God for this nation?"

Briefly, the well-known scholars exchanged inquiring glances. Was this a trick question?

"Answer me!" John demanded. "You are teachers in Jerusalem, and this is a simple question."

Rabbi Nicodemus stepped forward. "Every child in every synagogue school knows that Moses wrote the words of God, and those words are the law of God for every descendant of Abraham."

"Are all of the words in all five books of Moses equally law?" John bellowed his next question.

The men who managed the ferry boats stopped working and turned their attention to the dynamic and controversial preacher who had made their crossing his own arena. On the hillside, all eyes turned expectantly to the rabbi whose turn it was to speak. At the riverbank, children stopped playing in the mud, and beside the road, Jesus set his satchel of tools on the ground as he settled himself on the trunk of a fallen tree.

"All five books of Moses are the law," Rabbi Nicodemus confidently responded. "They are equally binding."

"Does the law of Moses bind the king?" John pressed.

Everyone sensed that a significant point was about to be made, and the exchange continued to hold the attention of every man, woman, and child who was close enough to hear.

Rabbi Nicodemus answered by quoting, "*When you enter the land the* L*ORD your God is giving you and have taken possession of it and settled in it, and you say, 'Let us set a king over us like all the nations around us,' be sure to appoint over you the king the* L*ORD your God chooses. He must be from among your own brothers…*" The rabbi paused for emphasis before he continued, "*When he takes the throne of his kingdom, he is to write for himself on a scroll a copy of this law, taken from that of the priests, who are Levites. It is to be with him, and he is to read it all the days of his life so that he may learn to revere the* L*ORD his God and follow carefully all the words of this law and these decrees and not consider himself better than his brothers and turn from the law to the right or to the left. Then he and his descendants will reign a long time over his kingdom in Israel.*"[5]

John turned away from Rabbi Nicodemus. His unblinking gaze settled on two wealthy men who sat near the top of the hill. "Has our king, Herod Antipas, written for himself a copy of the law?"

Both Manaen and Cuza were startled to find that they were now the focus of the interrogation.

Manaen stood and tersely responded. "Our king has a vast library, and within his library, there are several copies of the Law as well as the writings of all of the prophets."

"Does he read them?" John asked.

Manaen answered, "I have seen him read from the scrolls."

"Recently?" John pressed.

"Well, I do not recall a specific time when I observed that he was reading the sacred scrolls." Manaen struggled with his response.

The people snickered.

"By your responses, it seems you must have access to our ruler. Is that true?" John asked.

"Yes," Manaen replied. "I have been his companion since childhood."

"Then you will give him a message," John directed.

"You can be sure our king will get a full report on today's events," Manaen tersely responded.

"Speak these words to Antipas, the son of Herod the Great," John commanded. "*The LORD said to Moses, 'Speak to the Israelites and say to them, 'I am the LORD your God. You must not do as they do in Egypt,*[6] or as they do in Rome!'"

"Who are you to tell our king what he can and cannot do?" Manaen challenged. Cuza then rose to his feet to stand with his companion and reinforce their official presence.

Unintimidated, John continued. "I am the voice God has placed on this wilderness road to proclaim his words to this nation. His words are for the rulers and for the people. In the third book of Moses, it is written, *'If a man marries his brother's wife, it is an act of impurity; he has dishonored his brother. They will be childless.'*"[7]

Cuza gasped under his breath. "How does this man know?"

"The eyes of the LORD are everywhere, keeping watch on the wicked and the good."[8] John spoke the words the Holy Spirit poured into his mind.

"Can the man read my mind? Can he hear the words I whisper?" Cuza incredulously asked Manaen.

"I don't know," Manaen responded under his breath, "but we will hear him and report to the king."

"Yes," John responded again to their private communication. "Tell King Herod Antipas that the Lord says, 'I know you have put away the wife of your youth. I know you have broken the marriage contract that you made in my holy name with her father, the King of the Nabataeans. I know you have taken your brother's wife into your palace. There are no secrets that are not revealed in the throne room of heaven. I say to you, Repent! Return Herodias to her husband and take your wife back into your palace. You must keep all the *decrees and laws and follow them, so that the land where I have made you a king may not vomit you out. You must not live according to the customs of the nations… Because they did all these things, I abhorred them.*'"[9]

"The king has taken his brother's wife!" The words of the wilderness prophet were passed from person to person until the hill was abuzz with speculation and accusation.

"God knows!" John continued to direct his remarks to the officials from the court of Herod Antipas. "And now the people know! Tell your king both are waiting for his response."

"Are you the Messiah?" Nicodemus had stepped forward to pose the question. "Or are you a prophet like Elijah, a man who hears the words of the Lord for an evil king?"

John looked at the crowd. *The people were waiting expectantly and were all wondering in their hearts if John might possibly be the Messiah. John answered them all, "I baptize you with water. But one who is more powerful than I will come, the straps of whose sandals I am not worthy to untie."*[10]

As he spoke, John felt himself drawn to a man who was sitting on a fallen tree trunk not far from the crest of the hill. He looked directly at the man as he continued, "*He will baptize you with the Holy Spirit and with fire. His winnowing fork is in his hand to clear his threshing floor and to gather the wheat into his barn, but he will burn up the chaff with unquenchable fire.*"[11]

As John delivered the words of the Holy Spirit, he watched the man stand and then pick up his carpenter's satchel. A new message from the Holy Spirit suddenly burst into his soul and John shouted, "*I baptize with water…but among you stands one you do not know. He is the one who comes after me, the thongs of whose sandals I am not worthy to untie.*"[12]

John's voice trailed off. He could not speak another word at that moment. He knew that man. John had not seen his cousin Jesus since he was thirteen years old. Yet he was certain of the man's identity. Within his soul, the Holy Spirit confirmed he had correctly identified the man.

Briefly, Jesus waved his hand, acknowledging his cousin John and the Holy Spirit communication both men shared. Then, he turned and disappeared into the crowd.

"Repent! Repent! You are sinners who have desecrated the laws of God." John began to implore the people to make a new commitment to righteousness.

Chapter 10

Escape

So Herodias nursed a grudge against John and wanted to kill him. But she was not able to, because Herod feared John and protected him, knowing him to be a righteous and holy man. When Herod heard John, he was greatly puzzled; yet he liked to listen to him.

—Mark 6:19–20

In the predawn darkness, Joanna, with a small lamp in her hand, walked the long black corridors of Herod's Machaerus Palace. The palace was really an elaborate fortress high on a desert mountain not far from the Dead Sea. "Phasaelis?" Joanna called the name of her mistress over and over. The deposed queen was not in her royal suite. She was not in her luxurious bathing facilities.

Anxiously, Joanna hurried up the stairs that led to the top of the wall and to the three defensive towers guarding the royal dwelling. Near the first tower she saw another small light. "Phasaelis?" she anxiously inquired.

"Yes, Joanna, I am here."

Joanna hurried to her queen's side. Setting down her lamp, Joanna removed her own cloak and put it over the shoulders of her mistress. "It is cold out here. I was worried. The message from Antipas that we received last night—" Joanna spoke in short broken statements.

Phasaelis interrupted, "I am now a prisoner in this palace. My husband, who is no longer my husband, says I must remain here. He says he will provide for all my needs in this place. He does not understand my needs."

The sun began to rise in the east, a golden glow just above the craggy desert horizon. Both women paused and silently watched as the faint golden glow transformed into a glorious ball of fire resting on the brown landscape.

"What have I done that I should be exiled and imprisoned?" Phasaelis asked.

"You have been a faithful wife and an honorable representative for your people," Joanna loyally responded.

"For that, I have been rejected by the king. Now my heart longs for my home and my people," Phasaelis stated as she pointed toward the eastern desert, toward the Nabataean Kingdom bordering Israel.

"Antipas will not allow you to leave," Joanna cautiously stated. "He sent orders to the captain of the palace guard."

"I will leave," Phasaelis quietly but determinedly responded.

"How? Even if you slip out of these walls—the desert, the trek to Petra—it is impossible!"

"I am Nabataean," Phasaelis replied. "I know the ways of the desert."

"We sent your father a message," Joanna tried to delay the escape her mistress was planning. "Have you had a response?"

"No."

"Wait for his response," Joanna urged.

"I will wait a week, maybe two." Phasaelis looked directly into Joanna's eyes. "But one night, you will look for me, and you will not find me anywhere in this fortress. It has to be that way so you cannot be blamed." Phasaelis then smiled and added, "Anyway, you will be leaving soon. You have to return to Cuza your husband and your little boy Casper. You will not miss me."

"What about Lila?" Joanna asked.

"She is also Nabataean," Phasaelis answered. "We are making plans together. She would not fare well if I left her behind."

Joanna nodded her understanding. Then both women stood together in comforting silence as the rising sun warmed the barren landscape. With their eyes, they followed a small caravan of camels plodding steadily along the road from the land of the Nabataeans to the land of the descendants of Abraham.

A small royal contingent reined their horses to stop at the crest of the hill overlooking the river crossing where John was preaching and his disciples were baptizing. While dismounting, Cuza and Manaen exchanged quick glances that said, "We have brought Antipas to this place as he requested, but how will he react to the accusations of this man?" The captain of their guard quickly assisted Antipas in dismounting, and then the captain and his soldiers took the horses, leaving Herod Antipas, Cuza, and Manaen free to give all their attention to the charismatic preacher of the Jordan.

"Who did you come to the desert to see?" John asked as the Holy Spirit directed his attention to the new arrivals. "Did you come to see a man dressed in fine linen? That man is not here!" John held his camel's hair cloak out for all to see. "Did you come to see a man who guzzles old wine and speaks about things that make no sense?" John stroked his long uncut beard, an obvious symbol of his lifelong Nazarite vow.

"We came to hear Elijah!" an impudent voice shouted a response.

"This is the Crossing of Elijah!" John dramatically pulled his cloak off his shoulders and struck the water with it. "But the waters do not open for me. I wear woven camel's fur and a leather belt. I eat wild locust and honey, but those things do not make me Elijah the prophet," John responded.

John paused and then he continued. "Nevertheless, sit down and listen. I will tell you a story about the great prophet Elijah who went to heaven in a chariot of fire not far from this place."

"The man is a good speaker," Antipas commented. He turned to Manaen. "I have heard the great orators of Rome. This fellow could hold his own with them. There is a dramatic flare to his presentation. What is his name?"

Manaen politely replied, "The people call him John the Baptizer."

"I will spend this afternoon listening to what he has to say," Antipas announced as he settled himself down on an overstuffed cushion one of the soldiers had provided.

Cuza and Manaen, standing on either side of the king, once again exchanged glances over the king's head. Then they turned their attention back to the preacher.

John had taken a few steps closer to the crowd and was now telling the story. "There was a vineyard close to the palace of Ahab, king of Israel. It belonged to a man named Naboth. One day, Ahab said to Naboth, 'I want your vineyard for a vegetable garden. I am prepared to offer you money or another piece of land.'"

But Naboth refused to offer. "This vineyard is my inheritance," he protested.

Angrily, Ahab returned to his palace. Sulking and refusing to eat, he threw himself on his bed and would see no one.

His wife, Queen Jezebel, observed his sullen demeanor and asked, "What has happened to put you in such a foul mood?"

At that, point the Holy Spirit placed a memory in the mind of the king. Antipas remembered an afternoon spent with Emperor Tiberius, on the Island of Capri. Tiberius had looked up from his sumptuous meal and said to Antipas, "Why do you look so glum? You are not good company. Your sullen face has been in that bowl of wine for days."

Antipas then remembered his response, "My heart is longing for a woman I cannot have."

"There is no woman you cannot have," Tiberius had blithely responded.

"I cannot have my brother's wife," Antipas had wryly answered.

"Philip's wife? Herodias?" Tiberius had laughingly responded. "Am I not the emperor of Rome? I'll send Philip a letter commanding that he give his wife to you! Now be a good companion and keep me entertained!"

The Holy Spirit then pulled Antipas back into the story John was telling.

John's voice carried easily in the natural amphitheater, "Ahab answered his wife, 'There is a well-cultivated piece of land, a vineyard. I want it, but the owner will not sell it for any price.'

"Jezebel laughed. 'Let your despondency go! Eat, drink, and enjoy life because I will get that vineyard for you.' So Jezebel called the scribes. She dictated letters and sealed them with the king's ring. A feast was declared, and per her instructions, Naboth was given a seat of honor at the feast. At one point in the festivities, two well-paid scoundrels pointed to Naboth and declared that he had cursed both God and the king. Immediately he was taken out of the city and stoned to death. Once again, the Holy Spirit inserted thoughts into the king's mind, 'Tiberius did send a letter to Philip. It was a royal decree of divorce and a command that he not contest it.'"

Antipas squirmed a little uncomfortably on his cushion. Then he pushed the memories of Rome from his mind and continued to listen. After all, he had come to be entertained.

John was still dramatically telling the story. The elders of the city sent word to Queen Jezebel that her orders had been followed and Naboth's property was now the property of the king.

"Your half brother, Philip, has been commanded to give his wife to you. Should he object, he is as good as a dead man." The Holy Spirit was still speaking to Antipas.

Again, Antipas tried to force those thoughts out of his mind and focus on the literal story.

John's voice carried easily to the hill where Antipas sat. "When Ahab heard that the vineyard was now his own property, he left the palace and went to examine the land he had acquired. But the Lord had commanded Elijah the prophet to meet him in that place, to say to the king, 'Why have you murdered a man and stolen his property?'"

"Have you not broken your brother's heart, destroyed his marriage and seized his property?" the Holy Spirit loudly demanded.

Antipas cringed. He tried to focus on the words of the desert preacher.

John was repeating the judgment of the Lord on the house of Ahab. "Naboth was stoned. His blood spilled on the ground and dogs came to lick it up. Dogs will lick your blood also and the blood of your queen!"[14]

Herod Antipas rose to his feet. "It's time to go." He abruptly gestured to Cuza and Manaen as well as the small contingent of soldiers who had accompanied him.

Manaen and Cuza again exchanged silent questioning glances. As the men took the reins of their horses, John's voice seemed to increase in volume and authority. The king and his royal escort paused, compelled by the Spirit of God to listen.

"*Because you have sold yourself to do evil in the eyes of the* Lord. *I am going to bring disaster on you. I will consume your descendants and cut off from Ahab every last male in Israel—slave or free... because you have provoked me to anger and have caused Israel to sin.*"[1]

Herod Antipas stood beside his horse like his feet had suddenly become encased in bricks of dried mud. He no longer heard the name of Ahab. He now heard his own name as John pronounced the disasters the Lord would bring upon the sinful king. "There was never a man like Antipas son of Herod the Great who chose to disregard the laws spoken by the God of Israel and written by

Moses. Enticed by Herodias his brother's wife, he behaved in the vilest manner and disgraced his nation."[16]

Antipas wanted to mount his horse and gallop away, but he could not. The preacher was approaching. John's eyes were locked with the eyes of the king. When he came within an arm's length of the king, John placed a heavy hand on the king's shoulder and he said, "The Lord our God is a merciful God. For those who turn away from their sin, there is forgiveness. When Ahab heard the words of the Lord from the prophet Elijah, *he tore his clothes, put on sackcloth, and fasted. He lay in sackcloth and went around meekly. Then the word of the Lord came to Elijah the Tishbite: 'Have you noticed how Ahab has humbled himself before me? Because he has humbled himself, I will not bring this disaster in his day, but I will bring it on his house in the days of his son.'*[2]

"Humble yourself and repent." John's voice was low. Only the king could hear. "Return your brother's wife and take your own wife back into your palace. Then the Lord our God can have mercy on you and your generations."

Manaen stepped into the one-sided conversation. He removed the prophet's hand from the shoulder of the king. "This conversation is over," he announced as he turned the king and assisted him in mounting his horse.

From the height of his mount, Antipas seemed to regain his royal demeanor. The soldiers closed ranks while Cuza took a protective position at the rear. But before they could gallop away, John loudly challenged, "King Antipas!"

Every person turned to hear the exchange that was about to take place.

Antipas held his horse still, and for some reason no one could explain, the king's entourage waited to hear what the preacher had to say.

"The disaster you fear can be either reversed or postponed. But first, you must humble yourself before the Lord and repent. You must turn away from your sin. You must return Herodias to her husband, Philip. You must reinstate your wife to her rightful place beside your throne."

The Holy Spirit then stepped back and allowed Herod to exercise his free will.

"I will sleep on this matter," Herod disengaged himself as he added, "and I will hear you another time." With that, he wheeled his horse and galloped down the road leaving the rest of his contingent in clouds of dust.

From the desert plain, Kheti looked up at the crest of the towering brown crater called Machaerus. He could just make out the walls of the palace-fortress that had been built by Herod the Great. Now it was part of the kingdom of Antipas, son of Herod the Great.

"I tell you, Nodab, I am getting too old for journeys like this one! First, we take a message from the wife of King Antipas to her father, the king of the Nabataeans. Then soldiers take me from the market to the palace. Now I am helping the Nabataean general return the divorced queen to her father! When you return to Bethany, tell Toma he must recover quickly because this is my last trading expedition!"

Nodab chuckled. "You are just grumbling, old man. You love the caravan routes. You love to bring your goods to a market and to barter with the people. You even love the occasional adventure."

"Look at this trail," Kheti continued his complaints. "It is almost too narrow for a camel, and it winds around and around this barren mountain! Half of my caravan and most of my goods are still in Petra. If we get out of this place with the royal wife of Antipas, we still have to go all the way back through those winding desert canyons. I am an old man!"

Nodab chuckled again as he said, "Yes, you are an old man, a very clever old man. When it comes to the trading routes, there is no one who knows more. You took me in as a drover and taught me to be a merchant."

Kheti looked up to see two of Herod's palace guards standing in the road ahead of them. "Now, I will show you how to be a survivor," Kheti commented under his breath.

"Halt!" One of the soldiers took the reins of the lead camel. "This is a private road. It is not part of the trade route."

"I am carrying spices," Kheit replied. "Phasaelis, the royal wife of Herod Antipas requested that I bring them to her kitchen."

The two soldiers began to walk from camel to camel, looking in the baskets while Kheti called after them, "You may check the contents of each basket. You will find spices, salt from the Dead Sea, wine, Egyptian linen, dried sardines from Galilee." The voice of the experienced caravanner trailed off, and he whispered to Nodab, "The guards are checking to make sure we are not slipping some Nabataean soldiers into the fortress. Each basket could easily hide a man with his weapon."

"I'm glad you talked the general out of that maneuver," Nodab rejoined. Within minutes, the palace guards waved the caravan on. Nodab commented again, "We will have to get the royal wife off this mountain before the guards realize she is missing."

Kheti nodded in agreement.

Nodab and Kheti did not speak again until they had passed through the gate and come to the kitchen area. "We want to speak to Lila." Nodab spoke to several servants using the name of the one person they were to contact. Meanwhile, Kheti set to displaying his wares and bargaining with the overseer of the storehouses.

When Kheti had sold all of his salt, wine, and sardines, a slim Nabataean lady approached. Nodab went to her. "Lila?"

"Yes," she responded in a hushed tone.

From the folds of his robe, Nodab withdrew a hand-sized bundle. He pressed the clothbound package into the hands of the attendant to the queen. "This package of rare spices is to go directly to Phasaelis, the royal wife. It is a gift from her father, King Aretas. This gift is in a fragile container. It has made a long hard journey. Please ask the queen to open this package immediately and to send us a message to let us know that her father's gift has been delivered safely."

Kheti approached and added, "We will spend the night in the barns with our animals. When the first rays of morning light touch the desert floor, we will return to this kitchen area to pick up our baskets."

Kheti gestured meaningfully toward a stack of very large baskets that were waiting to be emptied. "As soon as we load them onto our camels, we will begin the descent from this mountain fortress to the plain below. Our caravan is returning directly to Petra."

Silently nodding that she understood, Lila took the small bundle and quickly disappeared into the clusters of buildings that made up the palace complex.

"That man! That desert varmint! He has publicly humiliated me!"

The voice of the new queen echoed through the stone corridors of Herod's new Tiberius Palace. The heavy curtains separating Cuza's office from the rest of the royal offices could not muffle the verbal outrage of Herodias.

"Antipas is not the man his father was," Manaen softly commented.

Cuza responded with raised eyebrows. "The king has been allowing her to rage about the preacher at the Jordan for days."

"His father would have silenced her," Manaen responded while drawing his finger meaningfully across his throat.

"He would also have silenced the preacher," Cuza added. "Rome does not like gatherings larger than five or six people. This man draws massive crowds every day. I am amazed the new governor, Pilate, has not ordered his arrest."

"This preacher is in the territory of Herod Antipas. He is not in Judea," Manaen pointed out.

"Put that wild man in jail! He is a troublemaker!" The shrill angry words of the king's new wife made both men involuntarily shiver.

"Be quiet, woman!" Herod Antipas broke his silence.

"Finally!" Manaen commented under his breath.

Cuza and Manaen listened as the king put a temporary end to his new wife's tirade. "Do you want trouble? Do you want the people to rise up against me? Let this man's popularity fade then I can take him, and few will notice. I will personally monitor his gatherings."

"I think we will hear this preacher many more times," Cuza commented.

"Antipas is really quite interested in him," Manaen added.

Both men heard quick female footsteps on the mosaic floor. The curtains suddenly flew open and Herodias made her angry entrance. "See to it that that freak of a preacher has no more to say about me!" As quickly as she had appeared, she turned on her heel and made a grand exit.

Both men gave quick respectful bows, but the queen had stormed down the hall without noticing their response.

"There are things about Phasaelis that Antipas is going to miss," Cuza commented.

Manaen nodded in agreement as the two men returned to accounting for the recent purchases that had been made for the palace.

Joanna put a fine woolen cloak across the shoulders of her mistress. She chose a heavy onyx broach to secure the cloak, but Phasaelis shook her head, "I will take nothing from this place that belongs to Antipas."

Joanna then took the decorative brass clip from her own cloak, "Then take this and remember our friendship."

Phasaelis smiled wistfully and nodded. "I will always hold you in my heart. Now return to your quarters. You must not know the things I am about to do."

Joanna understood. Silently, she embraced her queen. Then she embraced Lila before quickly turning away.

"Joanna?" Phasaelis called after her attendant. "Tell the servants to heat my bath. I want it ready at sunrise."

Joanna nodded and bowed. A little smile played at the corners of her lips. If the palace community thought the queen was in her bath, they would not look for her until at least noon. Antipas was a fool. This was a good and intelligent woman. Satisfied that her queen would survive and return to her own people, Joanna hurried to convey the queen's wishes to the servants.

There was no moon. Lila and Phasaelis felt their way from building to building. The baskets were waiting exactly as Kheti has left them. Lila quickly lined each one with a blanket, adding a small skin of water. She helped Phasaelis find a comfortable position, and then she closed and latched the lid before hiding herself in the other basket.

Kheti and Nodab had been watching. With the help of two of their trusted drovers, they moved quickly to load their camels. Years of working the trade routes allowed them to prepare their caravan without light. As blackness gave way to predawn grayness, Kheti led his caravan out of the desert palace called Machaerus. When they reached the road at the base of the mountain, Kheti turned his caravan into the glare of the rising sun. He knew Nabataean soldiers would meet him just as the trade route entered the maze of canyons that protected their capitol city of Petra.

Nodab fell into step with the old caravanner. "We are doing what is right," he commented. The law of Moses says if a man divorces his wife, she is to return to her father."

"Tell that to the soldiers if they come after us," Kheti rejoined.

"At Passover, my brother's friend, Jesus, shared the meal with us," Nodab began to relate a recent incident. "He told us when

Moses led the children of Israel from Egypt, Pharaoh's soldiers followed them to the Red Sea, but in that place, the God of the Hebrews made a wall of fire that separated the soldiers from the escaping slaves. When Jesus told the story, it seemed like God could do that today. I believe the God of the Exodus will take care of us."

"Jesus? That's Toma's cousin's son?" Kheti asked. "I haven't seen him since he was a very young man."

"He's a carpenter now, but he doesn't work all the time. When he visits my brother Lazarus, he explains the scriptures. He knows more than the rabbis in Jerusalem," Nodab continued the conversation.

"I'd like to hear him sometime," Kheti said. "Years ago, his father, Joseph, told Toma and me the strangest story about his conception and birth. Joseph believed he would grow up to be the Jewish Messiah."

A muffled cry of discomfort ended the conversation. Both men looked up and down the road. No one was in sight, so they halted the caravan and allowed the women to climb out of the baskets and walk beside the camels.

Chapter 11

Visiting Nazareth

And he went and lived in a town called Nazareth. So was fulfilled what was said through the prophets: "He will be called a Nazarene.

—Matthew 2:23

"Jesus! Jesus!" Enos, the eldest son of James, was the first to recognize the solitary traveler who briskly walked the narrow packed-earth road that led into the heart of the village of Nazareth. Still shouting the name of his favorite uncle, Enos raced ahead of the small flock of sheep he had been leading to the stone enclosure where they would spend the night. "I have been watching for you!" the boy ran into the open arms of his uncle.

Laughingly, Jesus responded, "Who told you I would be coming today?"

"Grandmother Mary talks about you every day."

Jesus laughed again and gave his nephew another hug. "Does your grandmother mention me every day along with a list of things she is waiting for me to do?"

"How did you know?" Enos seriously asked.

"It does not take a prophetic word to know some things," Jesus answered. "What are the most important things on my mother's list?"

"She wants you to write the marriage contract so Jose can get Deborah the shepherdess for his wife. Then you have to take it to her father."

Jesus smiled, "I can easily do that."

"We need more lumber. She says you always get the best wood for the price. My father gets mad every time she mentions it."

"I will take your father with me," Jesus responded to the family tensions. "We will get the wood together."

"Anything else?" Jesus asked.

"The addition to the synagogue is finished. Aunt Ruth had a baby girl. I have to get water for her family every day until her time of rest has passed." Looking quizzically up at his uncle he asked, "Why do women rest for eighty days after the birth of a girl? When a boy is born they only rest for forty days."

Jesus answered, "Do you remember the promise God gave to Eve? God said the One who would crush the head of the serpent would be the seed of the woman. The deliverer everyone has been waiting for will be born from a woman, but he will not have a human father. His father will be God. So females are special. They have to be protected. Beginning at birth, God has commanded a double time of rest and separation. That is part of his protection for them."

Enos nodded. "I knew you could explain it." Then he added, "I have to get back to the sheep. Everyone is in the vineyards or at the winepress except for my mother. She has been coughing too much."

"I will go see her before I help with the harvest," Jesus assured his nephew with another hug, and then he sent the boy back to his responsibilities.

Entering the quiet town, Jesus first came to the carpentry shop he shared with his brothers. Like every other place of business, it was temporarily closed so everyone could bring in the grape harvest and everyone could share in the wine supply for the year. Jesus lifted the familiar latch on the courtyard gate. Just inside the gate, he paused and listened. Yes, he could hear someone coughing. The sound was coming from the rooms he and James had added so James could marry and have a family.

"Father?" Jesus silently addressed his Father in heaven. "You have given me your heart for humanity. Your heart whispers health for my sister-in-law."

"Bring her a cup of water," God replied. "Speak words of health and life."

Eagerly, Jesus moved to carry out the healing instructions from heaven. Like so much of God's work on Earth, he knew the miracle would be unrecognized. His sister-in-law would think she had just recovered while he rejoiced privately with his Father. For so many years, Father and son had been secretly healing and helping. At times, they just sat alone together and shared big belly-laughs of joy over the miracles from heaven.

"Jesus!" It was early morning, and Jose was the first to welcome his oldest brother into the vineyards.

Like the rest of the men, Jesus was prepared to work from dawn to dusk through the long hot day. He wore a sleeveless short tunic that was loosely belted at the waist. He carried a large flat basket that he could fill and balance on his head for the short walk to the wine press.

Before beginning the steady work of gathering cluster after cluster, Jesus plucked a small handful of grapes and held them up as he prayed, "Blessed is the Lord God who gives us the fruit of the vine."

The harvesters around him responded, "Amen."

Jesus ate one of the grapes. He gave the rest to those closest to him, reminding each to gather with a grateful heart.

Then the work began. With a sharp flint in one hand, Jesus began removing cluster after cluster from the vines until his basket was filled. Easily balancing it on his head, he carried it the short distance to the winepress where the young men and some of the children were beginning the process of stomping the grapes. Back to the vineyard he went, filling his basket over and over until the sun was high and hot, and then all the men gathered at the winepress to drink cups of fresh grape juice and to eat warm barley cakes dipped in seasoned olive oil. While the harvesters rested the treading continued.

Accompanied by demons and evil angels, Satan slipped unnoticed into the midst of the relaxing laborers. For a long moment, the Evil One silently observed Jesus recovering from his morning labor.

To Raziel, his second in command, Satan snidely commented, "Yeshua, who calls himself Jesus, looks like any other man. He sweats. He needs food and water. His muscles need to rest. His body even requires sleep. It should not be so difficult to get him to speak a word against God or to get him to act on his own without regard to the plans of God."

"The Holy Spirit is with him," Raziel commented. "I can see the glory that we all knew in heaven hovering over him."

Satan responded through gritted teeth, "I would confront this man, Jesus, in the vulnerability of his humanity, but there is always the Holy Spirit with the Archangel Michael and the heavenly hosts. So far, I have been unable to stage a direct confrontation. I am forced to be satisfied to approach him through circumstances and the words of others."

Sitting a little apart from the other men, Jesus leaned comfortably against a stone wall. He was totally focused on conversing with the Spirit who casually informed Jesus that the owner of the vineyard had stopped by to see how the harvest was progressing.

Jesus looked up to see the landowners who had come from the nearby town of Seppharis to check on their harvest. Jesus knew that half of the wine would go into the owner's storage vats. The remaining wine would be shared by the families of Nazareth. For a brief moment, Jesus observed the owner and his son standing with several of the village men. But Jesus's mind was not with those men who conversed about the harvest and the amount of wine that could be expected. He was listening to instruction from the Spirit of God.

"My people, the sons and daughters of Abraham, are like a precious vineyard to me. Sing, Jesus, sing the song of my heart."

With a clear loud voice, Jesus began a traditional harvest song.

> *I will sing for the one I love, a song about his vineyard:*
> *My loved one had a vineyard on a fertile hillside.*
> *He dug it up and cleared it of stones and planted it*
> *with the choicest vines.*
> *He built a watchtower in it and cut out a winepress as well.*
> *Then he looked for a crop of good grapes,*
> *but it yielded only bad fruit.*
> *Now you dwellers in Jerusalem and men of Judah,*
> *judge between me and my vineyard.*[1]

It was a familiar song from the writings of Isaiah the prophet. Conversations died away. Spontaneously, other workers joined in. Everyone kept rhythm with their hands. Those in the grape trough beat the grapes in time with their feet. The red juice stained the hems of their work clothes while everyone sang.

> *The vineyard of the* LORD *Almighty is the house of Israel,*
> *And the men of Judah are the garden of his delight.*[2]

The song ended. The vineyard owner and his son departed, and one by one, the men picked up their baskets and returned to the harvest. Jesus grabbed his own basket and flint, adding his strength to the town's efforts. When darkness overtook the men as they worked between the rows of vines, everyone returned to the winepress. Then by the light of several bonfires, the treading continued.

Resting with his brothers and a few of his neighbors, Jesus sat close to the fire, staring at the flames and listening again as the Holy Spirit whispered his directions for the moment.

With a slight nod of his head, Jesus began a story, *"A man planted a vineyard. He put a wall around it, dug a pit for the winepress and built a watchtower."*

The conversations stopped. The relaxing men turned their attention to the storyteller.

Making eye contact with various neighbors, Jesus continued his story. "The owner then *leased his vineyard to some farmers and went away on a journey. At harvest time he sent a servant to the tenants to collect from them some of the fruit of the vineyard. But they seized him, beat him and sent him away empty-handed. Then he sent another servant to them; they struck this man on the head and treated him shamefully. He sent still another, and that one they killed. He sent many others; some of them they beat, others they killed. He had one left to send, a son, whom he loved. He sent him last of all, saying, 'They will respect my son.' But the tenants said to one another, 'This is the heir. Come, let's kill him, and the inheritance will be ours.' So they took him and killed him, and threw him out of the vineyard."*[3]

Jesus looked at the men around him and asked, "Now, what action will the owner of the vineyard take?"

"He will exercise the right of the kinsman to avenge the murder of his son," James quickly replied.

"Your response is too simple," Moshe chided James. "I have been listening to Jesus tell stories since he was a young man. There is always a deeper, less obvious meaning."

"And it is always rooted in Torah or the prophets," Salmon, the old olive grower, added.

The rest of the men nodded in agreement while expectantly keeping their eyes on Jesus's face. Even those treading the grapes paused to catch the deeper meaning.

"It is the song of the winepress," Jesus responded. "Israel, the nation chosen by God, is the vineyard. With mighty wonders, the God of Abraham broke the bonds of our slavery and brought us into this fertile land. He gave us the law, our watchtower, and he expected an abundant harvest. He sent his servants, the judges, and prophets. You know the history of our nation. Those men were tormented and finally killed. Now God can only send his Anointed One."

"We wouldn't kill the Messiah!" several men protested.

Jesus did not respond to their protests. Instead, he stood and tucked the back hem of his tunic firmly into the leather belt at his waist. Then he strode over to the winepress. Removing his sandals, he briefly washed his feet, and then he joined the young men who were stomping the juice from the grapes. With a loud clear voice, he began to sing.

> *I will tell of the kindness of the LORD,*
> *the deeds for which he is to be praised,*
> *According to all the LORD has done for us—*
> *Yes, the many good things he has done for the house of Israel,*
> *according to his compassion and many kindnesses*
> *He said, 'Surely they are my people,*
> *sons who will not be false to me'*
> *and so he became their Savior...*
> *Yet they rebelled and grieved his Holy Spirit.*
> *So he turned and became their enemy*
> *and he himself fought against them.*[4]

Suddenly, the song stopped, and Jesus stood motionless in the great vat of grapes. The abrupt silence pulled every eye to the tall, muscular carpenter.

"Ask me?" Jesus loudly demanded. "Ask me, why my garments are red?"

The other men in the vat stopped stomping on the grapes and looked uncomfortably puzzled at the man who was now the center of attention. One by one, they moved to the edge of the vat and stepped out, walking away with shaking heads. But one man paused and turned back, "Tell us carpenter, why are your garments red?"

"To answer your question, I will sing the song of the son that the owner sent to his vineyard." Jesus began to stomp violently and rhythmically. The juice from the grapes splashed on his linen tunic.

> *I have trodden the winepress alone;*
> *from the nations no one was with me.*
> *I trampled them in my anger*
> *and trod them down in my wrath;*
> *Their blood splattered my garments,*
> *and I stained all my clothing…*
> *I looked, but there was no one to help,*
> *I was appalled that no one gave support;*
> *So my own arm worked salvation for me,*
> *and my own wrath sustained me.*[5]

For a few minutes, the people of Nazareth watched their carpenter curiously. Then one by one, and in small groups they turned away.

In the shadows, Satan laughed. "No one understands his words. They think I have possessed his mind. That gives me some satisfaction!"

Mary heard her neighbors' comments.

"He's a good carpenter, but some of the things he says are disturbing."

"Joseph's son is crazy. Look at him!"

"He acts like he's the son of the owner of the vineyard."

"What does his story mean? Does he think we should attack the owner of this vineyard?"

"James?" Mary stepped over to her second son. "We need to get Jesus out of here before the whole town turns against us."

James turned to his eldest son. "Enos, go tell your uncle the family is going home."

Enos ran to the vat filled with smashed grapes. Jesus had finished his song and continued to rhythmically stomp on the grapes. "We're going home," Enos shouted. "Come with us!"

"Go with them," the Holy Spirit confirmed. "You will tell this story another time and those who hear the story will understand."

Bowing respectfully at the door to the home of Deborah the shepherdess, Jesus greeted her father. "I am here as the representative of my father, Joseph the carpenter of Nazareth. In his name, I offer this marriage contract for a union between Jose the third son of Joseph and your daughter, Deborah." Jesus placed the carefully penned scroll in the hands of Alon, a man who made cheese from goat's milk.

In response, the older man bowed and said, "Jesus, you and your brother are welcome in my home."

As the men sat on the floor beside a low table, they ignored the excited female scurryings in the household. With obviously subdued excitement, Deborah's mother placed three cups and a flask of wine on the table, and then she discretely withdrew. Jewish protocol insisted that marriage negotiations were properly left to the men.

"Before we read the contract, Jose would like to speak," Jesus initiated the meeting.

"I want you to know I do not intend to remain in Nazareth," Jose nervously said. "The village of Cana needs a carpenter, and should you accept this contract, I will immediately begin to build my shop and my home in Cana. The wedding will take place in Cana."

"Does Deborah know about these plans?" her father asked.

"Our meetings have been brief and proper," Jose said. "I have not shared this information with her."

"I am sure she has heard it now," Alon said as he glanced meaningfully toward the curtained doorway. It was obvious. All the women of the family had gathered behind that curtain.

"Deborah, come in here," the older man commanded.

Almost pushed through the curtain, Deborah stumbled shyly toward where her father sat at the table.

"I know that you know the purpose of this visit." Deborah's father nodded at Jesus, and his younger brother as he spoke.

Jose kept his eyes fixed on the table, but Jesus gave the girl a reassuring smile.

"I'm sure you just heard that Jose, who wants to marry you, is planning to make his home in Cana. Do you want to live in Cana with him?"

"It is a day's journey," Jesus offered.

"A day's journey is not far," Deborah responded. Then a little uncertainly, she looked back at the curtain where her mother stood with her sisters.

Deborah's mother nodded.

"Yes, if you find the contract suitable father, then Cana will be my home." Deborah gave a little graceful bow, and Jose let out a sigh of relief.

The reading of the contract was brief. In exchange for their daughter, there was the traditional gift of silver coins. Jesus offered to build an additional room on the family home. He further promised to inspect the construction of the carpenter's shop, and Jose's new home in Cana. Jose could not come and take his bride until Jesus had approved all the structures that needed to be built in Cana.

"Deborah, come in. Bring your mother and your sisters," Deborah's father called.

Excited, all the women burst through the curtain. The men stood. Jesus placed a cup of wine in his younger brother's hand. A little tentatively, Jose approached Deborah. He offered her the cup of wine. Everyone held their breath. They all understood if Deborah accepted the cup from his hand it would mean she accepted his offer of marriage.

First, Deborah gave Jose a modest smile. Then she reached out and took the cup. She drank from it, and then Jose drank from it.

Both families burst into congratulations. Wine was served all around and the marriage contract was signed.

Jesus spread his heavy cloak on the dry grass of the hillside that overlooked his hometown of Nazareth. He stretched out to enjoy the solitude of the warm night, the brilliant half moon and the tiny dots of light, distant suns created by the word of his mouth on the fourth day of Earth's history. With a rich baritone voice, Jesus began to sing one of the songs of King David.

"*The heavens declare the glory of God; the skies proclaim the work of his hands.*"[6]

In the courts of heaven, the Eternal Father called together his ruling angels. "Listen," God directed. "Listen to your Creator sing. Unless my Spirit pulls back the curtain that separates heaven from Earth, he cannot see my glory. Yet from the darkness of Earth, he praises me! His heart is always connected with my heart. His trust in me is so pure, so unshakable—"

"Haven't you guarded him since the moment of his conception?" Arrogant and mocking, Satan made a place for himself among the ruling angels as he spoke.

"It is our adversary!" Gabriel exclaimed.

Michael, the mighty warring cherub, drew his sword and placed himself between Satan and Father God.

God waved Michael aside and a heavy cloud enveloped the Almighty One as he said, "I will speak with my adversary. It will never be said that I am a ruler who ignores the complaints of his creation."

Turning His attention toward the leader of the fallen angels, God asked, "Tell me Satan, where have you come from?"

Satan answered, "I have been observing mankind on Earth."

"Did you notice my son?" God asked.

"Do you mean Yeshua the Creator, whom the mortals call Jesus the carpenter of Nazareth?" Satan sneered.

"He is the son of God and the descendant of Adam. There's no one else like him, a man who loves righteousness and hates evil!"[5] God exclaimed.

"If you would just allow me to touch those he loves," Satan protested.

The glory of God suddenly flared through the cloud. Balls of fire fell around the evil angel as God replied. "I took his father Joseph to the Place of the Dead and broke my son's heart. I have allowed you to poison the minds of the people of Nazareth. They ridicule my son day after day. Even in his own family, I have allowed you to spread your poison. Still, my son's heart is pure and his actions are perfect."

Slightly intimidated, Satan took a few steps backward, away from the potentially lethal balls of fire. With a little more submission and respect, Satan made his next request, "Since his conception, I have been required to test Yeshua through other people and circumstances. I have not been allowed to approach him as the ruler of the Earth. Unless I confront Yeshua who is representative of the whole human race, your claim to Earth and its inhabitants is invalid."

"As you say." The voice of God roared like thunder over an angry sea. "You may confront him. But at this time, you are limited to deception. You may not physically harm him."

On the hilltop overlooking Nazareth, a brilliant mist settled over Jesus, like the cloud of glory that would often come down on the tabernacle in the wilderness. From within the cloud, Jesus heard another voice, clear and golden, "Yeshua, heaven sends its greetings."

"Moses! How pleasant to see you again," Jesus sat up as he responded to one of the heavenly companions who often gave him direct instruction. Turning his head, Jesus could see Elijah had also come for this session.

"We have come to discuss the number forty," Elijah began the instruction.

"It rained on the earth for forty days and forty nights while Noah and his family remained sealed in the ark," Jesus began reciting the scriptural references he had memorized. "Jacob, after he died, went through the full forty day embalming process. Is forty a time of separation?" Jesus asked.

"I was separated from the tribes of Israel when I was on the mountain with God," Moses confirmed. "You remember, twice I went up on the mountain, into the thick cloud that hid the glory of God Almighty. Each time, I remained in that cloud with God for forty days and forty nights without food or water. The Lord sustained me."

Elijah continued, "The twelve spies separated from the people and searched out the land for forty days."

"They brought back an evil report. It was a test!" Moses interjected. "And all but two failed."

"Forty is a period of testing," Jesus said.

"Ten of those spies looked at the land through eyes of flesh," Moses informed. "Two spies looked through eyes of faith. The word of God was their reality."

"Do not forget the Evil One," Elijah asserted. "He is the one who filled those men with fear."

"How can I forget the Evil One!" Moses exclaimed. "For forty years, he walked among the tents of the Israelites. His suggestion was the root of every complaint and the cause of God's frequent righteous judgments."

"The giant Goliath taunted the Israelite army for forty days before the Spirit of the Lord brought forth David the shepherd boy to put an end to his proud boasting," Elijah recounted.

"So there may be confrontation and battle at the end of a period of forty," Jesus observed. "There could also be repentance and a stay of judgment. The people of Nineveh, when they received a warning from the prophet Jonah, repented for forty days and God spared their city."

"I traveled forty days, fleeing from Queen Jezebel," Elijah recalled. "My fear was so great that I did not consider the needs of my body, but God knew my flesh could not endure the trek. Twice he sent an angel with bread and water."

"At the end of those forty days, God met you at the mountain," Jesus added. "He showed you his power in the whirl wind and the fire."

"But dearest of all," Elijah recounted the incident with an emotional tremor in his voice, "was the tender, soft voice of God. I will never forget. At that moment, I experienced greater love and greater understanding than I could imagine."

Moses nodded as he looked at Jesus with empathetic understanding. He had lived on the earth for 120 years, and now, he was a citizen of heaven. He said, "To speak with God, to hear his response—it was all that sustained me during those wilderness years. I felt his love, like glorious waves flowing through my body."

"When my father Joseph died, I could not feel the love of God. I had to believe what I could not feel. I know it is that way with most humans, especially when life is difficult," Jesus responded.

Moses looked Jesus directly in the eye. "So you will understand when I tell you that no matter what you feel or do not feel, it is important for you to have complete trust that your Father God knows what you need. If you have a real need, it will be supplied without delay."

"I must warn you," Elijah added. "There is a mighty angel who left the throne room of God to seek his own glory."

"Many times since your conception, he has petitioned for opportunities to test you," Moses warned.

The Holy Spirit opened the memory of Yeshua the Creator.

Then Jesus said, "*How you have fallen from heaven, O morning star, son of the dawn! You have been cast down to the earth…You said in your heart, 'I will ascend to heaven; I will raise my throne above the stars of God'…But you are brought down to the grave, to the depths of the pit.*[7] I loved him. He was the most beautiful cherub."

"Do not be fooled. Now he is the adversary," Elijah informed.

"Satan has been my enemy since he deceived my daughter Eve," Jesus responded with grim matter-of-factness.

"Prepare to meet your enemy," Elijah warned. "Your preparation is a pure heart and a life that has met all the requirements of the law."

"Go to your cousin John at the Jordan crossing," Moses instructed. Just as I prepared Aaron and his sons, washing them with water in front of the entire assembly before they began to officially minister before the Lord, so you must publically cleanse yourself."

"I will leave in the morning," Jesus responded.

"The Holy Spirit will be your guide," Elijah added as both men vanished into the golden mist and the cloud lifted, getting smaller and smaller until it was only a wisp in front of the brilliantly white half moon.

Chapter 12

Bethany Beyond the Jordan

This all happened at Bethany on the other side of the Jordan, where John was baptizing.

—John 1:28

"Twice they tax us!" Peter complained as he led the little four donkey caravan loaded with dried fish toward the tax collector's booth at the Fish Gate entrance to Jerusalem.

His brother Andrew sarcastically responded, "Will they let us go on if we tell them Matthew already counted each fish and levied a tax?"

"As long as I can remember, either Matthew or his father has always met the fishing boats each morning as they unload their catch," John stoically lamented.

"Our father hates that family," James added. "He says if any one of the sons of Zebedee ever becomes a tax collector he will personally take him out to the middle of the lake, tie a stone anchor around his neck, and throw him overboard!"

"Is that all your father has said on the subject of tax collectors?" Andrew responded with his typical quick wit.

John answered, "After working for my father for the past few years, you know that is not all he has said about taxes and tax collectors!"

James approached the tax official, obviously a Jewish man assisted by Syrian soldiers in the army of Rome.

"What is your merchandise?" The tax collector squinted at the scroll where he was making an official record. He did not look up.

"I have four donkeys. Each donkey is carrying four baskets of dried sardines from Galilee," James responded.

"Look!" Under his breath, Peter complained to his brother Andrew. "That tax collector cannot even look an honest Jewish working man in the face!"

"Verify," the tax collector directed one of the soldiers to inspect the merchandise.

Quickly, the soldier thrust his arm into each basket, pushing to the bottom to be sure only sardines filled each basket. When he withdrew his hand the last time, he had a fist full of sardines.

"Sardines," the soldier confirmed the merchandise as he popped one of the leathery little fish into his mouth.

"Two bronze coins for each basket," the tax collector announced, still without lifting his eyes from the parchment scroll where he continually scratched figures using a pointed reed that had been dipped in ink.

"That's thirty-two coins!" James exclaimed. "We already paid the tax for these fish in Capernaum."

"That tax went to King Antipas. This tax goes to the governor from Rome." As the tax collector spoke, he stopped writing and looked up into the face of the young fisherman. "Thirty-two bronze coins or two silver drachma."

At that moment, Peter pointed at the soldier who had examined their baskets. "That man is eating our fish!" He exploded.

"Calm down, Peter." Andrew drew his brother aside and tried to speak reason. "He could have dumped all the baskets onto the ground, and then we would have lost more than the handful of fish he is now eating."

"Night after night of fishing, day after day of drying fish and repairing nets—we're not going to make any money on these fish!" Peter was loudly ranting.

"I don't have time for this," the tax collector stood as he spoke. "Escort these men down the road, away from Jerusalem. They are going to have to sell their fish some other place."

One soldier roughly grabbed James by the arm. Another soldier took the rope of the lead animal, and before Peter could make one more protest, he felt the point of a Roman spear directing him away from the tax booth at the Fish Gate.

"Jericho is a good market for fish," John suggested.

"They also have a tax collector at the gate," Andrew reminded everyone.

"At least the Jerusalem tax collector sent us away before we paid," James stated.

"Let's not pay any more taxes on these fish," Peter rebelliously suggested. "We can sell them in the villages between here and Jericho. And if we don't sell all our fish before we get to Jericho, we can cross the Jordan and sell in those villages. Agreed?"

"Agreed!" The four fishermen led their donkeys down the road toward Jericho.

"John?" the Holy Spirit called to the desert prophet just as the first rays of the morning sun began pushing the darkness westward.

Wrapped in his tattered camel's wool cloak, John sat up wiping sleep from his eyes and brushing gritty sand from his hair and his beard. In the encampment, animals were stirring. He could see a few small fires coming to life here and there, but mostly, he could sense that the Holy Spirit was moving through the mist that rose from the large pools of fresh springwater. It was calling him to immerse himself in everything God had for him that day. Without hesitation, John threw off his cloak and pulled the rough tunic over his head. Wearing only a linen loin cloth he walked into one of the nearby pools of spring water. Deeper and deeper, he waded into the cold, predawn water. John ducked beneath the dark chilly water, completely submerging his body. When he broke the water's surface, he paused and listened.

"I, even I, have spoken; yes, I have called him."

John recognized the familiar voice of the Holy Spirit.

"I will bring him, and he will succeed in his mission."[1]

"Who, Lord?" John asked. "Who are you bringing to this place?"

"You will know," the Spirit responded, "*The man on whom you see the Spirit come down and remain is he who will baptize with the Holy Spirit.*"[2]

John immersed himself again and again. He could no longer feel the coldness of the water. Instead, he felt the fire of the Spirit of God. It burned, filling him with excitement and anticipation. It burned like the golden ball of fire that had just risen in the east and now rested on the horizon of the desert floor.

Slowly, John walked out of the water. He threw the tunic he had slept in over his wet body. Geber was up, starting a small fire. He handed John a piece of flat bread. John broke the bread into two pieces as he loudly prayed, "Blessed are you, O, Lord our God and our Creator, who brings forth bread from the earth so man can realize his dependence on you."

John ate a small piece of the bread, and then he walked among his disciples who were waking up. He gave each of them a small piece of the bread as he quoted the words of Moses, "*Remember how the Lord your God led you all the way in the desert these forty years, to humble you and to test you in order to know what was in your heart, whether or not you would keep his commands. He humbled you, causing you to hunger and then feeding you with manna, which neither you nor your fathers had known, to teach you that man does not live on bread alone but on every word that comes from the mouth of the Lord.*"[3]

John then paused and surveyed the area that surrounded the spring that fed several pools of water and created an oasis just outside of the town of Bethany beyond the Jordan. It had become a camp ground. Men and women from every strata of society had come from all over Israel to hear the desert prophet. Enterprising villagers had turned one part into an outdoor market. There were fishermen from Galilee selling dried sardines. The prophet John walked past their baskets, and one of the men thrust a small cloth sack filled with little fish into his hands, "For you and your disciples," he said with a thick Galilean accent.

A woman piled some warm flat bread in his hands. Casually, John handed the food off to one of his disciples. Then he continued to walk through the camp until he sensed every eye was on him.

Suddenly stopping, standing in the middle of the camp, the desert preacher raised his voice and began to quote from the prophet Joel, *"Hear this, you elders; listen, all who live in the land. Has anything like this ever happened in your days or in the days of your forefathers? Tell it to your children, and let your children tell it to their children, and their children to the next generation.*[4]

"Weep because wickedness has invaded our land."

Peter and John stopped feeding their donkeys, completely captivated by the powerful preacher. "He's talking about the Romans," Peter stated with satisfaction.

"He's also talking about the coming of the Messiah" John added. "Listen to him!"

The desert prophet shouted, *"The LORD thunders at the head of his army; his forces are beyond number, and mighty is the army that obeys his command. The day of the LORD is great; it is dreadful. Who can endure it?"*[5]

"The fall feasts are just a month away," Peter exclaimed. "The trumpets will blow all day, like signals for war."

"You are too quick to jump to conclusions, brother." It was Andrew, placing a hand on Peter's shoulder. "This man is preaching preparation through purity. He's not impressed with your sword." Andrew gave a playful tug on the sword his brother always carried attached to his waist beneath the folds of his long robe.

"*Rend your heart and not your garments. Return to the* LORD *your God, for he is gracious and compassionate, slow to anger and abounding in love, and he relents from sending calamity. Who knows? He may turn and relent and leave behind a blessing—*"[6] As he preached, John the Baptist began to wade into one of the pools. His disciples also took their places in the various pools of water.

Facing the early morning crowd, John announced, "Now is the season of repentance! About thirty days from now, the trumpets will blow in Jerusalem, and the books of judgment will be opened in heaven. Repent, turn your life around now so your name will definitely be inscribed in the Book of Life, and you will not be left waiting and wondering for the next year."

Peter, with his brother Andrew, and James, with his brother John, left their donkeys and their baskets of dried fish. The fishermen hurried forward to proclaim their desire to be pure-hearted and to be immersed, sealing their commitment.

Cuza and Manaen reined in their horses as they approached the river crossing. Speaking to one of the ferryboat men, Cuza commented, "I see the desert preacher has moved."

"He has not gone far," the man replied. "He is at the springs near Bethany on the other side of the river. There is more room for people and the water is calm, clean, and plentiful."

"Is it a good place to camp?" Manaen asked.

"Oh, yes! It is the best water you will find between here and the next oasis."

Both men waved as they rode their horses into the river, forcing the animals to swim at the deepest point. On the other side, they dismounted, removed the leather saddles, and wrung out their horse blankets. "Antipas seemed rather relieved when he heard Phasaelis had returned to her Nabataean kingdom," Cuza commented as he tossed the damp blanket over a scrubby bush to dry in the hot sun.

"Yes, so now we have to prepare the Machaerus Palace for Herodias." Manaen responded. "The new queen seems obsessed with physically possessing every place the former queen occupied."

"Joanna is still there." Cuza added. "I will be glad to see her again."

"And your little boy, Caper?" Manaen asked.

"He is still in Capernaum with my mother. I had to get her another servant because Casper is wearing her out with all of his energy," Cuza answered. "If we are going to be at this palace for some time, I will send for him. I know my wife misses him."

"And how does your wife feel about waiting on the new queen?" Manaen asked.

"Knowing how loyal Joanna is, I am sure that she would prefer to retire from palace life," Cuza speculated.

Manaen checked the pouches that hung from each of the four horns of their leather saddles. "Our bread got wet," he announced as he tossed the soggy loaves on the ground. "We'll have to buy our evening meal in the village."

Both men sat on their saddles and waited for the blankets to dry so they could remount for the short ride to Bethany beyond the Jordan.

The coolness of the morning burned away. Some of the campers began their journeys back to their own villages. New people arrived. Cuza and Manaen rode into the oasis and set up their campsite under a tall date palm. Their plan was to allow their horses a full afternoon to feed on the grass and drink the water before, by the light of a full moon, they headed into the desert regions beyond this oasis. Sitting in the shade, Cuza asked Manaen, "What do you think?"

"That preacher could incite an uprising," Manaen replied.

"He doesn't talk like those who incite uprisings," Cuza countered. "He does not claim to be the Messiah. He is not calling the people to form armies or gather weapons. He is not talking about rebellion, civil disobedience, or opposing taxation."

"He is quoting the Jewish scriptures, and that alone can stir up extreme feelings of nationalism," Manaen responded. "I always knew Antipas was weaker than his father, but I never realized how weak until I watched him cower before this desert preacher," Manaen added.

"I don't think it was the man who intimidated him," Cuza ventured. "Every time I am near this man, I sense a power. I feel it now. I believe it is the power of Jehovah. Every ruler has to respect the power of Jehovah."

"You would not make that statement in front of the Great Herod, builder of the Jewish Temple and temples for many other gods."

"Herod the Great died an awful death," Cuza reminded Manaen.

"Yes, I saw him," Manaen admitted. "His body rotted while he lived. It was full of worms long before he died."

"The Jews believe God cursed him," Cuza stated.

"Maybe," Manaen agreed. Then, as an afterthought he added, "What will the Jewish God do to Herod Antipas for divorcing his first wife and taking the wife of his brother?"

As if the prophet had been part of their conversation, John the Baptist began to speak from the writings of the prophet Malachi, "'*If you do not listen, and if you do not set your heart to honor my name,' says the LORD Almighty, 'I will send a curse upon you.'*[7] *You ask, 'Why?' It is because the LORD is acting as the witness between you and the wife of your youth, because you have broken faith with her, though she is your partner, the wife of your marriage covenant. Has not the LORD made them one? In flesh and spirit they are his. And why one? Because he was seeking godly offspring. So guard yourself in your spirit, and do not break faith with the wife of your youth. 'I hate divorce,' says the LORD God of Israel!*"[8]

Manaen and Cuza carefully exchanged glances. Manaen spoke first, "When I was young, I trembled every time I was in the presence of the Great Herod who was the father of Antipas, but I think this desert prophet frightens me even more."

"The power of the Evil One was with the Great Herod, but the power of God is with this man," Cuza stated.

"It is amazing," Manaen further stated. "He draws every kind of man out to this desert oasis. Look, see that short chubby man?" Manaen pointed.

With his eyes, Cuza followed the direction of Manaen's finger. "Zacchaeus? The head tax collector for the Jericho region! Now I have seen everything!"

All afternoon, Cuza and Manaen watched people come and go. They watched people respond to the repeated calls to repent and be immersed. A tall craftsman entered the oasis. He seemed to know the fishermen from Galilee. He sat with them. He ate with them. He listened to the preacher, and then as the clouds of early evening moved across the sky, he went down into the water. He was the last man in a line of men who stood in front of the desert preacher, each waiting his turn to duck completely under the water and then to come up and hear the man of God speak words of new life into their souls.

Shortly after sunrise, John had taken his place in the water. Immediately, a line had formed. There never was an end to the men and women who were coming forward. Like a man without his own mind, John spoke to each person the words the Holy Spirit placed upon his lips. He spoke loudly, and every person in the vicinity of the pool where he was baptizing heard every word he spoke.

As the day progressed, John sensed the Spirit of God was speaking with greater and greater intensity. He felt the restlessness of the Spirit as it moved back and forth, over the pools of spring water, through the crowds on the hillside and then back to John. The desert preacher knew something of great spiritual importance was about to take place.

"Study each face and listen to me," the Sprit directed.

In front of him, the next man stepped forward. John looked directly into his eyes.

"Sins of the flesh, adultery, and lust," the Spirit informed.

"You are not to commit adultery in your thoughts or in deeds. Be sexually pure!" John commanded. "Do you repent and are you willing to turn away from your sins?"

Obviously shaken, the man stammered affirmatively.

"Then, wash and be clean."

Quickly, the man ducked completely beneath the water. As he stood, John placed both hands on either side of the man's head and said, "*When you and your children return to the LORD your God and obey him with all your heart…the LORD your God will restore your fortunes and have compassion on you.*"[9] Soberly, the man walked out of the water pondering the insight and the proclamation of the prophet.

The next man stood in front of John. John looked him squarely in the face and asked, "Are you repenting and truly turning away from your sins?"

"I am," the man replied.

"Dishonest scales," the Holy Spirit whispered.

"In heaven, the weights are accurate, and every attempt to tip the scales is recorded," John warned.

"How did you know?" the man stammered.

"There is nothing hidden from God," John answered.

"Then I repent!" the man exclaimed. "I will purchase accurate weights immediately."

"Then wash and be clean," John directed.

As the man ducked under the water, John sensed the weight of holy presence was increasing. It pressed against his shoulders like a heavy wet mantle. At the same time, John picked up on the spiritual excitement that seemed to fill the air he was breathing.

The man came up out of the water and stood dripping in front of John.

"*The* L*ORD* *your God will circumcise your heart and the hearts of your descendants, so that you may love him with all your heart…and live*,"[10] John blessed the man and motioned for him to step aside so the next man could come forward.

It was the end of the line. The last man stepped forward.

An overwhelming presence of holiness enveloped John.

"Your cousin," the Holy Spirit informed.

"Jesus!" John exclaimed as he embraced the son of Mary and Joseph.

Immediately, the Holy Spirit poured into him all the childhood memories—the stories his parents had told about his birth and his cousin's birth, the times they had spent together during the feasts of their childhood and adolescence.

"Why have you come to me like one from this multitude of sinners?" John asked as he gestured with his arm to include the entire baptismal scene.

"I am standing in the water in front of you to be baptized," Jesus answered.

"When I look into the eyes of men, I see their sinfulness. When they stand in front of me, the Holy Spirit shouts, "*God looks down from heaven on the sons of men…Everyone has turned away, they have together become corrupt; there is no one who does good, not even one.*"[11] But at this moment, I can hardly stand in the presence of the righteousness that lives within you. You should baptize me."

Jesus smiled as he shook his head, "No, let me stand in front of you now. Like every other man, I must obey the directives of the Holy Spirit. He sent me to this place to publicly participate in this demonstration of submission to my Father."

Then with his arm he gestured toward the people who surrounded them. "Everything God requires of the sons of Abraham, he requires of me."

Humbly, John bowed his head in submissive agreement.

"May I please you, Father," Jesus prayed and then he bent his knees and dipped beneath the surface of the water.

Without warning, the gray clouds seemed to split apart and a shaft of golden light shimmered directly on the spot where Jesus suddenly broke the surface of the water. All conversations and activities in the oasis stopped. Every eye was on the desert preacher and the man, dripping wet, standing in the golden light.

A sound like flapping wings—people pointed. Something white and graceful, like a large dove, was descending through the golden light. Momentarily, it hovered, and then it seemed to land on the man whose head was bowed and whose arms were stretched out to receive.

A voice like thunder—people trembled as they listened. "*This is my Son, whom I love; with him I am well pleased.*"[12]

All over the oasis, people began to ask? "Did you hear that?"

"It was thunder."

"No, it was a voice!"

"I heard, 'This is my Son.'"

"I think God spoke." Peter was the first of the fishermen to make a statement.

"God is pleased with our cousin, Jesus," John responded in amazement.

"I wonder what this means?" Andrew contemplated aloud.

"Look, Jesus is walking away. He's not coming back over here. He's headed for the desert road." James took a few steps toward the pool where Jesus had been baptized. "Jesus? Jesus?" he called.

In response, Jesus lifted his hand and waved, but he did not pause or turn. He continued walking. Jesus could see the shimmering essence of the Holy Spirit, and he was following him.

On either side of the road, heavenly warriors lined up and stood at attention. Silent and awed, they watched their Creator, like a warrior sent out alone to be the champion for his troops. The archangel Michael raised his sword in silent salute. Every angel followed the example of their angelic commander. Every sword was raised. Every angel stood in silent admiration.

John remained motionless in the water. He could also see the shimmering essence of the Holy Spirit as it led Jesus down the wilderness road.

As Jesus disappeared from sight, Geber called to John from the riverbank. "Your disciples have gathered at the fire. They have questions."

John nodded. Then he waded out of the pool and walked to the small fire his disciples kept burning day and night. He was almost at a loss for words, but finally, he managed to say, "*I saw the Spirit come down from heaven as a dove and remain on him. I would not have known him except that the one who sent me to baptize with water told me*[13] to look for that sign. He is the one I have been expecting."

"The Anointed One?"

"The Messiah?"

"When will he set up his kingdom?"

"Do we call for an army to drive the Romans out?"

John raised his hand for silence. "We wait on the commands of God. Until I receive a new directive from the Holy Spirit, we continue to call the people to repentance and direct them to demonstrate their repentance by being immersed in water. At this time, I have not received a new or a more aggressive directive. I remain a servant whose duty it is to prepare the way."

Chapter 13

A Wilderness Challenge

Then Jesus was led by the Spirit into the desert to be tempted by the devil.

—Matthew 4:1

Like a torch in the night sky, a full moon lit the wilderness road that skirted the base of a brown wind-carved mountain. Two riders, officials from the court of Herod Antipas, pushed their horses toward the desert palace not far from the Dead Sea.

The men rode in silence, concentrating on avoiding the unknown hazards of the road. Grotesquely shaped cliffs threw eerie shadows across the hard dirt. Gusts of wind whipped around the unusual rock formations, making travel uncomfortable for Cuza and Manaen. Mindful of their mounts, both men slowed, allowing their horses to fall into a slow walk.

"I've traveled this road many times, but tonight, it doesn't feel right," Manaen commented.

"There are lots of hiding places for bandits," Cuza added. "Maybe we were foolish to travel without an escort."

Responding to their uneasiness, Cuza and Manaen pushed their horses back into a steady pace. A cold wind unexpectedly gusted from a deep black gorge to their left. Both horses shied a little, but the men quickly brought their animals under control and then pressed them into a canter.

Again, Cuza and Manaen silently focused on the safety of their mounts as they rode quickly along the moonlit road. Both men felt a compelling urgency to get past the dry mountains with their rugged dark canyons and looming boulders.

After awhile, Manaen reined his horse down to a much slower gait. Cuza also slowed his mount. "Most of the places where bandits might hide are behind us," Manaen stated as he turned in his saddle to look at the road they had already traveled. Both men then rode slowly side-by-side, scanning the dark terrain on either side of the road as they continued their journey.

"What did you think about our day with the desert preacher?" Manaen asked.

"Honestly, I don't know," Cuza responded. "I was there. I saw and I heard. I have been questioning my senses ever since. Did you see a light from heaven and something like a giant white dove that floated down?"

"Yes," I saw it. I thought it looked more like a mantle. It came down and then fell across that man's shoulders like a piece of translucent fabric. I can't get the picture out of my mind, and I can't stop wondering what it means." Manaen responded.

A lizard darted across the road and a desert owl swooped down from the rocks to snatch his meal. Both horses shied and had to be brought under control again. "Our horses feel as skittish as we do," Manaen stated as he rubbed his horse's neck to calm her down.

Continuing at a slow and cautious pace, both men picked up their conversation, "Did you hear the voice or was it just distant thunder?" Cuza pressed for confirmation of his experience.

"This is my son. I am pleased," Manaen repeated. Then he quickly added, "Who was that man?"

"I don't know," Cuza responded. "I've never seen him before. I didn't hear his name. He looked like an ordinary village craftsman. He was friendly with the fishermen."

"I heard the prophet call him Jesus," Manaen said.

"Do you know how many men in Israel are named Jesus?" Cuza exclaimed. "It is one of the most common names!"

"Maybe we should return with a small contingency of soldiers and question the prophet?" Manaen suggested.

"Or maybe we should just drop by frequently," Cuza countered. "We can observe for now and see what develops. If we speak in the court of Antipas about what we have seen, our report will seem very unreliable."

"That's just a nice way of saying everyone will think we are crazy," Manaen stated. Suddenly, their horses stopped. With ears laid back, they began pawing and snorting. Both men struggled fiercely to keep their horses from turning to the right and running headlong into the rough terrain of the desert. "Something must be stalking us," Manaen stated. "I can hardly hold my horse."

"Could be a lion on one of those ledges." Cuza pointed to the rugged cliff that towered to the left of them.

"Let's get out of here," Manaen responded as he forced the head of his horse to face the road and dug his knees into its flanks. Cuza then spurred his own horse to catch up. Neither man mentioned their unusual day again.

Stalking eyes were peering out from a high ledge beside two wind-carved caves. They were not following the two riders from the court of Herod Antipas. They were watching the carpenter of Nazareth. Yeshua the Creator in human flesh had walked from the oasis to the base of this rugged mountain. Now he was sleeping.

Satan sneered as he muttered to himself, "O, how the Creator has limited himself. His body experiences fatigue and hunger. Like all the creatures of Earth, he needs water and food. I will wait until—"

A flaming sword of high-energy particles suddenly appeared in Satan's face.

Instinctively, the evil angel drew back. He respected the damage that weapon could do.

"Michael!" Satan growled the name of the angelic commander of the armies of heaven who was steadily advancing, pressing him back into the rock wall. "God gave me permission to approach and confront Yeshua."

"He did not give you permission without conditions," Michael responded. "We will be nearby, and we will be watching." Michael nodded toward the layers of rugged cliffs that made up the face of the mountain. Angels with drawn swords stood on each cliff.

"I should have expected a show of force," Satan responded. "My forces are also present."

"Hiding in the gorge." The Holy Spirit joined the encounter.

Beside the armed angel, a shimmering cloud materialized, and from within the cloud, the Holy Spirit continued to speak. "I have seen the former angels of God as well as your demonic spirits. They are drawn to darkness."

"My forces are stationed and under orders," Satan protested the inference that his army was fearfully hiding. "They have assignments. They must prepare."

The Holy Spirit brushed aside Satan's explanations as he stated, "We are heavenly observers."

"We are here to enforce the conditions laid out by God," Michael added.

"You may not physically touch your Creator," the Holy Spirit emphatically stated.

"I will not need to touch him," Satan arrogantly replied. "The elements he created—the wind, the heat—they will damage his human body. His flesh cannot survive without food and water. And the Creator placed within every human the desire to live. A man (and that is what Yeshua has chosen to be) will do anything to live."

"That is what we are here to see," the Holy Spirit replied. "I have called him to this desert place to fast and pray. He will not break his fast until his Father tells him it is time to eat. He will not leave this desert place until I lead him out."

Satan sneered, "So the great Yeshua does not have a mind of his own!"

"Yeshua-Jesus has completely surrendered his life to his Father God," the Holy Spirit responded. "He has submitted himself to the limitations God has placed on all humans."

Michael added, "He is demonstrating with every thought, word, and deed that the plans and the provision of God are totally sufficient for mankind."

"Ha! Even in their perfect garden home, Adam and Eve were easily moved to desire more than God was providing," Satan scoffed.

"And you," the Holy Spirit pointed a fiery finger at the evil angel. "*Once you were the model of perfection, full of wisdom and perfect in beauty. You were in Eden, the garden of God; every precious stone adorned you…Your settings and mountings were made of gold…You were anointed as a guardian cherub… You were on the holy mount of God; you walked among the fiery stones.*[1] But you were not satisfied with the provision of God."

Michael entered the conversation. "I knew you. Every morning, when you entered the throne room to greet your Creator, my heart swelled with admiration. *You were blameless in your ways from the day you were created till wickedness was found in you…. Then, you became filled with violence, and you sinned. So I drove you in disgrace from the mount of God, and I expelled you, O guardian cherub, from among the fiery stones.*"[2]

"That was only the initial battle," Satan retorted as he thrust his own evil finger in Michael's face. "Remember, you did not remove me from heaven without assistance."

"I was also in the battle." The glory of the Holy Spirit flared, and Satan fell back.

From the throne room, the words of God entered the confrontation making the desert mountains tremble. "*Your heart became proud on account of your beauty, and you corrupted your wisdom because of your splendor. So I threw you to the Earth.*[3] It all happened because you desired more than I had given you. *You said in your heart, 'I will ascend to heaven; I will raise my throne above the stars of God; I will sit enthroned on the mount of assembly, on the utmost heights of the sacred mountain. I will ascend above the tops of the clouds; I will make myself like the Most High.'*[4] See my son, Jesus."

Satan looked down at the carpenter from Nazareth. He was wrapped in his father's old cloak, sleeping on the packed earth of the desert floor.

God continued, "I love him because he is satisfied with whatever comes from my hand to him. His only desire is to do my will and experience my pleasure in his obedience."

Satan became speechless. How could it be? The Creator of the universe who had always lived in the splendor of heaven was really satisfied with life on Earth?

God broke the silence. "My son is yours to test on this point. You have forty days."

The early morning sun bathed the brown cliffs of the desert mountain with golden light. It threw sharp contrasting shadows across the entire face of the mountain. Jesus sat up and looked around, appreciating the rugged beauty of the wilderness.

Immediately, he recognized the voice of the Holy Spirit as it called to him from the barren mountain top. "Moses met God on the mountain. Elijah heard the still small voice of God in a high cave. Come up. Meet your Father God on this mountain. Enter his presence with prayer and fasting."

Without hesitation, Jesus hiked up his robes and secured them in his belt. He reached for the first jutting rock that would make a secure handhold and slowly, steadily, he began to climb the face of the mountain. Near the top, he could see a pair of caves behind a small ledge. Winded and sweating, he finally pulled his body over the ledge and into the shade of one of the shallow caves.

It had been more than a day since Jesus had enjoyed food or water. His mouth was dry and his stomach churned on its own juices, but Jesus refreshed himself with a psalm. Without the company of another human, he sang to his father, God.

I will exalt you, my God the King;
I will praise your name for ever and ever.
Every day I will praise you and
extol your name for ever and ever.
Great is the LORD and most worthy of praise;
his greatness no one can fathom.
One generation will commend your works to another;
they will tell of your mighty acts.
They will speak of the glorious splendor of your majesty,
and I will meditate on your wonderful works.[5]

He sang to the Holy Spirit.

The LORD is good to all; he has compassion on all he has made.
All you have made will praise you, O LORD;
your saints will extol you.
They will tell of the glory of your kingdom
and speak of your might,
so that all men may know of your mighty acts
and the glorious splendor of your kingdom.
Your kingdom is an everlasting kingdom,
and your dominion endures through all generations.
The LORD is faithful to all his promises
and loving toward all he has made.[6]

At the top of his lungs, Jesus sang for all of heaven to hear.

The LORD upholds all those who fall
and lifts up all who are bowed down.

The eyes of all look to you,
and you give them their food at the proper time.
You open your hand and satisfy the desires of every living thing.
The LORD is righteous in all his ways
and loving toward all he has made.
The LORD is near to all who call on him,
to all who call on him in truth.
He fulfills the desires of those who fear him;
he hears their cry and saves them.[7]

Satan heard the words of the song, and with clinched fist, he vowed, "Within forty days, you will choke on those words. Your food will not come in its proper time. Every cell in your body will scream for just a drop of water."

Then the evil angel looked around over his shoulder. His brooding eyes scanned the craggy ledges of the mountains. Where was the Holy Spirit? Where had Michael taken his angelic warriors? Satan could not see them. So he looked toward heaven and shouted to the throne room. "God, you have given me forty days and you must keep your word. You cannot intervene except to save his physical life."

The former archangel received no response, but he knew the character and the ways of God. He felt satisfied. God had heard his defiant rant, and he knew with certainty the Almighty Ruler of the Universe always kept his word.

After three days of quiet meditation, Jesus sat on the narrow ledge at the double mouth of the wind-formed cave. In this high and desolate place, for some unknown reason, Jesus was not experiencing the communication he usually shared with the Holy Spirit and his Father. It was alarming to feel so disconnected. With all his heart, Jesus cried, "Father God?" With every fiber of his being, he strained to reach past a sky that was like a mirror cast from bronze.

The beginning of a scripture suddenly ran through Jesus's mind. *"The Almighty is beyond our reach and exalted in power."*[8]

Jesus knew those words had not come from his own memory. "Even in this deserted place the spirit named Religion comes to distort the words of God," Jesus commented. Then speaking to the evil spirit, he completed the scripture. *"In his justice and great righteousness, he does not oppress. Therefore, men revere him.*[9] My heart is steadfast and confident that my Father will provide his presence at the right time."

With a controlling thought, Satan ordered the spirit to withdraw until the elements had further weakened Jesus. But he remained close enough to observe and listen.

Several days later, the evil angel heard Jesus pray, "Father God, the days and nights are passing. My throat is parched and my skin is blistered. My stomach has given up on its request for food. Still, I thirst. Even greater than my longing for water is my longing to hear your voice. Why is there silence?"

Satan listened closely, and then he called his spirits of Doubt and Abandonment. "Do your work," he commanded.

Immediately, both spirits began to project what seemed like the soft counsel of the Holy Spirit. "Examine yourself, Jesus. Have you displeased your Father? Has he turned his face from you?"

At first, Jesus ignored the thoughts.

But Doubt and Abandonment became louder and more insistent. "God is displeased with you, Jesus."

Like furious zealots, they hurled their verbal stones. "Your Father has abandoned and discarded you. You are in distress, but he does not care. The great God of the universe has no more use for you. He is going to let you die in this desert."

Raising the shield of scripture, Jesus answered the demonic thoughts that kept pummeling his mind, *"I say to myself, 'The* L*ORD is my portion; therefore I will wait for him. The* L*ORD is good to those whose hope is in him, to the one who seeks him; it is good to wait quietly for the salvation of the* L*ORD.'"*[10]

Projecting his command, Satan temporally withdrew those demons to wait until the sun and the elements had furthered weakened the human body of Yeshua-Jesus.

Again and again, the sun passed its zenith and moved toward the western horizon. Each day, it illuminated the whole Jordan valley in the vicinity of Jericho. From the mountain top, Jesus could see Jericho with its beautiful date palms and lush clumps of vegetation. The Jordan valley near Jericho looked like emeralds tossed on a cloak made from camel's wool.

On the twelfth morning, Jesus looked out across the Jordan, observing the farms and fields around Jericho. He had another thought, and he knew it was not his own. There was a challenging edge to the question. "Almost like Eden, do you remember that beautiful garden?"

In response, Jesus began to quote from the vast amount of scripture he had memorized. "*Now the* L*ORD God had planted a garden in the east, in Eden; and there he put the man he had formed. And the* L*ORD God made all kinds of trees grow out of the ground—trees that were pleasing to the eye and good for food.*[11] *The* L*ORD God took the man and put him in the Garden of Eden to work it and take care of it. And the* L*ORD God commanded the man, 'You are free to eat from any tree in the garden: but you must not eat from the tree of the knowledge of good and evil, for when you eat of it you will surely die.'*"[12]

A slight rubbing sound drew Jesus's attention to the mouth of the second cave. A poisonous viper slid from the shadows into the warmth of the late afternoon sun. The snake paused and looked at the man who had taken possession of his high ledge.

Jesus looked directly into the amber eyes of the snake and said, "I see you, Lying spirit. Once again, you have chosen to hide in a serpent. It is written, '*Now the serpent was more crafty than any of the wild animals the* L*ORD* *God had made.*'"[13]

In response, the snake coiled and then lifted his head. His forked tongue tested and retested the heated atmosphere.

Jesus did not move. Neither did he take his eyes from the snake. Suddenly, the snake projected another challenging thought, "Did the Spirit of God really lead you to this high deserted place? Did he bring you to this ledge so I could sink my fangs into your heel and send my poison throughout your entire body?"

"I know to whom I speak," Jesus answered. "Relay this message to your master. As the Creator, I cursed you and said you would *crawl on your belly and…eat dust all the days of your life.*[14] We are enemies."

In response, the snake submissively lowered its head and slithered away, down the rugged slope.

After that encounter, Jesus slumped back against the mountainside. His head was throbbing from dehydration and the work-hardened muscles of his arms and legs were cramping.

"Father?" He called for the hundredth time. When it became obvious there was no immediate response, Jesus repeated the words of Jeremiah, "'*Let him sit alone in silence, for the* L*ORD* *has laid it on him.*'[15] Blessed be the name of the Lord. I will be thankful and satisfied to wait in silence."

After the serpent slithered off the ledge, the Holy Spirit approached Satan again. "It could have been that simple in the garden, if Eve had just repeated the words of God. If she had just stated that she was satisfied with the provision of her Creator and turned away—"

"But she didn't," Satan forcefully countered. "It may take a little longer to make Yeshua-Jesus realize he needs more than God is offering him. But I have time—another twenty-eight days."

The Holy Spirit cautioned, "Jesus is aware of your presence. He knows sin is crouching like a hungry animal, and it desires to have him. He has known that since he was a child."

"When his flesh is weak, it will not matter," Satan arrogantly replied. "I have taught all of humanity to value their flesh above the Spirit that lives within them and connects them with God."

The Holy Spirit paused and listened. Then he said, "I am always drawn to the praises of God." Quickly, he turned and left the Evil One.

From the high dusty ledge, Jesus sang with a parched, cracking voice,

> *One thing I ask of the Lord, this is what I seek:*
> *that I may dwell in the house of the Lord all the days of my life,*
> *to gaze upon the beauty of the Lord and to seek him in his temple.*[16]

The Holy Spirit settled over Jesus, bathing him in waves of love.

This touch from heaven, it was worth the thirst and the discomfort of twelve days on the mountain. "Your presence is like getting cool water from these rocks," Jesus responded. Then with a clearer voice, he continued the psalm.

> *For in the day of trouble he will keep me safe in his dwelling;*
> *he will hide me in the shelter of his tabernacle*
> *and set me high upon a rock.*[17]

At Bethany beyond the Jordan, Peter and Andrew checked all their baskets. "Empty!" Peter announced. "We sold all the sardines."

"Do we go back to Galilee, now?" James asked.

"No," his brother responded. "In just two weeks, everyone will begin the journey to Jerusalem for the Feast of Tabernacles. Let's stay here and learn from the prophet. We can return to our fishing boats after the feast."

"Every time this desert prophet speaks, my heart burns for the Messiah to come and run the Romans out of our land," Peter concurred. "He breathes life into the scriptures. I have never heard a man with such fire and anointing."

"Our father has fire without anointing. We will hear about wasting two weeks when we could have been fishing," James warned.

"Zebedee is like a storm on Galilee, sudden and fierce, but it ends quickly," Andrew reasoned.

"We can withstand the gale," John rejoined. "I will reason with him."

"So, we stay!" Peter announced. "Let's go sit with the disciples of the prophet. He is teaching them." Without waiting for the others, Peter hurried to sit on the rocks close to John the Baptist and his disciples.

"We are in the season of repentance," John the prophet shouted. "Soon, the trumpets will sound and in heaven the judgment will begin. Repent!"

The desert prophet stepped into the pool, wading back and forth in the water as he taught, "Repent for Adam who loved the pleasures of the flesh more than the directives of his Creator. He desired to keep his mate, so he ate the fruit."

With an open heart and an eye that appreciated the beauty of this wasteland, Jesus studied the desert sky. The stars seemed close enough to touch. Some star formations looked like dippers that could be filled with cool water. Insistently, his body reminded him that every cell needed water. And every demon hiding in the gorge repeated, "You need water. You need water." Their chant went on endlessly, like the steady marching of the hob-nailed sandals of a legion of Roman soldiers.

Resisting the demands of his body, Jesus continued to study the night sky. He noticed the moon had nearly disappeared. The thin crescent that remained appeared like a cup that could hold a refreshing drink of water.

"Wouldn't you like a drink? It's not a long walk to the Jordan River."

As he had done many times since entering this arid region, Jesus again rebuked his flesh as well as the Demanding spirit that seemed to never fade into silence.

He was not leaving this mountain to look for a cup of water. Patient and determined, Jesus waited. His Father, through the Holy Spirit, had called him to this place. He would remain on this arid ledge until heaven commanded that he move on.

It was the twenty-fifth day. Jesus carefully positioned his body so his head faced Jerusalem. He stretched out on the flat ledge. With a raspy voice, he began his early morning prayer, "*Give ear to my words, O LORD, consider my sighing. Listen to my cry for help, my King and my God, for to you I pray. In the morning, O LORD, you hear my voice; in the morning I lay my requests before you and wait in expectation.*"[18]

What are you expecting? Once again, Satan's demons shot their thoughts into the mind of Yeshua-Jesus.

Jesus answered the voices in his head, "I am expecting my next directive from God. Until then, I continue following his last instruction."

"His last instruction?" the spirit called Rebellion probed, hoping to stir some independent thinking that would lead Jesus into disobedience.

"I am to fast and pray in this barren place," Jesus restated his instructions.

In a desert like this, men can quickly lose their minds and their lives without water, the spirits of Self-Preservation and Fear pressed their thoughts into the mind of Jesus.

Jesus answered, "When Israel came out of Egypt into a desert like this, they saw no water so they allowed themselves to be captured by Self-Preservation and Fear. With their complaints, they tested God until Moses struck the rock and water flowed."

After that statement, Jesus reached out and rubbed his hand over the rough surface of the mountain that had become his home. "Water can come from this rock if it is the will of God. He knows my needs. I will not test him with complaints. I will not allow either Fear or Self-Preservation to take possession of my mind. *Though he slay me, yet will I hope in him.*"[19] Weakly, Jesus closed his eyes, allowing the climbing sun to pass over him into the relative coolness of evening.

Thirty times, the sun had passed over Jesus, burning the life out of his body. On a few occasions, he had seen distant thunderclouds and dusty whirlwinds. Desert animals had approached, some curious and some hungry. Now as another evening announced the beginning of a new day, Jesus again appreciated some relief from the burning sun.

Looking up, he saw the first three stars and then signal fires blazed, one after the other across the distant hills, and Jesus knew that a new month had begun. The faint sound of ram's horns drifted from villages at the edge of the wilderness. It was the Feast of Trumpets, a day filled with the sounds of ram's horns and trumpets, a day of warning and preparation.

In the recesses of a nearby canyon, Satan trembled. He hated the sound of trumpets. In heaven, the trumpets had announced every move of the Eternal Father, Yeshua the Creator, and the Holy Spirit. On Earth, they were prophetic declarations.

Satan looked up to see Jesus weakly pulling himself to a standing position, supporting himself by leaning into the rock wall. He was responding to the trumpets. In a voice that was only a whisper, he was repeating the words of the prophet Joel, "*Blow the trumpet in Zion; sound the alarm on my holy hill. Let all who live in the land tremble, for the day of the LORD is coming. It is close at hand.*[20] *The LORD thunders at the head of his army; his forces are beyond number, and mighty are those who obey his command. The day of the LORD is great; it is dreadful. Who can endure it?*"[21]

"Who can endure?" Satan repeated as he watched Jesus sway with weakness and then crumple into a sitting position.

Quickly, the Evil One moved close enough to assess the physical condition of Yeshua-Jesus. This man, once the Creator of the universe, had slumped into unconsciousness. The Evil One knew Jesus had not urinated for at least a week, and he was quite certain his kidneys had stopped functioning.

Evening suddenly rushed across the barren landscape. Like a comforting blanket, darkness covered the ledge. The bats that daily attached themselves to the ceiling of the high shallow cave exited in a stream of dark beating wings. They would have a meal of flying insects before returning to their daytime shelter, but Jesus would eat nothing.

"My son," It was the voice of God calling him back into consciousness. "You have waited through the long hot day." With a thought, God restored the function of Jesus's kidneys and stabilized the electrolytes in his body so his flesh would not die before he completed this forty day test.

Immediately, Jesus sat up and responded, "Your voice is my refreshment, and your instruction is my bread and water."

"Do you know what day it is?" God asked.

"The beginning of a new year," Jesus answered. "It is the Day of Trumpets."

"It is the anniversary of the day Adam was given dominion over the Earth," God reminded Jesus.

At that moment, the Holy Spirit drew back the curtain of time and made available to Jesus the memory of Yeshua the Creator.

"The trumpets of heaven announced the event," Jesus recalled. "Adam's first administrative act was to name each animal and assign it a habitat."

"Each animal came before him with its mate and when every animal had been named, Adam asked for his own mate," God added.

"Eve—she was beautiful and intelligent, a perfect partner for Adam," Jesus wistfully stated.

"On the day of her creation, we made the first entry in the Book of the Earth's Population," God recalled. "Adam's name was the first to be inscribed. He was the ruler. Then we added Eve's name."

"There came a day, after Eve had been deceived and Adam had willfully chosen to disobey, that I had to temporarily cross out Adam's name and write the name of our adversary," Jesus said. "I remember, I vowed to challenge Satan for rulership of the Earth."

"You are here in the place of Adam," God informed. "You have come to show the Evil One and all who dwell in the universe that it is possible for a created being to chose to live in perfect submission to me and to the laws of my kingdom."

"*Oh, how I love your law! I meditate on it all day long,*[22]" Jesus responded. "You have taught me to wait on your directives and not to move ahead with my own plans," he added.

"The Evil One thinks there will come a point in your life when you will not wait for direction from heaven. Then you will reason as a man who puts himself above God and makes his own decisions. Our adversary believes he can force you to doubt the scriptures as well as the things we have done together. He thinks he can manipulate circumstances causing you to fear and then to step back into your independently divine role. Every human who has ever lived has fallen into one of his snares. Our enemy feels very confident that you are no different."

"What is it that the Eternal One asks of his creation?" Jesus rhetorically asked. "It is nothing more than to *fear the LORD your God, to walk in all his ways, to love him, to serve the LORD your God with all your heart and with all your soul, and to observe the LORD's commands and decrees.*[23] They are for the good of mankind. I want nothing more than to serve you."

"*Shout it aloud, do not hold back. Raise your voice like a trumpet. Declare to my people their rebellion and to the house of Jacob their sins.*"[24] John the Baptizer quoted from the writings of Isaiah. "You have heard the trumpets. From sunset to sunset they have sounded a warning—prepare for judgment!"

Peter, John, James, and Andrew found large flat rocks at the edge of the pool. They sat down and dangled their sandaled feet in the water while they listened.

"Right now, the books of heaven are open. When you were children in the synagogue schools, you were taught these books are opened on the Day of Trumpets and they are closed on the Day of Atonement. You only have ten days to plead before the God of heaven. Where will your name be written—the Book of Life or the Book of Death?"

Gradually, more people arrived and found places to sit and listen to the prophet. Dressed in his rough camel's wool tunic, John the Baptizer stepped away from the pool and began to walk among the people as he continued, "The life of each man and woman passes before the Eternal One. He is like a shepherd who counts the sheep as they enter his fold. Only the healthy sheep get to walk under his rod into the safety of the stone enclosure. Those who are riddled with the disease of sin must stay outside where lions and bears can tear them to pieces."

"Hear my voice when I call, O Lord; be merciful to me and answer me. My heart says of you, 'Seek his face!' Your face, Lord, I will seek,"[25] Jesus called to his Father, repeating the same scripture over and over. His mind did not seem to have an original thought.

Time had become confusing. Jesus no longer heard the trumpets. At times, his mind slipped in and out of deep nothingness. Never in his life had he imagined that a human body could experience such weakness. Certainly, he no longer had the strength to climb down and walk back to civilization. Jesus leaned weakly into the strength of the mountain. He felt his heart slip into an irregular rhythm, and a wave of dizziness washed over his body.

To distract himself, Jesus looked down toward the base of the mountain. On the rocks below, a small herd of wild goats moved nimbly from rock to rock. The animals brought a weak smile to Jesus's face. They moved with such gracefulness, and their horns curved majestically into half circles. The animals stopped to strip the leaves from a lone scraggly shrub.

Moving close, Satan whispered, "Watch."

Jesus's eyes were immediately drawn to the sleek body of a mountain lion, crouching on the rocky ledge that was just above the goats. In less time than it took to exhale, the lion sprang and took one of the goats by the throat.

The rest of the flock fled, scattering over the rough terrain while the lion tore into the body of the helpless animal.

O Adam, Jesus addressed the first man in his mind, *the whole creation has been groaning as in the pains of childbirth right up to the present time.*[26] I hate death.

"Yeshua, my son." God spoke into the horror of the moment.

"You will establish a kingdom without death, without predators, or prey. You left your heavenly throne to face death, to experience death, and to overcome death," God informed.

"Now?" Jesus asked. "Is this the time of my death?"

God did not answer.

The horror of predator and prey continued on the rocks below.

Jesus closed his eyes and whispered, "*You brought me out of the womb; you made me trust in you even at my mother's breast. From birth I was cast upon you; from my mother's womb you have been my God.*"[27]

Intently, Satan studied Yeshua-Jesus. Once again, his flesh was failing. The evil angel looked around, hoping that heaven would restore the function of his body so the torment could continue.

"Michael!" Satan called the name of the commander of the angelic host. "Look at your Creator. His physical body will soon give out."

Materializing from behind a craggy boulder, Michael responded, "The Spirit of God that lives within him is stronger than his human body."

"Are you going to let his body die? Right here?" Satan asked. "I have not had my face-to-face challenge yet!"

"Five days remain. You may approach him any time," Michael answered.

"In two days, it will be the tenth day of the seventh month," John announced. You must show the Lord that you recognize your sin. You must deny yourselves all food and water. Do not do any work. Do not even feed your animals. It is a day to fall on your face before the Creator of Earth and hope he will have mercy and write your name in the Book of Life for another year."

Cuza and Manaen reined in their horses under the shade of a date palm. It had been nearly forty days since they had left this oasis on the king's business.

"We cannot stay and listen," Cuza stated.

"I know," Manaen responded. "We have to escort Antipas and his entourage to Jerusalem for the Feast of Tabernacles."

"From there, we move everyone to his desert palace near the Nabataean border," Cuza added.

"Prophet, should we go to the Temple?" a man shouted his question.

John the Baptizer answered, "That is the place that God has chosen for atonement to be made for you. Two goats will be chosen. One will become a sin offering for the people. Its blood will be carried into the Most Holy Place and sprinkled behind the veil. The sins of the people will be placed on the head of the other goat, and it will be led into the wilderness to die."

"Will all sins be forgiven?" another man asked.

Cuza and Manaen exchanged glances. Both men were silently wondering about the sins of Antipas.

"No!" the preacher shouted. "It takes more than blood and ritualistic words. Every sin must be recognized. Every sin against another man must be made right. There must be repentance and a heart that is set on never repeating that sin."

"What about King Antipas? He brings a caravan of offerings and sacrifices to every one of the Lord's festivals."

Cuza looked to see that one of the fishermen was asking the question.

"*Does the LORD delight in burnt offerings and sacrifices as much as in obeying the voice of the LORD?*" John answered. "*To obey is better than sacrifice, and to heed is better than the fat of rams.*"[28]

"The message of this prophet has not changed," Manaen commented.

"Those are dangerous words he speaks," Cuza added as both men wheeled their horses and continued their journey back to the palace of Antipas in Galilee.

It was the hottest part of the day. Jesus slowly shifted his position on the ledge. The muscles in his legs were painfully cramping again. He tried to move, but his head seemed so light and fuzzy that he was not even sure where the ledge dropped off. Searching for some clarity, he began to recite scriptures. *"As for God, his way is perfect; the word of the LORD is flawless."* Jesus's voice was only a dry whisper. *"For who is God besides the LORD? And who is the Rock except our God? It is God who arms me with strength and makes my way perfect. He makes my feet like the feet of a deer; he enables me to stand on the heights."*[29] Exhausted, Jesus dropped his head and let it rest on his chest.

"Stand on the heights!" Satan sneered. "Yeshua, you cannot stand at all. It has been forty days, and you are close to death."

Immediately, the Holy Spirit moved in to counter, "Yeshua is resting in the strength of the Rock. Have you noticed that he is not demanding food or water? He knows he can trust his Father to provide. Even near the point of death, he waits on God."

"Rouse him," the Evil One demanded. "I will confront Yeshua in his human form now!"

With unexpected suddenness, Jesus felt strength flowing through his body. He became alert. His senses came alive to the painful stinging of his sunburned skin, to the unbearable dryness of his throat, to the overpowering odor of the decaying carcass on the rocks below. A large shadow passed over the ledge, and Jesus watched as a black vulture swooped down to tear scraps of rotten meat from the remains of the dead goat. A wave of nausea rolled through his body. Jesus heaved, but his stomach was empty. Then, without warning he became ravenously hungry. His hands trembled and his body shook as it demanded nourishment.

A soft glow developed beside Jesus, and out of the radiance came a voice, "You need to eat." Hidden in artificial glory, Satan tried to mimic the benevolent tone of heaven. "*If you are the Son of God, tell these stones to become bread.*"[30]

The stones, no bigger than a man's hand, were within reach, but Jesus recognized the deceitful premise of the suggestion. He answered, "I will not question the things my Father has spoken to me. Before I came into this wilderness and climbed this barren mountain, I heard God say, '*This is my Son, whom I love; with him I am well pleased.*'"[31] Jesus paused, leaning hard against the rock wall of the mountain as he fought back waves of intense hunger and nausea.

At that moment, Satan burst out of his glory cloud, displaying all of the radiance that remained in his degenerating body.

The brightness was momentarily stunning. With one hand, Jesus weakly shaded his eyes. Then he said, "I have seen the glory of heaven. I have seen the angels of God. You are not from heaven, and you are not an angel of God." Then gathering all his strength, he added, "*It is written: 'Man does not live on bread alone, but on every word that comes from the mouth of God.'*[32] I will live on the word of God. When my Father God commands that I eat bread, bread will be provided. Then I will eat it."

"So, you know who you are? Do you know who I am?"

Confidently, Jesus answered, "Once, before you challenged the authority of God, you were called Lucifer. Your radiance was much greater then."

"How much do you know about angels?" Satan probed. "Did you see the angels that lined the road as you walked to this place? They wait to do your bidding."

Jesus nodded. "There have been many times when the Holy Spirit has drawn back the curtain that separates the earthly from the heavenly realms. I have seen the angels. I have seen those who are loyal to me and those who have fallen with you."

"Come with me!" With the permission of the Holy Spirit, Satan whisked Jesus away from the wilderness to stand on the highest point of the Temple in Jerusalem. From that spot, they could both look out, viewing all the city with its surrounding valleys and mountains. They could look directly down and see all the activity in the various courts of the beautiful Temple Herod had restored. But most significantly, they could see the angels patrolling the walls of the city.

For a long moment, both Satan and Jesus stood side-by-side looking directly at the heavenly angelic force. The fiery chariots stopped making their rounds, and every angelic warrior came to attention. The warring seraph, Ophaniel, who commanded this segment of the Lord's army, raised his sword, silently saluting his Creator.

"Your army stands ready to serve you." Satan gestured toward the magnificent force that stood just above the city walls. *"If you are the Son of God," he said, "throw yourself down. For it is written: 'He will command his angels concerning you, and they will lift you up in their hands, so that you will not strike your foot against a stone.'"*[33]

With great effort, Jesus turned to face his enemy. "How arrogant are your words! I know the position I have willingly taken on Earth, and I know my position in heaven. I am Yeshua your Creator. By the words of my mouth, you were formed. By the words of my mouth, all the beings of heaven were created. *I am who I am.*"[34] Ignoring his own physical weakness, Jesus looked directly into the eyes of his adversary. Divinity flashed as Jesus answered him, "It is also written: *'Do not put the Lord your God to the test.'*"[35]

For a moment, the Evil One fell back almost losing his own balance on the edge of the precipice. With an angry swish of his wings, Satan quickly regained his balance and brought Jesus back to the mountain top.

Upon touching the ledge, Jesus felt his legs buckle beneath him.

Satan, an angel of fading light, towered over him. "Since you remember your heavenly role, I assume that you remember the plan you made with the Holy Spirit and the Eternal Father."

"Yes," Jesus softly answered. "I have come to live as a man, completely submitted to the plans of God and the laws of his kingdom. Then I will die."

"And what is the purpose of this noble sacrifice?" Satan sneered.

"I am taking the punishment for the sin of Adam and the curse that he brought upon all mankind," Jesus answered. "I will then take the place of Adam as ruler of this world."

"Rulership of this world—it does not have to be so difficult." Satan shook his head in mocking admonition. "Look!" With a wave of his hand, Satan filled the sky with scene upon scene—the seven hills of Rome, the acropolis of Athens, the pyramids of Egypt, and Jerusalem set on Mount Zion. Every physical accomplishment in every civilization was on display for Jesus. "*All this I will give you*," he said, "*if you will bow down and worship me.*"[36] Before Jesus could reply, Satan was showing him a lavish banquet. Emperor Tiberius and his guests were gorging themselves on meats, breads, and fruit. Quickly, the Evil One changed the scene. Now Jesus saw a beautiful Roman bath where men of means lounged in pools of tepid water while they drank wine from silver goblets. "I know you are thirsty. I know you are hungry," Satan whispered. Then with a deceptively sweet voice he added, "But I know there is something you want more than anything I have shown you."

Abruptly, Satan changed the scene and Jesus saw armies marching, bloody battles—violent death, starving children, and lepers. Then scene after scene of natural disasters: fires, earthquakes, floods, and famines. "As ruler of this world, you could end wars. You could end sickness and death. You could control nature—that's what you want, isn't it? You want Earth to be like heaven. Just recognize me as a god—equal to God. Worship me."

Drawing on the last of his physical strength, Jesus said to him, "*Away from me, Satan! For it is written: 'Worship the Lord your God, and serve him only.'*"[37]

The whispered Word hit the evil angel with a supernatural power that threw him off balance. With a sneer, the fallen angel tried to step forward to tempt Yeshua again. Immediately, the Holy Spirit, like a protective wall of fire, materialized between the Creator and his enemy. A trumpet blast pierced the air and Satan found himself falling backward from the ledge.

Knowing his time with Jesus had come to an end, Satan flared his wings defiantly and then turned to flee.

Responding to Michael's signal, the angelic army drew their swords. Michael pursued Satan while the rest of his warriors swooped through the canyons and caves to rout the army of evil beings from their hiding places.

On the ledge, Jesus had collapsed. His lungs had nearly stopped. It seemed each shallow breath might be his last.

"My son!" the heart-moving cry of the Eternal Father pierced the atmosphere.

Ministering angels hurried to the spot with basins of cool water as well as the sweet bread of heaven.

For several days, the angels hovered over their Creator-in-human-form. They bathed him. They fed him and brought refreshing water to his lips. They shaded him and fanned him with their wings. He slept with his head on an angelic lap. The angels stayed with him until his strength returned. Then he was able to climb back down the steep face of the mountain and return to his cousin John who was still preaching and baptizing at the oasis at Bethany beyond the Jordan.

Chapter 14

Look, the Lamb of God!

I have seen and I testify that this is the Son of God.

—John 1:34

Evening was falling. As Jesus walked along the road to Bethany beyond the Jordan, he could just make out the tall date palms that grew near the freshwater springs. There were a number of small campfires around the oasis, but Jesus did not go to any of them. By the white light of a moon that was growing toward total fullness, he gathered some branches and made a three-sided shelter, crawling beneath it to sleep the remainder of the night.

At dawn, John and Geber were washing in one of the pools of water when *John saw Jesus coming toward him and said, "Look, the Lamb of God, who takes away the sin of the world! This is the one I meant when I said, 'A man who comes after me has surpassed me because he was before me.' I myself did not know him, but the reason I came baptizing with water was that he might be revealed to Israel."*[1]

Geber responded, "I saw the white mantle that fell from heaven and landed on his shoulders like a dove. I heard the voice, so I know God is with him like he is with no other man. But this man is not a warrior or a political leader."

"He is God's choice," John replied. "We will wait and watch."

As John finished his sentence, Jesus slipped out of his tunic and waded into the pool of spring water. He ducked beneath its cool surface and came up rubbing the desert grit from his beard. Over and over, he ducked beneath the water, scrubbing his body, enjoying the freshness of feeling clean once again.

"Cousin!" When Jesus had finished washing he came over to John and embraced him.

"I was wondering if I would see you again," John said.

"I go where the Holy Spirit sends me," Jesus answered.

"And where did the Holy Spirit send you?" Geber joined the conversation.

"Into the desert for forty days," Jesus replied.

Geber merely nodded. He understood the significance of forty days.

"And now?" John asked.

"I will stay here for a few days and listen to your teaching," Jesus answered. "I will go to Jerusalem for the feast and then return to you until I am directed to move on."

"Shouldn't I learn from you?" John questioned.

"For a time, God willed that Elisha was to be a servant for Elijah. Then when the time of Elijah's ministry ended, God poured out on Elisha a double anointing," Jesus responded.

"Then let it be that you will remain with me until the time that my ministry declines," John said. "In my heart, the Holy Spirit testifies that your words are true. Your ministry must increase while mine decreases. Blessed be the name of the Lord." John dropped his head for a moment and then he looked up into the eyes of his cousin. "I have been waiting for this day. I must admit, I expected there would be more drama—not just our quiet conversation."

Jesus reached out and placed his hand on his cousin's shoulder. "God has given you enough fire and drama for both of us. Keep calling this nation into the Kingdom of God through repentance. I will call to these people who are the sons and daughters of Abraham in mercy and compassion—maybe they will hear."

"Mercy and compassion," John echoed. "The people do need mercy and compassion, but those men of sin who oversee the Temple—they do not deserve any mercy or compassion!"

Longinus looked up as his assistant entered.

His first officer said, "A representative from the Temple is here to receive the official vestments for the high priest. He has a request. He wants to be allowed to keep the vestments overnight for the next seven nights because the rituals for this occasion are day and night."

"Does the high priest ever sleep?" Longinus rhetorically asked.

"I'm sure he does," the first officer responded.

"Then when he prepares for bed, the robes are to be returned to the fortress."

"They want to just keep the robes in the same room where the priest is sleeping," the officer informed.

"Have you seen those robes?" Longinus asked. "They are covered with more precious gemstones and gold than the emperor has in his entire wardrobe. No, the officer at the gate will receive them every night." Longinus dismissed his officer with an annoyed sigh. "Those Jews are forever requesting exceptions to the procedures."

Pilate entered the room and Longinus stood, saluting in acknowledgment.

"How many people are in the city for this feast?" Pilate asked as he strode over to look out the window at the Temple complex.

Longinus replied, "I do not have a count, but the streets are crowded and people are still arriving. They are building booths on hillsides and rooftops. It looks like the whole city is camping out."

"What about the water situation?" Pilate asked. "Just a week ago, for their Feast of Trumpets, the fortress ran out of water. I could not even bathe."

"We have not had rain and there are more people," Longinus answered.

"Send some men out into the elevated countryside, toward Bethlehem. Find a source of water for the city and a route for an aqueduct. Get the engineers to draw up plans." Pilate made himself comfortable, sitting at the table where Longinus had been working. "But the soldiers are not to tell anyone what they are doing. These people are too easily upset."

"How are you going to pay for this project?" Longinus asked.

"Have you seen the money that comes into this Temple, especially during their celebrations? I have been watching their treasury boxes. The money never stops coming."

"Yes," Longinus concurred. "This is the celebration of their final harvest. Over the next week, vast amounts are expected."

"I'm going to appropriate some of that money for an aqueduct and a new water system for this city," Pilate stated.

"How are you going to get them to agree?" Longinus asked.

"Agree? They are not going to be asked." Pilate stood and walked over to the window again. "After this religious holiday, I am going to march in and take half of their gold and silver coins."

Longinus looked squarely at the governor of Judea as he asked, "What if they complain to Rome?"

"I have already prepared a letter to the emperor explaining the critical need for water in this city and the responsibility of the local government"—Pilate pointed toward the Temple before finishing his statement—"to pay for it."

"Are you going to wait for the emperor's response?" Longinus asked.

"No, I want a new water supply for this city before their spring festivals begin. Now get the men to bring extra water into the fortress. It's going to be a long week."

"Susanna!" In the governor's apartment, Procila greeted her new friend from the court of Herod Antipas. "I'm so glad you could accept my invitation."

"It was not easy," Susanna responded. "I had to make an excuse to get away from Herod's palace here in Jerusalem. Herodias is so demanding, and she has a very jealous nature. If she knew we had a friendship, she would assume I was betraying her."

"I know," Procila nodded her head affirmatively. "I have lived in Rome. Among the ladies, there is a ruthless competitiveness that can be just as dangerous as the politics of men. Come look." Procila led Susanna over to a table beside a window in the wall of the Antonio Fort that overlooked the Temple courts. "Ever since I came to Jerusalem with my husband so he could fulfill his duties for this festival season, I have been glued to this window. So many different rituals and sacrifices—I want to understand what I am seeing.

Susanna sat in a chair beside the window. From that height, she could see the Court of the Women, the fifteen steps and the gate that was the entrance to the Court of the Israelites. She could see the area that was just for the priests, the altar of burnt offering, the laver, and the steps that led into the Holy Place. "I will never get used to seeing so much of the house of the Lord," Susanna spoke with reverence.

"I can see this place means a lot to you," Procila commented.

"Oh yes," Susanna answered. "This Temple is the place where we come into the presence of our God. We live by his laws. He is our personal and our national identity."

"We have many gods and many different temples," Procila stated.

"But it is different when you have only one God," Susanna countered. "Our one God is everything that all your gods are and more."

Procila leaned closer to the window. "All the people are carrying branches and a yellow citrus fruit. There are tall willow branches around the altar. What is happening down there?"

"It is the Feast of Tabernacles. The city is full of booths made from tree branches. For the next seven days, no one will be living in their own homes. Even Herod Antipas has a booth in his courtyard."

"Is Herodias living in a booth made of branches?" Procila coyly asked.

Susanna laughed. "She and Antipas have separate booths. Both are quite luxurious. It is hardly like camping on a hillside."

Both women laughed as they imagined the haughty new wife of Antipas camping in a typical booth made of branches.

Susanna pointed to the altar. "If you get up when the trumpet sounds at dawn, you will see the people bring fresh willow branches to place around the altar. Then the priests will march around the altar once. On the seventh day of the feast, the priests march around the altar seven times blowing their trumpets. This commemorates the destruction of Jericho, when our people first entered this land. Another service also takes place each morning. A procession of priests goes down to the spring and they bring back a golden pitcher filled with water. When it is time for the wine offering, both the wine and the water are poured at the same time into the receptacles on the side of the altar. Then the choir will stand on the steps and sing."

"I have heard the choir," Procila commented.

"This is a time of great rejoicing," Susanna continued, "because all of the harvest is in. People are bringing their first fruits and the tithes. It is also a celebration of hope. We wave our branches before the Lord and pray for rain to begin the next crops." Susanna pointed to an area of the Temple where there were animal pens and a pool of water for washing the animals. "There will be lots of animal sacrifices—seventy bulls will be sacrificed for the sins of the nations of the world. Tonight at sundown, there will be a blast from the silver trumpets. Most people will have a special meal in their booths, then at midnight"—Susanna pointed to the four tall golden cauldrons of oil—"those lamps will be lit. The gates of the Temple will be thrown open and all the people will come to celebrate. The important men of the city will dance and juggle torches."

"Can you stay and watch with me?" Procila asked.

"The other women watch from those balconies that have been built just for this festive occasion, so I can watch from here," Susanna agreed.

"Did your master, the prophet, go up to Jerusalem for the feast?" Upon returning from Jerusalem, Andrew approached one of John's disciples.

"On this side of the Jordan, we are no longer in the land God gave to Abraham, so it is not a requirement for us," the disciple replied.

"But the distance is not great," Andrew protested. "My brother and I walked it in only two days. We built our booth and went to the Temple as required by the law."

"Most of the men left this oasis and went to Jerusalem for the feast, but I believe John remained. Let's ask him to explain."

Both men walked over to the desert prophet. At that same moment, Jesus came walking by. John completely ignored their question about the feast. Instead, he pointed to Jesus and said, *"Look, the Lamb of God!"*

When the two disciples heard him say this, they followed Jesus.

Turning around, Jesus saw them following and asked, "What do you want?"

They said, "Rabbi, where are you staying?"

"Come," he replied, "and you will see."[2]

"Jesus?" Andrew who knew Jesus from Capernaum asked, "After you were baptized, why did you leave us and where did you go?"

Pulling a few branches aside, Jesus invited the men into his three-sided shelter. "Here, sit in the booth that I have made for this season, and I will tell you about my forty days in the wilderness." Jesus made himself comfortable. "I spoke with God and with the enemy of God. I saw wild animals, and heavenly angels brought me bread and water."

The stars were out and a glorious half moon bathed the oasis in white light. Andrew and John's disciple left Jesus, hurrying away to tell about the man who spoke to God and who defied the Evil One.

The first thing Andrew did was to find his brother Simon Peter *and tell him, "We have found the Messiah." And he brought* Simon Peter *to Jesus.*

Jesus looked at him and said,[3] "I know you. I have sailed on Galilee with you and repaired your fishing boat. Your family works for Zebedee. Everyone calls you Simon son of Jona, but I call you Peter, the rock."

For a moment, Peter looked stunned. He was silent, studying the face of a man who had been in his village often.

His brother Andrew gave him a good-natured shove. "The Messiah has been with us for some time, but we didn't know it."

"I always knew there was something special about the way you taught us the scriptures." Peter finally found his voice. "But where is your sword? How are you going to rout the Romans? When will you declare your kingship?"

"Did you hear the voice of God when I came to John to be baptized?" Jesus responded.

"Yes," Peter answered.

"God speaks to me often. His Holy Spirit is my constant companion." Jesus smiled a little at the impatience of the man before him. "I do nothing except I get a directive from heaven. My Father knows the time. I will wait for his directive."

"Tell us," Peter and Andrew spoke almost in unison. "What is the word of God for this moment?"

"We will return to Galilee, and to anyone who will listen, we will speak the same message that John the Baptist has been speaking. 'Repent because the God of Israel is coming to live among you.' I will leave in the morning."

The next day, as Jesus prepared to leave for Galilee, he saw Philip and *he said to him, "Follow me.* I am going to Galilee. As we make the journey, I will be teaching many things regarding the Messiah and the Kingdom of God."

Philip responded, "I have been close and listened as you spoke with the prophet and with Geber who helps him. I want to hear more. I will come, but first I must tell my friend."

Philip, like Andrew and Peter, was from the town of Bethsaida. Philip found Nathanael and told him, "We have found the one Moses wrote about in the Law and about whom the prophets also wrote—Jesus of Nazareth, the son of Joseph."

"Nazareth! Can anything good come from there?" Nathanael asked with undisguised incredulity

"Come and see," said Philip. There was a bit of a challenge in his voice.

Nathanael could not ignore the challenge.

Peter and Andrew were standing with Jesus. *When Jesus saw Nathanael approaching, he said of him, "Here is a true Israelite, in whom there is nothing false."*

Nathanael heard the comment.

"How do you know me?" Nathanael asked.

Jesus answered, "I saw you while you were still under the fig tree before Philip called you. You were praying for a pure heart, for a life that would invite the Spirit of God."

Then Nathanael declared, "Rabbi, you are the Son of God; you are the King of Israel."

Jesus said, "You believe because I told you I saw you under the fig tree. You shall see greater things than that." He then added, "I tell you the truth, you shall see heaven open, and the angels of God ascending and descending on the Son of Man."[4]

Chapter 15

Misunderstood

And they took offense at him. But Jesus said to them, "Only in his hometown and in his own house is a prophet without honor."

—Matthew 13:57

It was evening when Jesus, Peter, and Andrew along with Phillip and Nathanael walked into Capernaum. Zebedee's fishing boats were preparing to leave their moorings. The four fishermen tossed the cloth sacks that contained their extra clothing near the gate of Zebedee's house. They ran for the boats.

James and John who had returned earlier stood in their boat and called, "Hurry, or you will have to swim! We're going to the warm springs in the sea where the large fish are beginning to gather." With jovial greetings, the men found their places in the fishing boats. Jesus watched as they set out.

"Jesus?"

Jesus turned to see his Aunt Salome standing in the open gate to her courtyard.

"It is going to be a chilly night. Come, stay in the house." She stepped aside and Jesus entered the home of his mother's sister who lived in Capernaum.

"I saw your mother and brothers in Jerusalem," Salome said as she placed some flat bread and roasted fish in front of her nephew. "Your mother said she is concerned because the people of Nazareth think you are strange."

"Some of them think I am crazy," Jesus responded. Then he added, "What did you tell her?"

"I told her the fishermen love to hear you teach. I told her you are the only one Zebedee trusts to repair his boats."

"Did your words comfort my mother?" Jesus asked.

"Yes," Salome sat across from Jesus. "Your mother thinks it would be best if you made Capernaum your home." She stopped talking and waited for his response.

"It is written in the prophets that God will honor Galilee of the Gentiles, by the way of the sea, along the Jordan."[1]

Aunt Salome looked at Jesus a little strangely, then she said, "That's what disturbs the people of Nazareth. You speak of yourself as if the scriptures were written about you."

"What do you know about my birth?" Jesus asked.

"I was there when your mother told our father, Heli, about the angel. I was there when your mother told Joseph that the Spirit of God was your Father," Aunt Salome answered. "Joseph did not believe her. Our father had doubts, but I believed her."

"Then why is it so difficult to accept the fact that the scriptures are written about me?" Jesus gently challenged.

"I guess because in all other ways, you are so normal," Aunt Salome replied.

"You believed my mother when she said the Spirit of God was my Father." Once more, Jesus quoted scripture, *"Who has gone up to heaven and come down? Who has gathered up the wind in the hollow of his hands? Who has wrapped up the waters in his cloak? Who has established all the ends of the earth? What is his name, and the name of his son? Tell me if you know!"*[2]

"You're the son?" Salome asked with a hint of skepticism.

"God is my Father," Jesus added clarification. Then returning to the subject of making Capernaum his home, Jesus said, "Tomorrow evening, I will worship in the synagogue. On the first day, I will travel to Cana to help Jose build his house and his carpenter's shop. After that I will go to Nazareth. I will gather the scrolls from my grandfather's house and my personal belongings. Then I will move to Capernaum."

"We have a room for you," Salome offered. "Zebedee said I could invite you to live with us."

Darkness was creeping over the Sea of Galilee. Every fishing boat was tied to its mooring. All the nets were hanging or spread upon the rocks. One by one and in groups of two or three, the men of Capernaum left their homes and walked with silent respect to the synagogue in the center of the town. Each man wore the clothes that were reserved for Sabbath, the only clothes that did not smell like old fish, and each man carried a small oil lamp, which was placed along the path so there would be illumination when they returned to their homes after sunset.

Walking with the men from the family of Zebedee, Jesus entered the synagogue and took his place on one of the stone benches surrounding the bema. The president of the synagogue knew Jesus. Many times, the quiet carpenter had spent the Sabbath in this fishing town. His presence in the synagogue always seemed to make the worship service sweeter.

"May I call you up to read?" Jairus, the president of the synagogue, approached Jesus before the service began.

"Read," the Spirit of God confirmed.

Jesus nodded affirmatively. Then he pulled his prayer shawl over his head as he shut out the daily life of the community and opened himself to everything God wanted to say to him.

"My son, I look down from heaven, and I want you to know that you are the one who brings joy to my heart. You are humble, and for you, my written and spoken word is the rule of life. I have heard the words the people of Nazareth have spoken against you. Their accusations and judgments have come before my throne.

*So, hear the word of the LORD, you who tremble at his word: "Your own people who hate you, and exclude you...have said, 'Let the LORD be glorified...*that Jesus the carpenter no longer worships in our synagogue.*" Yet they will be put to shame.'"*[3]

"It pains me, Father, to be so misunderstood," Jesus responded.

"You did nothing to cause this misunderstanding," God replied. "Our adversary has whispered lies throughout the town. He could not defeat you in the wilderness. So now, he is increasing his verbal attacks as he tries to discredit you in your family and among the people who have known you since childhood."

While Jesus listened to the words of his Father, the service began with a responsive chant. "Bless the Lord!"

"Blessed is the Holy One for all eternity," the men responded.

Then the president of the synagogue read, *"The Israelites are to observe the Sabbath, celebrating it for the generations to come as a lasting covenant. It will be a sign between me and the Israelites forever, for in six days the LORD made the heavens and the earth, and on the seventh day he abstained from work and rested."*[4]

"Do you remember?" God asked.

From beneath his prayer shawl, Jesus responded, "The first Sabbath?"

Then the Holy Spirit opened the memory of Yeshua the Creator.

Like the other men in the synagogue, Jesus swayed back and forth. In soft unison, the men chanted the prayers of their ancestors. While they chanted, Jesus whispered to his Father, "I spent the first Sabbath with Adam and Eve. I told them about each day of creation. I told them how I thought and planned every aspect of Earth's creation just for them. Oh, how we celebrated!"

"These fishermen appreciate the Sabbath," God commented. "It is the only day they do not have to go out on their boats."

"These are good men," Jesus responded. "They work hard, and they do not leave places for our enemy to inhabit their lives."

From the bema the president of the synagogue intoned, "Jesus, the carpenter from Nazareth, come forward to the Torah."

Respecting the traditions of the synagogue, Jesus came forward, bowing, chanting the reader's prayer, and kissing his fringes after they touched the scroll. From the writings of the prophet Isaiah, Jesus began to read, *"If you keep your feet from breaking the Sabbath and from doing as you please on my holy day, if you call the Sabbath a delight and the LORD's holy day honorable, and if you honor it by not going your own way and not doing as you please or speaking idle words, then you will find your joy in the LORD, and I will cause you to ride on the heights of the land and to feast on the inheritance of your father Jacob. The mouth of the LORD has spoken."*[5]

Stepping back from the open scroll, Jesus spoke to the fishermen who had gathered to honor God as the sun had set and Sabbath had begun. "Tonight, the God of the universe has smiled on this little town. His Spirit is present. He knows that you really do welcome this day of rest. He knows you welcome the words his servants have written, and you desire for these scriptures to become the life you live. God will fulfill his promise to you. The inheritance of your father Jacob is yours. Jacob saw God face to face, yet his life was spared."

"Did you hear that?" Peter nudged his brother Andrew. "We're going to see God face-to-face."

"Really?" Andrew's tone was slightly mocking.

"Jesus is always right about the scriptures," Peter defended his statement. "We are Sabbath keepers. The scripture says that the inheritance of Jacob is ours, and Jesus is right. That inheritance is not just the land of Israel. It is also seeing God face-to-face."

Several days later, Jose and Jesus raised the beam that was to be the main support for a new house in Cana. They let it drop into the hole they had previously dug. While Jose steadied the beam, Jesus stabilized it by packing the dirt and adding a pile of rocks.

Both men then stepped back to check the vertical line of the beam and to drink from the waterskin that lay on the floor.

Jose looked at his older brother and spoke what had been on his mind, "You have not been home since before the Feast of Trumpets, yet people are talking about you as if you were there annoying them every day. Even James has nothing but critical words."

"At creation, God placed two trees in the garden. Division is the fruit of the tree of the knowledge of good and evil. Unity and peace are the fruits from the tree of life," Jesus answered. Both men sat for a brief rest and Jesus continued, "The enemy of God offers each man in every age the fruit from the evil tree. He tries to deceive all mankind. Satan wants each man to think he can obtain knowledge that no one else possesses. Once the thoughts that lead to division are planted in a man's mind, the man feels it is his duty to share his unique knowledge so that everyone will admire and appreciate his brilliance."

Jose looked a little puzzled.

Jesus clarified, "Throughout Nazareth the Evil One has spread many lies about me. He wishes to bring division between me and my family and between my family and the town's people. Because I speak the words of God, he works to make my message ineffective."

Jose nodded. "Toma stopped to rest his camels and spend the night. He told mother that he could not recover from the beating the bandits gave him until you came to visit. He believes you healed him." Jose looked questioningly at his older brother.

"God in heaven heals," Jesus answered. "But sometimes, I have been present to see how much he cares for his children."

Jose continued, "Toma said you touched him, and he felt healing power surge through his body. Immediately, the pain was gone and he could move."

"That was the power of God," Jesus repeated. "I hear a voice in my head. It is a voice I am very familiar with. It is the voice of God. If God says touch, then I touch. If healing power flows through me, it is God not me. Most things I do are very normal." Jesus pointed to the wooden beam that stood upright from the ground. "God told me to help you build this house, but so far, it has been your sweat and my sweat—nothing more."

Jose laughed. "If we are not getting any heavenly help, we had better get back to work. I want to get my wedding party together and bring Deborah into this house before Passover."

Jesus grabbed the shovel and went back to work digging the hole for the next upright beam.

Jose began to plane the next beam. As he worked, he began one of the antiphonal songs that was typically sung as families made their way to Jerusalem for the annual feasts. *"Unless the LORD builds the house, its builders labor in vain."*

Jesus sang the next phrase, *"Unless the LORD watches over the city, the watchmen stand guard in vain."*

The brothers sang the rest of the psalm together, *"In vain you rise early and stay up late, toiling for food to eat—for he grants sleep to those he loves."*[6]

The heavy drapes that separated the administrative offices from the other rooms in the desert palace of Herod Antipas were suddenly thrown open. Somewhat startled, Manaen and Cuza looked up. Antipas stood in front of them, agitated and eager.

"The new governor, Pilate, has done it now!" Antipas gloated. "Get a parchment. Prepare a letter to Tiberius."

Cuza scurried to get the writing materials, while Manaen asked, "What has the new governor done?"

"He marched into the Temple complex when the treasury boxes were being emptied, and he took half of the money!" Antipas announced. "I have been in conference all morning with emissaries from the high priest. I am sending a letter to the emperor introducing a delegation from the Temple and personally recommending that Pilate be relieved of his duties. Judea needs to be governed by someone who understands the Jewish culture."

"Do you have someone in mind?" Manaen boldly asked.

"My father ruled Judea as well as Galilee," Antipas answered. "I think I am the obvious choice."

"There is no doubt your father was an effective ruler," Manaen replied. "Do you know why Pilate took the money?"

"He's building an aqueduct to bring water from Bethlehem into Jerusalem," Antipas answered. "But Pilate does not understand. Money that has been dedicated to God cannot be used, even for good projects. Now the whole city of Jerusalem is in an uproar."

"And you are in a position to discredit the new governor from Rome," Manaen added.

"I learned from my father," Antipas stated with satisfaction. "He never missed an opportunity to place the careers of his enemies in jeopardy while securing his own position in the empire."

With a parchment and reed, Cuza began writing the formal greeting: "To Tiberius ruler of the Roman Empire." All three men bent over the table as the complaint was carefully worded.

The winter rains were steadily falling. Jesus and Jose walked through the house that had been completed, checking the sod and thatch roof for leaks. "Looks good," Jesus stated as he continued to reach up and test the ceiling for moisture. "Why don't you return to Nazareth for the Feast of Dedication? You might see Deborah. You and James can make some furniture and bring it back."

"What about you?" Jose asked.

"I am going up into the hills around Galilee to spend the eight days of the holiday in prayer," Jesus replied.

Jose looked at his oldest brother a little skeptically. "I know you follow the laws of Moses more carefully than any other man in our village. I have seen you, very early in the morning, strapping the leather boxes to your arm and to your forehead. I have heard you recite the required prayers. Shouldn't that be enough?" Jose shook his head as if the movement would straighten his thoughts. Then he added, "Eight days of prayer—how can anyone pray for eight days? When I was younger, I used to think you were just getting away from the responsibilities of the carpentry shop, but now, I believe you really were spending all that time praying."

Jesus chuckled, appreciating the frankness of his younger brother. "Prayer is not a one-sided conversation. God through his Holy Spirit responds. He shows me things."

Jose interrupted, "Do you mean visions, like the prophet Daniel had?"

"Sometimes," Jesus answered. "At times, I seem to go to heaven in a trance like Isaiah did. I experience the presence of God like Moses did. You know, Moses and God had conversations just like you and I talk. I have visited with heavenly beings—angels, Moses, Elijah."

"I cannot begin to imagine!" Jose exclaimed. "Why do you get this kind of communication with God? You're not a priest. You are not part of the Temple elite. You are just a carpenter from Nazareth."

"Do not envy me. The greater the revelation, the more difficult will be the calling of God on my life. Think about the prophets who wrote the holy books," Jesus answered. "They were ordinary men, often persecuted. Those who had prophetic visions, those who saw heaven, those who led the nation—each had a great price to pay. The gossip and slander in our hometown of Nazareth is just the beginning of the price I will pay. But before I pay the ultimate price, I will give God's message to this nation. Both men and women from this nation will then carry it to every part of the world. *The law will go out from Zion, the word of the LORD from Jerusalem*."[7]

With a puzzled expression on his face, Jose replied, "All through the history of our people, the prophets have been killed. I don't want you to die."

"I will not die until I have spoken every word God has for me to speak and I have done every deed he has commissioned me to do." Jesus smiled at his brother. "I am confident my time has not yet come."

Dawn broke through the gray mists drifting over the surface of the Sea of Galilee. It was the first day of the Feast of Dedication. Sitting up from his resting place in the mouth of a shallow cave on the side of one of the hills that over looked the lake, Jesus began his morning routine. From a cloth pouch, he pulled the two black leather boxes with straps. It had been made by his grandfather, Heli. He remembered watching his grandfather as he carefully penned the scriptures that fit into little compartments in each box. Holding the boxes he recited, *"Consecrate to me every firstborn male… Commemorate this day, the day you came out of Egypt, out of the land of slavery, because the LORD brought you out of it with a mighty hand.*[8] *This observance will be for you like a sign on your hand and a reminder on your forehead that the law of the LORD is to be on your lips.*[9]

"Father, *Oh, how I love your law! I meditate on it all day long*,"[10] Jesus began his conversation with God.

God responded, *"Great peace have they who love my law, and nothing can make them stumble."*[11]

Jesus sighed. The voice of his Father was like warm waves rolling through his body and his emotions.

God continued, "Let us speak of Israel, your bride. Remember my words through the prophet Hosea, 'You are going to allure her and speak tenderly to her. You will be a doorway that leads her away from trouble.'"

"How can I allure all of Israel when my own hometown rejects me?" Jesus asked. "I feel their words like knives cutting my flesh. Even their glances bring me pain. My mother feels humiliated. My brothers do not understand."

"Speak the words that were written by the prophet Hosea. They are your own words," God answered.

Jesus spoke the scripture that rolled through his mind. *"In that day… Israel will call me 'my husband'; she will no longer call me 'my master.' I will remove the names of other gods from her lips; no longer will their names be invoked."*[12] Then he paused and waited for his Father to comment.

"Your own spoken word brought this planet into existence. Your word will bring both the adopted and the natural sons of Abraham into your arms," God confirmed.

Satisfied that Father God knew his heart, Jesus picked up the first black leather box. He slipped it over the bicep of his left arm so that it rested next to his heart. As he wrapped the straps around the box and down onto his bare forearm, he quoted the traditional verses, "*I will betroth you to me forever; I will betroth you in righteousness and justice, in love and compassion. I will betroth you in faithfulness, and you will acknowledge the LORD.*"[13] In his mind, he could see his bride, a mass of ageless people. They were beautiful, wearing white and standing before the sapphire throne.

Reverently, he fitted the second leather box above his forehead. It was the tangible demonstration of having the law of God imprinted on his mind, directing every thought and movement. He completed wrapping the leather strap on his arm around his hand and middle finger. Then in the tradition of his people, he began to sway and chant, "Blessed are you, Lord our God… who sanctifies us with his commandments and has commanded us to *tie* your word *as symbols on our hands and bind them on our foreheads.*"[14] For Jesus, these were not idle words. He said them every weekday morning. The leather boxes and straps as well as the rituals that accompanied the words added emotional depth.

It was as if the leather straps bound him to his Father God, and at the same time, they bound him to his people, Israel.

It was the third day of the Feast of Dedication. For three days, Jesus had remained at the mouth of the cave speaking to his Father, reciting scripture, meditating on the words written by men as they were dictated by the Holy Spirit. "It is the season of remembering the dedication of your Temple, the kindling of the fire on your altar of burnt offering and on the seven branched lampstand in the Holy Place. Father, what do you want to show me regarding these things?"

In response to his question, the shimmering cloud of the presence of God wrapped itself around Jesus. The Holy Spirit pressed in and said, "Remember the words of Solomon at the first dedication service for my Temple. *'Will God really dwell on earth? The heavens, even the highest heaven, cannot contain you. How much less this temple I have built!'*"[15]

In the mind of Yeshua, Jesus recalled the beautiful Temple that Solomon had constructed. His heart was moved by the generous preparations made by King David as well as the purity that his son Solomon had displayed throughout the building and the dedication. "The people gathered. They were filled with appreciation and awe," Jesus reminisced aloud. "So reverently, the priests carried the ark, the symbol of the Eternal One living among them. They brought it into the Most Holy Chamber. *The cherubim spread their wings over the place of the ark and overshadowed the ark and its carrying poles.*[16] *When the priests withdrew from the Holy Place, the cloud filled the temple of the LORD. And the priests could not perform their service because of the cloud, for the glory of the LORD filled his temple.*"[17]

"Alas, the glory did not remain," the Holy Spirit sighed and Jesus felt both his tears and his warm breath.

"Over time, the kings and the people ignored the commandments that were given to Moses, and the glory departed," Jesus stated.

"The Holy Spirit then reopened the curtain of history, and Jesus saw Jerusalem surrounded by the siege works of Nebuchadnezzar.

"My people, my city, my Temple-." Jesus wept the tears of Yeshua. He felt the same heartbreak he had experienced so long ago.

"First, the holy vessels and all the nobility of Jerusalem were taken." As horrific scenes of devastation scrolled across the mind of Jesus, the Holy Spirit narrated, "Years passed and then Nebuchadnezzar returned. He *marched against Jerusalem with his whole army...and built siege works all around it.*[18] *The famine in the city* became *so severe that there was no food for the people to eat. Then the city wall was broken through, and the whole army fled at night*[19] The king was captured. *Then they put out his eyes, bound him with bronze shackles and took him to Babylon.*[20] Years later, Nebuchadnezzar sent troops again. *He set fire to the temple of the Lord, the royal palace and all the houses of Jerusalem. Every important building he burned down. The whole Babylonian army... broke down the walls around Jerusalem and carried into exile the people who remained in the city.*"[21]

"Jerusalem, Jerusalem, how often I would have shielded you, but you would not come under the shelter of the laws I gave to Moses." Once again Jesus experienced his own preincarnate heartbreak. "Solomon's Temple was my Temple. I loved its bronze columns. I appreciated the dedication and the workmanship that went into a dwelling place for my presence. It's gone. It's gone, and the ark of my presence is also gone."

"Hidden by faithful Jeremiah," the Holy Spirit informed. "It is under the city in a sealed tunnel that extends beyond the walls of the city."

Then the Holy Spirit encouraged, "Take heart. Remember, my words give life to those things that appear to be dead. '*In the first year of Cyrus king of Persia, in order to fulfill the word of the* LORD *spoken by Jeremiah, the* LORD *moved the heart of Cyrus...to make a proclamation throughout his realm and to put it in writing: "This is what Cyrus king of Persia says: 'The* LORD*, the God of heaven, has given me all the kingdoms of the earth and he has appointed me to build a temple for him at Jerusalem in Judah. Anyone of his people among you—may the* LORD *his God be with him, and let him go up.'"*[22]

"Ezra brought the first group of faithful Jews back to the land. They carried with them the gold and silver basins and utensils that had been taken from Solomon's Temple," Jesus recalled.

"I was with them," the Holy Spirit added. "An army of angels led the way and protected the rear."

"The first thing the returning exiles did was to build the altar and reestablish the sacrificial services," Jesus said. "There was a dedication service, and the fire that was never to be extinguished was rekindled on the altar. It took many more years, but finally, the people finished rebuilding the Temple."

"There was such excitement in heaven!" The Holy Spirit seemed to enjoy sharing memories with Jesus. "The Temple had to be built by men. It was the tangible evidence that they really desired for God to live among them."

"And they had to submit to the laws of the kingdom of heaven," Jesus stated. "The blessings of living in the kingdom are acquired through submission."

"You have come to Earth to teach by word and example," the Holy Spirit reminded.

"Submission to the laws of God is the way to the kingdom," Jesus repeated. Then he began to recite part of Nehemiah's beautiful petition, "*Remember the instruction you gave your servant Moses, saying, 'If you are unfaithful, I will scatter you among the nations, but if you return to me and obey my commands, then even if your exiled people are at the farthest horizon, I will gather them from there and bring them to the place I have chosen as a dwelling for my Name.*"[23]

"That prayer brought all the resources of heaven and Earth together," the Holy Spirit stated.

"The city walls were rebuilt. Through the teaching of God's law, the priesthood and the people were brought back into relationship with God," Jesus said.

"Time passed, generation replaced generation. The writings that contained the words of God were pushed aside, and men began building their own kingdoms based on their own ideas." The Holy Spirit was still laying out the history of the Temple for Jesus.

"When the laws of God are ignored, the Evil One invades," Jesus stated.

"Antiochus, the Greek king of Syria marched through the land." The Holy Spirit showed Jesus the armies of the wicked king as they set a statue of Zeus up in the Temple and desecrated the altar of burnt offerings by sacrificing a pig.

"Those were dark years." Jesus felt his heart ache as he viewed the hateful acts of his enemy. "The Temple services ceased. A penalty was attached to everything that was part of the Law of Moses. Even mothers were killed if their babies were circumcised. "Holy Spirit, where were you?" Jesus asked.

"I was stirring the hearts of devoted men, like the old priest in the little town of Modiin who refused to sacrifice a pig," the Spirit answered.

"Every Jewish boy knows that story," Jesus responded. "It was the beginning of a revolution, years of guerrilla warfare that culminated in the restoration of Temple worship."

"The Feast of Dedication is officially the celebration of the cleansing and rededication of the Temple at that time," the Holy Spirit informed. "But"—the Holy Spirit sounded sad and weary—"The stones of the Temple were old and worn. The fabric was faded. The cedar had dried and splintered. In places, the gold was flaking and the roof was leaking. In the hearts of the men whose lives were supposed to be dedicated to the service of the Temple, there was jealousy, covetousness, dishonesty, and even murder."

Jesus shook his head sadly as he remembered the more recent history of his people. "My people opened the door for another invader—Rome."

The Holy Spirit continued the account, "And Rome appointed Herod whom God gifted with great architectural talent. He rebuilt the deteriorating Temple. He made it into the magnificent structure that you often visit. Herod thought he was creating a monument to himself. Actually, he was preparing the most magnificent structure on Earth for Yeshua the Creator, who has chosen to become a descendant of Adam."

At that moment, the Holy Spirit took Jesus to the Temple, and he viewed it from every angle. There was not a chamber he did not see. Nothing was hidden.

"This is my house, the place where I will represent God on Earth." Jesus kept looking, moving from place to place within the vision. "It is a very large structure, but there are very few places I could easily occupy," Jesus observed.

"Go to the people. Teach on the porches and in the courtyards that are open to the public. I will go ahead of you and make a place," the Holy Spirit said. "This is the message you are to give: *Reform your ways and your actions, and I will let you live in this place. Do not trust in deceptive words and say, 'This is the temple of the LORD, the temple of the LORD, the temple of the LORD!'* [24] *Will you steal and murder, commit adultery and perjury…, and then come and stand before me in this house, which bears my Name, and say, 'We are safe"-safe to do all these detestable things?' Has this house, which bears my Name, become a den of robbers to you? But I have been watching.*"[25]

"John has been calling the nation to repent. The ordinary people seem to respond, but those who represent the Temple question and then ridicule him," Jesus responded. "I do not expect they will receive the same message from my lips."

The Holy Spirit answered, *"Therefore this is what the Sovereign* LORD *says: 'My anger and my wrath will be poured out on this place, on man and beast, on the trees of the field and on the fruit of the ground, and it will burn and not be quenched.'"*[26]

The eyes of Jesus widened, and with both hands, he gripped his tunic just over his heart. The cloth ripped, and Jesus fell on his face sobbing in the dust. "My city, Jerusalem," he moaned. "I can see your future. The faces of your dead children will now haunt me. When I see the Romans who occupy our land, I will also see their swords piercing the innocent, their torches lighting the Temple tapestry. The Spirit of God has shown this to me during the Feast of the Dedication of the Temple, and I am devastated. The flames leap into the sky and the gold that covers the cedar planks melts. It runs into the crevices between the giant blocks of stone. And after it cools, the soldiers, motivated by greed, pry the stones apart and scrape the gold into their pouches." Grieving, Jesus rocked and cried again and again, "Oh, my people...oh, my city...oh, my Temple, I will give everything, even my life so you can be the people of God who live in the city of God and worship eternally in his holy presence."

At dawn on the eighth day of the feast, Jesus left the shallow cave on the side of the hill that overlooked the Sea of Galilee. In the flesh, he was weary. Intercession had taken a toll on his body. At the home of Zebedee, he stopped and ate a simple meal, and then he began the two-day walk to Nazareth.

Chapter 16

A Wedding in Cana

On the third day a wedding took place at Cana in Galilee. Jesus' mother was there, and Jesus and his disciples had also been invited to the wedding.

—John 2:1–2

"Put the water jars into the wagon first," Mary directed as three of her sons hauled six large stone jars out of Heli's courtyard.

"We're going to need a second wagon," Jesus observed. "Jose should take all of grandfather's furniture and tools to his new home. I only need the scrolls." Jesus felt the insides of the jars to make sure they were completely dry, and then he filled them with the carefully rolled scrolls—the books of Moses, the writings of the prophets as well as books of Jewish history. Most of those scrolls had been copied by his grandfather Heli.

"I hate to see my father's house empty," Mary commented. "Salome and I grew up here. It was a good home."

"This house has been empty for years," James cuttingly remarked. "Jesus was supposed to live here, but he is never in town. Mother, we should rent this place. It will be additional income."

"After the wedding," Mary brushed her second son's suggestion aside. "Jesus"—Mary turned to her eldest son—"we will go to my sister's home at Capernaum first. We can spend the Sabbath there. On the first day, we will go to Cana. I want to set up the house so it will be completely ready for Deborah. I do not want her parents to think our family cannot provide for their daughter."

"Yes, Mother," James inserted himself into the conversation as he heaved the sixth stone jar up into the wagon. "Not many families start out with six water jars."

After a little time in the shed behind the house, Jesus carried some tools to the wagon. He showed them to Jose. "You can use these in your new carpentry shop. If there is anything you don't have, be sure to ask Simon the blacksmith. He can make it for you."

"Have you contacted the wedding coordinator in Cana?" Mary stopped sweeping out the empty house and broke into her sons' conversation.

"Jose and I made all the arrangements before the Feast of Dedication," Jesus answered.

"Will we have enough food? What about the wine?" Mary fretted. She used a corner of her mantel to wipe the sweat from her face. Then talking more to herself than to her sons, she said, "I don't think we have enough money set aside for this wedding. People are coming from Nazareth, from Capernaum, and all of Cana will be invited. I wish your father was still alive." She started to sweep again, and then she stopped and turned to Jesus one more time. "Will there be enough food? What about the wine?"

Jesus looked directly into his mother's eyes. "Mother, we have used everything God has put at the disposal of our family so it is enough."

"I am not assured," Mary pressed for a more definitive response.

"I am sure my Father God makes sufficient provision for everything," Jesus answered.

"Well, I'd like to see you provide a little more muscle for this project," James sarcastically interrupted. "Take the end of this feeding trough and help me lift it into the wagon."

By midmorning, two wagons, Jesus and three of his brothers, along with Mary, began the journey that would culminate in a wedding.

In the governor's palace in Caesarea, both Pilate and Longinus stared out the window that overlooked the harbor. "A delegation from the Temple is boarding one of those ships and departing for Rome," Longinus informed. "They are carrying an introduction to the emperor as well as an official complaint signed by Antipas."

"Antipas has used this situation to his advantage," Pilate ruefully stated. "Somehow, I need to get to the emperor before this delegation gets an audience."

"You know, this is not really about using the Temple money so Jerusalem can have an adequate water supply. It is about the fact that Antipas wants to rule over all of Israel like his father did." Longinus paced the floor considering various options, and then he said, "I have received reports that the king of the Nabataeans is preparing an army to attack Antipas."

Pilate sat up and waited for more details.

Longinus continued, "Phasaelis, the divorced wife of Antipas, has returned to her father, King Aretas. I have heard he plans to avenge the honor of his daughter."

"That is foolishness," Pilate stated. "He may defeat the few soldiers Antipas commands, but Rome will then come and annihilate the Nabataeans."

"Here is the point," Longinus explained, "Rome wants its rulers to be wise enough to prevent and not instigate wars. You need to write to the emperor to inform him that the foolish marital escapades of Antipas have put the nation in danger. You must show that Antipas, who claims to understand Jewish customs, has broken their laws and put the regions of Galilee and Perea in danger."

"Is your information accurate?" Pilate asked.

"I question the caravanners regularly," Longinus replied.

"Then let's write the letter. I have friends in Rome who will get it to Tiberius before the Jewish delegation can get an audience." With an abrupt gesture, Pilate called for a military scribe.

"Is everything ready?" Jose interrupted his mother as she directed the two servants who had been hired for the wedding to fill the water jars and arrange the tables.

"By the time you return with your bride, these tables will be covered with food. The wine will have been delivered. The bridal chamber is already prepared." Mary beamed with excitement. "Get your brothers, your cousins, and their friends. Take the torches, and go get your bride."

"What about the wedding invitations?" Jose asked.

"When we were in Capernaum, I invited Zebedee and his family. The wedding coordinator sent a runner ahead to Nazareth. All of Deborah's friends and family will be invited. I have told everyone in Cana about this wedding. Do not worry."

"Mother has done enough worrying for all of us," James stated as he clapped his younger brother on the back. "We are ready. On the way, I will tell you everything you need to know about married life."

Jesus joined his brothers. His cousins James and John, the sons of Zebedee, were with him, along with their work associates, Andrew and Peter. "You're not the only married man in this wedding party," Jesus announced. "Peter has been married for two years. He may also have some advice."

The men started out the gate walking at a brisk pace. Peter was the first to begin the traditional advice to the groom. "You will probably find that it was good to move away from your wife's family. We still live with my wife's family—"

Peter's brother Andrew interrupted, "Peter has to do a lot of apologizing. It seems he has a habit of saying the wrong thing and then the whole family gets in an uproar."

"You didn't have to say that," Peter protested.

"You do have to be careful what you say," James reiterated. "A happy wife makes a happy home."

Jesus then spoke, "When Adam and Eve were put out of the garden, God made Adam to be like an extra layer of protection for Eve. A wife is to come under the covering of her husband's protection." Jesus turned to Jose as he spoke, "You must not fail to provide for your wife and protect her."

Peter interrupted, "Jesus, when will you take a wife?"

"You saw my home near where John is teaching and baptizing. I only constructed a three-sided booth with palm branches for a roof. I don't think my booth would qualify as a home for a bride. And in Capernaum, I store my belongings in my uncle's home and sleep wherever I lay down."

At that moment, the Holy Spirit showed Jesus the plans that were waiting in heaven for mansions on streets of gold.

After a little silent walking, Jesus added as if thinking aloud, "When I have completed a home that is fit for my bride, I will come for her."

By the time Jesus made the statement, it seemed a little out of place. The men were slightly puzzled, but they accepted his statement and said no more about it.

It was nearly midnight when the six men entered Nazareth. "The bridegroom is here! Come out to meet him." Jesus was the first to announce their mission. Shouting and laughing, the men went straight to the home of Deborah the shepherdess.

Throughout the town, lamps were lit. People poured out of their houses and swelled the procession. Somehow, everyone knew and everyone was prepared to walk the rest of the night back to Cana.

Deborah was ready, standing in the courtyard of her father's home. Her face was covered with a fine linen veil. A sedan chair waited on the ground beside her. By the light of burning torches, Jose approached his bride. He took her by the hand and helped her into the chair. The four fishermen immediately hoisted the chair to their shoulders.

Above the laughter and chatter, Jesus shouted, "Today we remember the words of the prophet Jeremiah, '*There will be heard once more the sounds of joy and gladness, the voices of bride and bridegroom…saying, "Give thanks to the LORD Almighty, for the LORD is good; his love endures forever.*"'[1]

It was a familiar psalm. The fishermen carrying the bride sang the next verse. "*Give thanks to the God of gods. His love endures forever.*"

The women sang the next verse. "*Give thanks to the LORD of lords: His love endures forever. To him who alone does great wonders, his love endures forever.*"[2]

Back and forth, the men and women sang. By torchlight and lamplight, they walked the hard dirt road from Nazareth to Cana. A wedding—it was a reason to break the pattern of village life, a time to celebrate.

"I am so happy." Jesus overheard Deborah's mother. "I used to think I would never have the joy of Deborah's wedding."

"Thank you, Father," Jesus spoke to God as he remembered the afternoon when he had touched the hump on Deborah's back, and it had disappeared. Then, he walked up beside John and asked, "May I carry the chair for a while?"

Without pausing or tipping the chair, John passed the carrying pole over to Jesus. "There are plenty of strong men in this procession," Jesus announced. The sons of Moshe, Ahaz and Harim, were walking close to the sedan chair. Jesus commandeered them, "Relieve Andrew and Peter." Then Jesus's youngest brother,

Jude, ran forward and tapped James the brother of John on the shoulder, taking his pole. So it went through the night, the men trading off and carrying the bride to her new home in Cana.

It was dawn on the third day of the week when the wedding party made its noisy entrance into the sleepy town of Cana. Everyone in the town had expected the bride to arrive that morning so most had already cared for their animals and done those things that were necessary so they would be free to join the celebration.

Mary was standing in the doorway to the courtyard, nearly jumping with excitement. For a moment, she left her post and ran to find the servants. "Here"—she breathlessly positioned both servants by the water jars—"as each person enters, pour water over their hands and their feet. Then they will be clean and able to eat and drink right away." She turned to return to the doorway, but then she stopped and turned back. "Greet each person as they wash, and then direct them to the food and wine. Everyone will be hungry and thirsty after their long walk." Mary ran back to the gate arriving just in time to swing it wide open for the bearers of the sedan chair.

The friends of the bride drew back the curtains of the chair and Deborah remained properly seated until the guests had passed by offering her their well-wishes. Then Deborah's mother, along with Mary, helped her out, escorting her to the women's bath not far from the house. With the assistance of both mothers, Deborah completely undressed and combed out her long hair.

As unobtrusively as possible, Mary studied Deborah's bare back, running her eyes up and down the length of the girl's spine to make sure there was no hint of the horrifying hump that had been there during childhood. Satisfied that Deborah was both healthy and perfectly formed, Mary held out her hand to help the girl as she stepped down into the pool.

But Deborah didn't need Mary's assistance. She eagerly skipped down the steps, quickly ducking beneath the surface of the water. She remained under the water until she could not hold her breath another moment. Then she broke the surface overwhelmed with laughter and excitement.

"You were a child when you stepped into the water, and now, you are a woman," Deborah's mother exclaimed as tears of joy rolled down her cheeks.

"Here, here." Mary rushed forward with a large piece of white fabric. "We have to help you dress and fix your hair."

"What is Jose doing right now?" Deborah asked as she finished dressing.

"His brothers have taken him to the men's bath," Mary answered. "I have given him his father's white robe and prayer shawl."

"The guests have probably eaten all the food that was out for their morning meal," Deborah's mother commented. "Let's hurry."

When Deborah entered the courtyard, her father Alon, joined her mother, and together, they escorted their daughter to her seat of honor.

"It is the time of our rejoicing!" Deborah's father announced.

Jose then came over. His eyes met the eyes of his bride. Then he covered her with the linen veil that had been laid aside so she could wash. "As I cover you with this veil, I promise to cover you with provision and protection. I separate you from the eyes of the world and reserve you for my eyes only."

Mary with Jesus, the representative of his father Joseph, along with Deborah's parents, took their places on either side of the bride and groom. They escorted the couple to the place where James, Simon (the brother of Jesus), and Jude along with Moshe (the lifelong friend of Joseph) each held a corner of Joseph's prayer shawl to create the huppah under which the couple would be married.

"May your offspring be as the stars of the sky—too numerous to count," the local rabbi greeted the couple.

Deborah began the traditional circling of the groom. She moved gracefully. Everyone could see that even though she was veiled, her face was always toward her bridegroom.

"In the beginning God created the heavens and the earth."[3] The rabbi from the synagogue at Cana began the traditional retelling of the creation story. "In seven days, God created the Earth. His creation was complete in six days, and he rested on the seventh day. Today, the hand of the Creator and his spoken word through the Torah are both active in the creation of this new home."

Deborah finished the seventh circle and then stopped. One of her witnesses came forward and lifted her veil so that she and Joel could share their first cup of wine.

"Who will read the marriage contract in the presence of these witnesses?" the rabbi asked.

Jesus stepped forward. He spread the beautifully penned marriage contract on the table. The fine parchment with its decorative script was his gift to the couple. Then he read, "On this day, Jose son of Joseph the carpenter of Nazareth said to Deborah the shepherdess and daughter of Alon, 'Be my wife according to the laws of Moses and Israel. I promise to honor, support, and maintain you in accordance with the custom of all respectable Jewish husbands. I have brought you silver coins, the tangible symbol of my pledge. In addition, I promise to provide you with food, clothing, and all the necessities of life. I understand my obligation to come to you as Adam came to Eve so you can be fruitful and bear children.' The virgin Deborah has consented to be the wife of Jose. This contract has been signed and witnessed."

The rabbi then lifted a second cup of wine. "By sharing this second cup in front of your friends and family, you, Jose, agree to aggressively implement this contract and you, Deborah, become a partner in this contract."

With nervous hands, Jose took the cup first and drank. One of Deborah's witnesses lifted her veil for the second time, and Deborah took the cup from Jose and drank.

Everyone cheered. Then Peter shouted, "Bless this marriage!"

Moshe was the first to respond, "My friend Joseph did not live to see this happy day, so I will say the first blessing for him." Taking a big breath, he began to chant, "You are blessed, Lord our God who created everything, including this marriage. Jose and Deborah, be blessed and give glory to the Creator."

Deborah's father loudly invoked the second blessing, "Blessed are you, Lord our God, who created man so that my daughter could have a husband."

The rabbi then said the third blessing, "Blessed are you, Lord our God, who created man in his own image. You made man and woman with the ability, when joined together, to reproduce. Blessed be your name."

James, the brother of Jose, added the fourth blessing, "May the town of Cana rejoice because today, there is a new home and a new family. Blessed is the Lord who adds new families to Israel."

Mary stepped to the front. She stood in front of the couple and said, "Let this couple be very happy just as Adam and Eve were happy before they had to leave their garden home. Blessed be the Lord who makes the bride and the bridegroom happy."

Jesus then stepped up beside his mother. He raised both hands toward heaven and with great tenderness and affection, he proclaimed, "Blessed is the sovereign God of Israel and all the nations. He is the one who has created our joy. He is the one who will bring pleasure and delight to both the bride and the bridegroom. To everyone who has gathered in this place, he gives brotherhood, peace, and friendship."

The master of the wedding nodded to the servants, and cups of wine were quickly passed around. Together, everyone said the final blessing, "Blessed is the Lord our God who is the Creator of this world and who made the fruit of the vine for the pleasure of man."

As friends and family were drinking to the bride and bridegroom, Jesus and Mary, along with Deborah's parents, came forward to escort the couple to the wedding chamber. Jose and Deborah stepped out from under Joseph's prayer shawl and walked through their friends to the room where they would consummate their marriage.

The wooden door closed behind them shutting out the merriment in the courtyard. At first, they stood, a little stunned at the sudden solitude. Then, Deborah boldly asked, "Do you know what to do?"

Jose answered, "As we walked to Nazareth, my married brother James as well as Peter the fisherman gave me more information than any man could use. But my brother Jesus who is not married gave me the best advice."

Jose stepped forward and removed Deborah's veil so he could see her face clearly. "Jesus said to love you like I love my own life. He said to be as careful with your body as with the body of a newborn baby. Jesus told me every word and every touch carries its own message. I am to make sure that message is always love and respect."

"I have heard many people in the town speak negatively about Jesus, but I have found him to be very wise and helpful." Deborah paused and then added, "He isn't in this room, and this is sort of an awkward moment, but I find his words very encouraging."

"Would you like to eat?" Jose pointed to the food that had been left for them on a low table.

"I'm starved," Deborah laughed as she sank down onto a cushion near the table. "Who ever came up with the idea that the bride and the groom had to fast on the day of the wedding?"

"I don't know, but let's break our fast now!" Jose picked up a piece of flat bread that was covered with crushed almonds and honey. He handed it to Deborah. "My mother made this. She makes it for every special occasion."

In the courtyard, Mary was busy overseeing the food for the wedding feast. The guests were at the water jars, pouring water over each hand twice, observing the purification rites of the Pharisees. Jesus was visiting with Simon the Zealot, his boyhood friend, while James, John, Peter, and Andrew stood nearby waiting for their turns to wash.

Out of the corner of his eye, Jesus noticed his mother speaking first to the servants, then to the master of the wedding ceremony. After that, he saw her hurrying from place to place with her mantle flapping like the wings of a bird that was trying to fly but just could not get off the ground. Finally, he saw her approach him with a steady gait and a determined look in her eye.

"Father?" he silently asked to be forewarned.

"I have heard your mother," God responded. "I will provide what she needs."

There was no time for further conversation. Mary was standing in front of her son. "They have no more wine. I have looked in every possible storage place. Our guests have finished every drop of wine that we purchased for this wedding. Jose has come out of the wedding chamber, so it is time to start the feast and we have no wine!"

"Mother, why are you bringing this problem to me? I have told you many times that the provision of God is sufficient."

"Well, I have spoken to your Father," Mary responded. "I heard him answer in my heart. He said, 'Go to Jesus.'" So Mary turned and said to the servants who were standing by the water jars, "My eldest son will tell you what to do." Without another word, she returned to the wedding celebration.

"Father?" Jesus waited for clarification.

"Remember the blessing over the wine." Jesus heard the Holy Spirit. "The Lord God is the Creator of the fruit of the vine. Now is the time to demonstrate this truth. Your closest friends will see and understand. Others will see and not understand. Most will not know what you have done."

"What are you going to do, Jesus?" Simon the Zealot was asking the question, while Peter, James, John, and Andrew were listening for his response.

"Watch and see," Jesus answered.

Then Jesus turned to the servants. "Bring more water and fill all six jars to the brim."

"Jesus," Peter protested, "what are you going to do with all that water? That is more than 150 gallons of water!"

"You can't serve these guests water," Simon the Zealot admonished.

Ignoring his companions, Jesus walked along the row of water jars reverently, repeating the blessing that was always said over the wine, "Blessed are you, Lord our God, King of the Universe, who creates the fruit of the vine." Then he said to the servants, "From one of these jars, dip out a cup and take it to the man who is overseeing the banquet."

The servants moved quickly, hurrying away with a filled cup.

"Jesus!" Peter protested.

"Would you like a closer look?" Jesus put the dipper into one of the jars. He brought it up full of deep purple wine, which he poured back into the stone jar so his friends could see that the water had now changed into wine.

"I need a taste!" the Zealot exclaimed.

"Not until I hear what the master of the banquet has to say," Jesus answered. With that statement, he walked close to where the servants were presenting the wine to the man the family had hired to coordinate the event.

The master of the banquet tasted the water that had been turned into wine. He did not realize where it had come from, though the servants who had drawn the water knew. Then he called the bridegroom aside and said, "Everyone brings out the choice wine first and then the cheaper wine after the guests have had too much to drink; but you have saved the best till now."[4]

When Jesus returned to the water jars, he saw that Simon, Peter, James, John, and Andrew were deep in conversation. Unnoticed, he stepped back, allowing them to continue.

Peter was leading the discussion, "We say the blessing over the wine every time we drink wine. The blessing says that God, the Creator and king of this world, is the one who makes the fruit of the vine. Jesus just made the juice that comes from the fruit of the vine. Does that mean he is God?"

"Blasphemy," James fearfully stated. "You cannot say a man is God. You can be stoned for saying that!"

"What if the man is the Messiah?" John asked.

"Do you remember," Andrew spoke up thoughtfully. "We saw the mantle like a dove float down from heaven."

"We heard the voice," Peter recalled. "This is my son. I am pleased."

"John the Baptist said Jesus is the one we have been waiting for," Andrew asserted.

"Every time I am around Jesus, I feel something like an energy no one else has," John continued in a quiet almost secretive voice. "It radiates from him like heat, but it isn't heat."

"I know what you mean," Simon the Zealot said. "I thought it was like love that you could feel."

"I have felt it," James admitted. "I thought it was just a glow of righteousness."

Peter put his little finger in the jar of wine, and then he licked the drop. "This is good wine. This is real. Now, every time I bless the wine, I will think of Jesus as the Creator of the fruit of the vine."

(This, the first of his miraculous signs Jesus performed in Cana of Galilee. He thus revealed his glory, and his disciples put their faith

in him. After this he went down to Capernaum with his mother and brothers and his disciples. There they stayed for a few days.)[5]

Jesus stood in the gate of his Uncle Zebedee's home. He watched as his mother along with his three brothers James, Simon, and Jude began the two-day walk back to their home in Nazareth. His cousin James came up from behind and slapped him on the shoulder. "Want to go out fishing with us tonight?"

"No," Jesus shook his head as he spoke. "I need to go back to where John is teaching and baptizing."

James looked a little disappointed. "I wish we could go with you, but this is one of the most important fishing seasons of the year. We won't be free until a few days before it is time to leave for Passover."

"Well, walk down to where John is teaching." Jesus threw his arm across his cousin's broad shoulders. "You know the place. I'll be there, and we can go up to the feast together."

"We will all come." Peter, Andrew, John, and James began to get excited. "We'll bring Phillip and Nathaniel."

"I'll see you there." Jesus waved as he began his own journey away from the northern coast of the Sea of Galilee, taking one of the less traveled roads around the western side of the lake until he reached a main road that went south through Samaria in the general direction of Jerusalem.

Chapter 17

Before Passover

If someone forces you to go one mile, go with him two miles.

—Matthew 5:41

Longinus slowly dismounted. With a sinking feeling, he walked around his mount, lifting each hoof, checking for stones or deep cracks. Finally, he straightened up and patted his horse on the flank. "No one is going to be riding you for a while."

He turned to the small squad of foot soldiers accompanying him as he returned to the Antonia Fortress in Jerusalem after a week with Pilate in the palace at Caesarea. "Carry my bags and the saddle."

Longinus took his horse by its leather reins and led it slowly down the road until he saw a house where a man was watering a small flock of goats. "Shalom." Longinus tried to use the typical Jewish greeting, but the word felt unnatural on his tongue.

The Jewish man looked up and his body obviously stiffened.

Longinus continued to approach with his limping horse. "I would like to pay you to board and care for this horse until the deep split in its hoof heals." Longinus watched the body language of the man. It seemed to soften a bit.

"A split hoof?" The Jewish man left his goats and approached.

"There are embedded rocks that need to be removed," Longinus continued.

"I have cared for donkeys and oxen." The man bent over and examined the horse's hoof. "This animal will need several weeks of rest."

"I am authorized to pay a full day's wages for each week that you board this animal," Longinus offered. As he spoke, he pulled several coins from the pouch that hung from his leather belt. "This will cover three weeks. At that time, I will send a soldier to check on this horse."

"I will care for your animal." The man took the coins.

Longinus turned to walk down the hard dirt road toward Jerusalem. He was not unaware that the foot soldiers behind him were getting a little pleasure from the fact that their commander was now walking. In a way, he had just become their equal.

"Fall in!" He ordered his small troop into formation as he set the standard marching clip for Roman soldiers. He was mindful that one man was carrying his bulky saddle. Another man was carrying his horse blankets. And still, others were carrying the bags that had been strapped to his saddle horns. He knew this extra baggage put his squadron at a disadvantage if they should need to get to their weapons quickly.

Keenly aware of their vulnerability, the Roman centurion who was the highest ranking officer under Pilate made his eyes constantly scan the countryside as well as the road ahead. He noticed a Jewish man walking the road ahead of them. From behind, Longinus observed he was young and strong. "Wait!" Longinus called.

Jesus stopped and turned to see who was calling.

"You." Longinus strode quickly to where Jesus was standing. "Carry this saddle and these bags." He pointed to a soldier who threw the saddle across Jesus's arm and to another soldier who piled two heavy bags on top. Without further discussion, Longinus led his soldiers down the road. Jesus followed.

Both men knew the law—a Roman soldier could only conscript such service for one Roman mile. When Longinus and his men reached the next mile mark, they stopped and waited for Jesus, who walked up to the Roman commander. With a big smile on his face, Jesus passed the commander, continuing to carry the saddle and the bags.

Longinus hurried to catch up with him. "You don't have to carry these."

The Roman commander was in his face, and Jesus was grinning. "Friend, I will gladly carry your saddle and these bags for another mile."

By now, the two men were walking side by side, each matching the other's determined stride.

"Why?" Longinus asked. Then he quickly looked around to see if bandits were waiting to leap from behind rocks to attack them.

"There is nothing to fear," Jesus spoke to the centurion's unspoken thoughts.

"Why?" Longinus pressed for an answer.

"The Kingdom of God is near. It is starting like a mustard seed. It will grow and become an enormous plant."

"What are you talking about?" Longinus questioned. "Another kingdom? Is this treason?"

"I am talking about a kingdom that has no land and no boundaries. Every man, woman, and child can belong to this kingdom because it is a kingdom of the heart. The citizens of this kingdom live to show kindness without any conditions."

"I heard a man, a strange hairy man, speak of the Kingdom of God. He was at the crossing of the Jordan River not far from Jericho. Is his kingdom the same as the kingdom you speak of?" Longinus asked.

"Yes," Jesus answered. "We speak of the same kingdom."

"Does your kingdom have an army?" Longinus asked. "Do they fight and take territory?"

"Actually, the kingdom has come to take back what has been captured." Jesus could see the puzzled expression on the centurion's face so he continued, "Are you familiar with the Hebrew Scriptures?"

"A little," Longinus answered.

"The first book of Moses tells the story. The God that we worship made this Earth and the first people. His enemy tricked the people. That enemy captured their thoughts. He enslaved their bodies with illnesses and death. I am here to free the minds and the bodies of the people who have been captured. Then they can live righteous lives that will be pleasing to God."

"Can a Roman live a life that is pleasing to God, or is this just for Jews?" Longinus asked.

"You heard the preacher at the river. He told you the Kingdom of God is for every man: ordinary people, tax collectors, soldiers.

It is easier for a man who understands simple right and wrong to be part of the kingdom than it is for those who fill their heads with so much theology that they have no compassion for humanity." Jesus paused and looked deeply into the eyes of the Roman centurion. He answered the question that Longinus had not spoken. "I will tell you how you can be part of the Kingdom of God. One day, go to the river. Find that preacher you were telling me about. Repent for all the men you have mistreated or killed. Repent for moments of dishonesty. Go under the water and come up a new man. Begin a new, clean life."

"Is it that simple?"

"It is that simple," Jesus answered.

The sun was beginning to set. Jesus could see the centurion was looking around for a place to camp for the night. Jesus repeated the words of the Holy Spirit. "Walk one more mile, and you will find a wayside inn. You will be able to spend the night and rent a horse to complete your journey."

They came to an intersection of roads, and Jesus set the saddle and bags carefully on the road. "I will leave you now," Jesus said. "But maybe I will see you again in Jerusalem at the Passover Feast." Jesus then turned and continued his journey on the road that led to the area near the Jordan River where John was teaching and baptizing.

Geber carefully pushed the hot coals to the side and laid a round flat piece of dough on the heated rock. He watched the bread bake. Then he quickly flipped it so it would cook on both sides. John sat beside him, twisting his long hair into locks that could be tied back out of his way.

Geber broke the silence. "I've been thinking about your message, 'Repent for the kingdom of heaven is at hand.' What does it mean? I mean, how will repentance bring about the reestablishment of the throne of David?"

John thought for a long moment, and then he said, "It is the message God through his Holy Spirit has given. I believe God himself is coming to the land, and he cannot come if the people are full of sin."

Both men heard a noise and looked down the moonlit road. Someone was approaching.

"I cannot imagine who would be traveling the desert road at night." Geber stood to get a better look. After a time, he said, "I think it is the man you baptized, the one that you said was the son of God."

"Jesus?" John stood up and began hurrying to meet the man who was almost close enough to come into the light from their fire.

"John!" Jesus hurried forward to embrace his cousin.

Together, they walked to the fire and sat down. Jesus pulled a small cloth bag from his belt. "Jose got married. It was quite a wedding feast. I saved you some roasted almonds." He gave the bag to John.

"I was wondering when we would see you again," Geber broke into the conversation.

"I plan to stay awhile and sit at the feet of the teacher," Jesus responded as he nodded toward John.

"Sit at the feet of the teacher?" John shook his head. "I'm not much of a teacher. I do not understand the words I say. We were just trying to figure out how the kingdom will come."

"Adam and Eve lost the kingdom when they disobeyed. Doesn't it stand to reason that man can regain the kingdom through obedience?" Jesus said.

"That is very simple," John responded. "Is that all there is to the kingdom, obedience?"

"Those Jerusalem teachers, the very ones who come out here to argue points of the law, think their meticulous obedience makes them superior to all men and guaranteed a life in God's kingdom," Geber said.

"Those snakes!" John hissed. "Their hearts are as black as these ashes."

"I am not talking about the letter of the law," Jesus said. "I am talking about the Spirit of God. He comes into our lives and writes the character of God on our hearts. Then men will think God's thoughts and do his deeds, and the Evil One will have no more power."

"*The* L*ORD your God will circumcise your hearts and the hearts of your descendants, so that you may love him with all your heart and with all your soul, and live*,"[1] Geber quoted from the fifth book of Moses.

"And what will be the visible signs of the kingdom?" John asked. "Will our armies rise up and rout the Romans out of the land? Will we have a new and righteous government?"

Jesus answered, "First, ordinary individuals will seek God with all their hearts, then signs will follow. Remember the words of Isaiah. '*In that day the deaf will hear the words of the scroll, and out of gloom and darkness the eyes of the blind will see. Once more the humble will rejoice in the* L*ORD; the needy will rejoice in the Holy One of Israel.*'[2] When you see these things, then you will know that the Kingdom of God has invaded Earth. The invasion is beginning in the land, among the descendants of Abraham, but it will spread throughout all the nations."

"Many peoples will come and say, 'Come, let us go up to the mountain of the LORD, to the house of the God of Jacob. He will teach us his ways, so that we may walk in his paths.' The law will go out from Zion, the word of the LORD from Jerusalem."[3] Geber quoted from Isaiah.

The fire burned down to coals. The three men continued discussing the kingdom as it was described in the books of Moses and in the prophets. At dawn, the people gathered, and John called for repentance. He called the ordinary people to publically repent. He called the Temple leadership to publically repent, and he called the king and his new wife to publically repent.

The ordinary people came forward, confessing their sins and dipping under the water.

Representatives from the Temple watched. They huddled together, discussed, and criticized every word John said.

Soldiers from the court of Antipas listened and commented among themselves. They had met the new queen, and they did not expect her to repent anytime in the near future.

Jesus sat under a palm and some of John's disciples sat with him, listening to his commentary on John's preaching.

Childish feet ran along the mosaic floor of the Jericho palace. Cuza and Manaen looked up from addressing the invitations to the banquet that Antipas planned to host at his Jerusalem palace on the second night of the Passover. Suddenly, the little five-year-old daughter of Herodias burst through the curtains that separated their offices from the royal quarters.

"No, Salome!" The men could hear the little girl's wet nurse calling and hurrying down the corridor in search of the giggling, mischievous runaway.

Trembling with the excitement of her successful escape, the five-year-old grabbed a corner of the curtain and twirled around, wrapping herself in the hanging drapes. The curtains swayed and shook as the child was in constant motion, unable to contain her excitement.

With quick bows and apologies, the wet nurse ran into the offices and pulled Salome out from within the heavy drapes.

Cuza and Manaen chuckled.

As the wet nurse left with the little girl, Manaen commented, "She is a beautiful child."

"Even though Antipas is only her stepfather, he is quite taken with her," Cuza added. "He treats her like the child he never had."

Both men then returned to their task, discussing the political pros and cons of each invitation.

"Pilate and his wife?" Cuza waited with poised pen.

"They will be at the fortress for the entire feast," Manaen stated. "We have to invite them."

"The ranking centurion who commands the fortress?" Cuza asked.

"I have met him. He is a career man from Rome. I believe his name is Longinus," Manaen responded. "Yes, he knows how to mingle with royalty."

"How about someone from the Jewish community?" Cuza asked.

"I don't want anyone who is pushing agendas," Manaen countered.

Cuza responded, "I know a wealthy member of the Sanhedrin who keeps his own council and seems to know his own mind, Joseph of Arimathea. He is from a merchant family. He has done some traveling outside of Judea. My family has known his family for years. I think he and his wife could represent the Temple without making anyone uncomfortable."

Cuza looked up again from the invitations. "I have received word that Philip is coming to Jerusalem for Passover. He is inquiring about staying at his father's palace."

Manaen winced. "He and Antipas are half brothers. They have equal rights to the palace, but—"

Cuza finished Manaen's thought, "Herodias used to be married to Philip, and now, she is married to Antipas."

Both men could hear little Salome running up and down the stone corridor just outside their offices. Manaen commented, "Salome is the daughter of Philip and Herodias."

"According to protocol, Philip should be invited not only to the banquet, but also to stay in the royal residences for the entire time that he remains in Jerusalem," Cuza informed.

Manaen sighed, "Put that invitation aside. I'll talk this over with Antipas."

Chapter 18

Events at Passover

Now while he was in Jerusalem at the Passover Feast, many people saw the miraculous signs he was doing and believed in his name. But Jesus would not entrust himself to them, for he knew all men. He did not need man's testimony about man, for he knew what was in a man.

—John 2:23–25

When it was almost time for the Jewish Passover, Jesus went up to Jerusalem.[1] James and John—the sons of Zebedee—Peter and Andrew as well as Philip and Nathanael who were fishing partners all walked with Jesus. They traveled together from the place where John, the prophet of the Jordan had been teaching and baptizing to the city where all Israel was gathering for the Passover Feast.

From a safe distance, Satan shadowed Jesus and his companions. In the wilderness, he had not been able to cause the son of God and descendant of Adam to disavow either his parentage or his purpose. Now he must find a weakness. He moved a little closer and listened.

"Jesus?" Nathanael began his question. "I have been listening to the prophet at the river. He always speaks about the kingdom, but he never calls for an army. How will the kingdom come if we do not rally an army and drive the Romans back to Rome?"

"Does God need an earthly army?" Jesus replied. Then he began a song.

Your throne, O God, will last for ever and ever;
a scepter of justice will be the scepter of your kingdom.
You love righteousness and hate wickedness;
therefore God, your God, has set you above your companions
by anointing you with the oil of joy.[2]

It was a familiar psalm, and the men who walked with him easily joined in.

"What did we just sing about?" Jesus asked as the last baritone note drifted into the countryside.

"The Kingdom of God," Nathanael answered.

"We did not sing about armies," Jesus expounded. "We sang about conquest through righteousness and victory demonstrated in joy. We sang about the battleground of the heart. The Kingdom of God is inside you." With his index finger, Jesus lightly poked Nathanael in the chest. "When you open yourself to allow the Spirit of God to push out the evil and replace it with righteousness, then the Kingdom of God has been established in you. Nothing in this physical world can shake the inner joy that will be yours."

"But what about the throne and the scepter?" Peter asked.

"When every heart is ruled by righteousness, then the nation will be righteous, and God will set his government in place," Jesus answered. "First, we lay the foundation of righteousness."

Philip pointed to the walls of the city and the golden spires of the Temple that were just ahead. "I was taught the righteousness of the land is in God's house."

"We are going there," Jesus responded. "We will look for righteousness."

The men entered one of the many enclosed pools that had been strategically built around the Temple mount so visitors from all directions could immerse themselves in fresh water before entering the Temple courts. This pool was a place where only Jewish men were allowed.

Without pausing for permission, Satan entered the pool area behind Jesus and his companions. This was familiar territory. The demonic spirits of Religion and Pride controlled most of the Temple establishment. He had set up both principalities and powers to control the Temple, the city of Jerusalem, and the entire Jewish world. Satan settled himself into a dark corner to watch.

The Temple guards were walking the perimeter of the pool, observing the men undress, unobtrusively noting that each man had been circumcised and that no one entered who had an obvious body deformity or disease.

When Jesus and his friends arrived, at least one hundred men were in the pool and more were on the periphery dressing and undressing. Jesus approached a pair of Temple guards and asked, "Are you the guardians of righteousness in this place?"

"Yes," one guard gruffly answered. "We enforce the code of the Temple."

"On the edge of the pool, there is a man with a deep running sore on his leg," Jesus informed as he pointed.

The guard moved quickly and apprehended the man just as he was about to step into the water. With no regard for the man's nakedness, he brought him back to where Jesus was standing with his friends. "Is this the man?" the guard asked.

Jesus pointed to the infected gash on the man's leg. "Is it lawful for this man to enter the Temple?"

"A priest will have to decide," the guard answered as he gestured for another guard to go get a priest.

Jesus turned to his friends. "We are looking for righteousness. I believe many wash in this pool and remain unclean. They enter the courts of the Temple infected and unchallenged."

In the corner of the room, Satan smirked as he nodded his head, agreeing with Jesus's statement.

A priest hurried into the pool area. Both Jesus and the Temple guard pointed to the pussy gash on the man's leg.

The man protested, "I was kicked by my cow. The priest in my local village saw the wound, and he said it would not prevent me from coming to the Temple."

The Temple priest held a lamp close to the wound so he could see clearly. "It is infected, unclean," the priest pronounced. "You may not enter the Temple. Return to your city and remain outside for seven days, then show yourself to the local priest. He will sprinkle you with the water of cleansing."

"But I have traveled all the way from Alexandria to celebrate this Passover in Jerusalem. I may not be able to make this trip again," the man pleaded.

"May I have a look?" Jesus reached for the lamp in the priest's hand and brought it close to the infected gash. With his free hand, Jesus picked up the fringe of his own prayer shawl. He touched the fringe to the oozing wound as he spoke, "*But for you who revere my name, the sun of righteousness will rise with healing in its wings. And you will go out and leap like calves released from the stall.*"[3]

The priest gasped, then he snatched the lamp back from Jesus and held it close to the man's perfectly healthy skin. "Is this some kind of profane magic trick?" he asked.

"The man's leg is healed!" Peter exclaimed.

"How can healing be profane?" the guard rhetorically asked.

"It is profane! It is profane!" Satan silently shot his lie into every mind that would receive it.

The companions of Jesus were taking their own close look. "Did you see the man's wound a moment ago?" John asked his brother James. "Jesus touched the sore with the fringes of his prayer shawl. His shawl was spread out like a wing!"

James responded, "He spoke of righteousness. Jesus said when righteousness comes, healing will follow!"

The other men in the pool area began to come over to hear the story and look at the man's leg.

Totally excited, the man began to jump around and test his healed calf.

Puzzled and exasperated by the events, the priest left.

In the corner of the room, Satan trembled with anger and frustration as he realized that Jesus, this son of God and son of man, had now moved from rural Galilee to the Temple in Jerusalem.

Unobtrusively, Jesus stepped away from the excitement. He removed his prayer shawl, kissed it, and carefully folded it. Then with genuine respect for Temple protocol, he completely undressed and stepped into the pool to wash. Those with him also washed, but they could not stop talking about what they had just seen.

The beggar, Ichabod, watched as wave after wave of worshippers climbed the steps to be in the Temple for the evening sacrifice. People from all over the world had come for the Passover, which was only a day away. This had been a good day for receiving alms.

For one surprising moment, the waves of people paused, and a group of men stood near the spot where he always begged. One of the men stepped closer and bent down.

"Friend?"

Ichabod recognized the face of the carpenter.

"How is your chair?"

Ichabod grinned back. "I am sitting in it, and it is still very sturdy."

"Do you need me to replace the leather?" Jesus asked.

"Maybe in a few months," Ichabod replied. "But for now, it is good."

"I will check with you again," Jesus said as he dropped a few coins in the beggar's bowl. Jesus started to walk on, but he stopped and turned back to the beggar. "We are looking for righteousness in the house of the Lord. You sit here every day. Have you seen righteousness?"

The beggar chuckled as he pondered the unusual question.

"I don't know that I have seen righteousness, but yesterday, I saw royalty. Antipas, his new wife, and her little daughter brought his personal sacrifices to the Temple. The high priest, Caiaphas, met him at this gate. I have heard the stories about how King Antipas divorced his first wife and took his brother's wife. The high priest did not say one word to Antipas about that. He welcomed him and fawned over both his wife and her child."

Jesus replied, "The prophet Samuel said to King Saul what the high priest should have said to King Antipas. *'Does the LORD delight in burnt offerings and sacrifices as much as in obeying the voice of the LORD? To obey is better than sacrifice, and to heed is better than the fat of rams.'*"[4]

"If the appearance of the Messiah depends on righteousness in this Temple, I don't think he can come!" Peter exclaimed.

Ichabod looked a little startled at the intrusion into his conversation.

But Jesus quickly responded by saying, "Let me introduce you to my friends. We often discuss the scriptures, and they are always ready to offer their opinions. This is Peter and his brother Andrew. I believe you have met my two cousins, John and James the sons of Zebedee. Philip and Nathanael are fishermen. All these men work together."

Ichabod grinned up at Jesus. "Look at you! I know a rabbi with his disciples when I see him. You used to be just a carpenter. Now you are like the teachers who come here with their little flocks of students." Then Ichabod spoke to the men with Jesus. "If this man teaches the scriptures as well as he makes chairs, you had better learn from him."

Good naturedly, Jesus patted Ichabod on the shoulder. "I'll see you another time, friend." And Jesus, along with his companions continued into the Temple.

The Beautiful Gate opened almost directly into the Court of the Women where the offering boxes were lined up in cubicles according to the designation of the offering. Jesus found a place where he could stand and watch the people as they brought their offerings and poured them into the various boxes. After a little time, he asked his disciples, "Can you tell who is righteous by the offerings that they bring?"

"The wealthy make a big show, clanging and banging so everyone will notice them," Nathanael commented.

"And the ordinary people walk up quietly, almost like they are ashamed of their modest offerings," Peter added.

"Only God, who looks at the heart, knows," James commented.

Jesus watched a little longer. As he watched the parade of the wealthy, the Spirit of God opened up the ledgers of heaven, showing page after page to Jesus. Jesus took a decisive step toward the offering boxes. With his hand, he made a sweeping inclusive gesture as he spoke, "Thieves and robbers, how boldly you rob God in your tithes and offerings!" The books of heaven are open. The angels of God record every financial transaction accurately. Not one of these offerings is an honest ten percent. *You are under a curse—the whole nation of you—because you are robbing me. Bring the whole tithe into the storehouse, that there may be food in my house.*"[5]

The men who were with Jesus noted that some of the wealthy who were bringing large offerings heard what Jesus had said. Peter nudged Andrew and pointed toward the men who clutched their gifts while looking both startled and alarmed. One man quickly poured his offering into the box, and then he hurried off to confer with a priest and one of the Temple guards.

Peter was about to speak a word of warning to Jesus, but to his surprise, Jesus was no longer focused on the ostentatious parade of donors. He had turned to a woman who was waiting for the commotion around the treasury boxes to die down. Moving closer, Peter heard Jesus say, "God, who sees you in your humble home, is ready to pour out a blessing on your home and your crops. He will restore the health of your husband and increase your childbearing years because you have honored him with ten percent. Return to your home. Your husband is out of his sickbed and working with the animals."

"Is your husband sick?" Peter stopped the woman as she moved away.

"How does this man know?" the woman asked. "My husband has been in bed for three days with pain in his back." Then she hurried away, quickly dropping her coins in the treasury box and then running for an exit that would put her on the road to her home.

Very deliberately, Jesus began walking again, turning his head from side to side, taking in all the sights and sounds of the Temple preparing for Passover. He was very keenly aware of the Holy Spirit's instructions. He was equally aware of an extremely evil presence in the Temple. As Jesus walked, his friends followed, wondering what would happen next.

Approaching the entrance to the Court of the Israelites, Jesus stopped at the base of the fifteen curved steps that led to the ornate brass gates. The gates stood majestically open. Looking through them, the men could view the building, which housed the Holy and the Most Holy Place. On one section of the steps, the Levitical choir was gathering. On the lower steps, several men were standing, bending their knees and repeatedly bowing toward the Holy Place. Jesus paused and turned to those who were with him. "Is righteousness standing on these steps?"

"I see men praying," Philip stated.

"And I see men preparing to praise God," Andrew added.

Jesus responded, "God spoke to Solomon at the dedication of his Temple. *'If my people, who are called by my name, will humble themselves and pray and seek my face and turn from their wicked ways, then will I hear from heaven and will forgive their sin and will heal their land. Now my eyes will be open and my ears attentive to the prayers offered in this place. I have chosen and consecrated this Temple so that my Name may be there forever. My eyes and my heart will always be there.'*"[6]

The men who were with Jesus watched in amazement as Jesus then mounted the steps and began walking among the praying men. Moving selectively, he reached out and touched man after man with the fringes of his prayer shawl entangled in his fingers. Each man, once touched, immediately praised God and left the steps laughing and staggering like a drunk.

A small cluster of priests gathered in the open doorway at the top of the steps. They were pointing at Jesus and talking among themselves.

Peter looked hard at them and then he informed the others, "The priest doing all the talking is the one who came to the pool where we bathed."

Philip added, "One of those priests was near the offering boxes."

Jesus briefly glanced at the priests. He saw the spirits of Satan directing their conversation, and he turned his back to them.

When no man was left praying on the steps, Jesus returned to his friends and continued walking through the Court of the Women. Briefly, he stopped by the chamber of Wood. Priests were busily examining the wood and discarding those pieces that were rotten. Jesus commented, "Only those pieces of wood that are without disease can be burned on the altar before the King of the Universe. *When a king sits on his throne to judge, he winnows out all evil with his eyes. Who can say, 'I have kept my heart pure; I am clean and without sin'?*[7] I tell you now, every man will come before the King of the Universe. Some men will be discarded." Jesus glanced over his shoulder. The men who were with Jesus followed his glance with their own eyes. The small group of priests that had been talking near the top of the steps was following them.

The men with Jesus exchanged alarmed glances, but Jesus did not show any reaction.

Continuing his stroll, Jesus led his group to the Chamber of the Nazirite. There, several men were in the process of completing their vows, shaving their hair, and washing. Jesus and those with him stopped to watch. Behind them the Levitical choir began to sing.

> *The Mighty One, God, the LORD,*
> *speaks and summons the earth*
> *from the rising of the sun to the place where it sets*[8].
> *Gather to me my consecrated ones,*
> *who made a covenant with me by sacrifice.*
> *And the heavens proclaim his righteousness,*
> *for God himself is judge.*[9]

Without comment, Jesus moved on and his friends followed. He led them to the covered colonnade where sheep and goats were kept in makeshift pens, where live doves had been crammed into covered baskets, and where men haggled over the price and quality of sacrificial animals like they were in a country market.

For a long moment, Jesus stood and observed. Normally, the Temple market operated at the far end of this wide corridor. But for this Passover season, it had been expanded so vendors and merchants filled the area, consuming the space where rabbis usually taught the people.

Aided by the Holy Spirit, Jesus could see the spirits named Greed and Dishonesty moving from vendor to vendor, weighing in on each transaction. Hovering over those spirits, Jesus saw the controlling spirits of Religion, reigning as if the Temple of God was their own palace. And high above the sanctuary, he saw Satan conferring with Raziel, the evil principality over Jerusalem.

Above the music from the Levitical choir and orchestra, over the bellowing and shouting of the animal market, Jesus heard the voice of his Father, "I am not welcome here."

Jesus spoke to his friends, "Is God honored in this place? Or is this just a man-made shrine to Greed and Dishonesty?"

He sensed the mocking laughter of those evil spirits who worked through the men who ran the Passover market. Within his heart, the Holy Spirit raised a sense of righteous anger.

Deliberately walking back through the area where doves were being sold, Jesus studied the floor. It was covered with bird droppings and feathers mixed with scraps of twine and strips of leather. Here and there, he bent over, picking up carefully selected leather cords, a piece here, a piece there. As he wandered back and forth through the market, he began to braid the leather strips until he had a substantial whip with three knotted strands. His deliberate meanderings brought him to the place where all currency was exchanged for Temple coins so each male could pay the half shekel tax and purchase animals to sacrifice.

The men with Jesus immediately produced their coins, exchanging them for the Temple coinage.

"Wait!" Nathanael suddenly protested. "I gave you more than the value of the half shekel. Where is my change?"

The man at the money exchange mockingly laughed, "We only exchange here. We do not make change."

Frustrated, Nathanael turned away, complaining to the others.

"A half shekel! A half shekel! If you have not already paid for the year, you must pay now. A chanting money handler thrust a demanding hand toward Jesus. "I will change your money into Temple coins so you can pay the Temple tax."

Behind the man, Jesus could see Satan himself saying, "I run this Temple, and you will pay me!"

Like in the wilderness, Jesus stood and looked right through the demanding man to the one who was manipulating him. "God says: '*What right have you to recite my laws or take my covenant on your lips? You hate my instruction and cast my words behind you.*'"[10]

Then, speaking to the money changer, Jesus challenged, "Do you change coin for coin, or is there an uneven exchange?"

One of the Temple guards stepped up. "Is there a problem here?"

Jesus turned to him.[11] "When you see a thief, do you arrest him or join with him?"

With one free hand, Jesus suddenly reached out and flipped the money table on its side.

The Temple guard and the money changers dove for the scattering coins, but they could not stop them from rolling across the pavement. Neither could they stop Jesus angrily striding from table to table, tipping each one over while he brought his homemade whip smartly across the hand or back of anyone who tried to stop him.

Moving on to the animal pens, Jesus quickly opened the gates and shooed the beasts in the direction of the melee. With his whip, he incited the animals to run into the demolished area of the money changers where the animals came to a bellowing halt with coins under their hooves and frantic men crawling between their legs.

The doves were next. Jesus threw the woven lids off the baskets. With his free hand, he reached in, grabbing handfuls of birds and tossing them into the air. For a moment, Jesus was obscured by wildly flapping wings. Then the flock rose into the air and soared to freedom.

Dumbfounded by the unexpected actions of Jesus, his friends watched.

A crowd gathered—a cheering, laughing, pointing group of ordinary people. The Temple guards scattered, hurrying to get directions from the officiating priests.

Jesus threw his whip on the Temple floor and walked to the section of Solomon's porch that should have been reserved for the rabbis. The people followed. His friends followed. There, he sat down and began to teach, "You have come to this place to meet God, to bring your offerings, and to pray. You did not come to be robbed or taken advantage of."

"My heart beats with such excitement when I hear Jesus teach," John commented.

"There are others who seem less excited," James pointed to the priests who had been following Jesus. The captain of the Temple guard stood with them. "They know they should not have allowed the market to spill into the area of instruction."

"They would run everyone out and set it up again, but they are afraid of the people," Peter responded to the comments of his friends. "There must be two hundred people listening to Jesus teach, and more are coming.

"Look"—John pointed to one well-known rabbi—"that is Nicodemus, one of the most important teachers in the nation. He is sitting down to listen and his disciples are with him."

In the Roman fortress that was attached to the Temple, Longinus received a messenger from the high priest.

"A man has entered the area where money is exchanged and animals are sold. He has ransacked the place. What are you going to do about this?" the messenger asked.

"Did he steal money or animals?" Longinus asked.

"No," the messenger replied. "But money is all over the floor, and the animals are loose."

"Is the man Jewish or another nationality?"

"He is Jewish, maybe from Galilee," the messenger answered. "He has shown complete disrespect for the Temple and the Temple authorities."

"Disrespect for the Temple and the Temple authorities? Is that all?" Longinus demanded.

"He has gathered a crowd." The messenger pushed to make the situation sound menacing.

Longinus gestured to one of his men who hurried out of the room to observe from the wall that overlooked the Temple

In a short time, the soldier returned to report, "There is a large crowd: men, women, and children. They are all calmly standing and sitting around a very ordinary man. The man appears to be teaching."

With an irritated shake of his head, Longinus said, "This has nothing to do with the politics or interests of Rome. This is about your own Jewish nonsense. You have a force of men to keep order in your Temple. That should be sufficient. I will not intervene unless the empire is threatened."

Pilate walked into the room just as Longinus indicated that the messenger be escorted back to the stairway that led to the Temple courts.

Pilate looked questioningly at his commanding centurion.

"Someone has overturned the money changers' tables and freed the animals," Longinus explained. "Now they want Roman troops to come in and deal with their problem. I won't have anything to do with their Temple money."

"After the complaint they made to the emperor about Temple money in the hands of uncircumcised gentiles!" Pilate agreed, "we will never touch a Temple coin again."

Pilate tossed a small rolled parchment on the table. "We have been invited to a banquet at Herod's palace for the second night of Passover."

"That should be an interesting evening," Longinus responded.

"I expect it will be long and boring," Pilate replied.

Chapter 19

The Second Night of Passover

Now there was a man of the Pharisees named Nicodemus, a member of the Jewish ruling council. He came to Jesus at night.

—John 3:1–2

It was the second night after Passover. In Herod's palace, there were two receiving lines at the entrance to the banquet hall. Antipas, along with Manaen and Cuza, stood where the draperies had been tied back. With proper bows, they greeted Pilate, Longinus, Joseph of Arimathea, and a few others. In the women's receiving line, Herodias, Susanna, and Joanna greeted Procila and the wives of the other married men. Servants then assisted the men, pouring water over their hands and washing their feet. Perfumed oils were offered. Then each man was escorted to his place of reclinement around the table. Likewise, the women were offered water and perfumed oils before they were escorted to their own section of the banquet hall where each lady was offered a straight-backed chair positioned so soft polite conversation was possible while observing and listening to the male interaction in the same room.

Procila leaned toward Herodias. "Last night, I tasted some of the foods that are typically eaten during the Passover meal." She broke off a piece of the unleavened bread that a servant offered her. "I had never tasted bread made without yeast. It has a refreshing mild flavor."

Herodias responded, “For the rest of this week, it is the only type of bread that will be found anywhere in this city and throughout the nation.”

“I know,” Procila replied. “I have been studying the Jewish faith and how it unites the people of this land. One God, one set of laws to govern both religion and life—there is nothing like it anywhere else in the empire.”

“There are advantages and disadvantages to the Jewish world view,” Herodias pragmatically answered. Then she turned her head away from Procila to focus on the conversations of the men.

“Have you heard the prophet at the Jordan near Jericho?” The commander of the Antonia Fortress was speaking to Joseph of Arimathea, a member of the Jewish Sanhedrin.

The rest of the women followed the example of Herodias. They stopped their own conversations to focus on the men.

“I have heard him,” Joseph replied. “He is not calling the people to rebel; rather, he is calling them into obedience to the law of God.”

Pilate entered the conversation with a pointed remark. “I have heard that he is publically calling the king of this region to live by the ancient laws of Moses.”

Antipas cleared his throat and took a sip of wine as he mentally groped for a face-saving response. After a second sip of wine, he responded, “I have heard the man in person, and I find him fascinating. He is a picture of every prophet that has come to our land throughout the history of our people. When I hear him, my heart is moved to remember the unique history of the Jewish nation. I consider him a national treasure.”

In the women’s section of the banquet room, Herodias sat motionless with stunned indignation. She could feel the eyes of the other women on her reddening face. Then she heard Pilate’s wife, Procila, whisper to the wife of Joseph of Arimathea. “The prophet has great condemnation for Herodias and her new marriage to Antipas. He has announced God's displeasure to the entire nation."

"All of Jerusalem has heard," Joseph's wife quietly replied. "Everyone expects God will punish Antipas and his wife for breaking the sacred laws and not heeding the warning from the prophet." Both women turned away from Herodias and leaned toward the table where the prophet was still the focus of conversation. They heard the commander of the Antonia Fortress speak up.

"I have had reports that the king of the Nabataeans is building up his army so he can attack you and avenge the honor of his daughter."

"I didn't know the Nabataeans had an army," Antipas responded with a gesture that indicated he was brushing the threat aside.

Procila leaned toward Herodias and commented, "A war over your marriage to Antipas—that would be the talk of the empire. You and Antipas could become more famous than Cleopatra and Mark Antony."

"There will be no war," Herodias hissed. "This is nothing but the rantings of a crazy man. No one should listen. He should be silenced!"

Across the room, Pilate added another goading comment. "I know the emperor would never allow such public condemnation of his wife to take place in Rome. Men have died for less."

Herodias trembled, waiting for her husband's response. Futilely, she tried to catch her husband's eye so she could demand with her own eyes that he defend her honor.

After an awkward silence, Antipas, with his eyes fixed on the rim of his wine cup, growled, "This is not Rome. Rome wants me to keep the peace, and in this part of the world, you do not kill popular prophets and keep the peace. But—" Antipas then looked up, directly at Pilate, and he raised a challenging eyebrow. "If you consider the man a threat to Rome, you should act."

"On the contrary," Pilate chuckled as he spoke. "I find the man to be most useful. He is fearless, direct, and correct in his interpretation of your laws. I would not kill him or even put him in prison."

In the women's section, all the ladies gasped. Then they held their breath, waiting for Antipas to defend himself and his wife. There was only uncomfortable silence.

The silence was broken when Herodias stood red-faced, regal and fierce. "I will have the prophet's head!" she announced. Then she turned on her heel and left the banquet.

Cuza nodded toward his wife, Joanna. She quickly got up and followed Herodias out of the room. Manaen steered the male conversation to crops and weather. While in the ladies' corner, there was much speculation about a king who feared a desert prophet and a woman who had to defend her own honor.

On the bridge that spanned the Kidron Valley going from the city to the Mount of Olives, a prominent rabbi named Nicodemus wrapped himself in a dark cloak. By the light of the full moon, he crossed the bridge, heading toward a grove of ancient olive trees. He had been informed that Jesus, the carpenter from Nazareth, who had caused such uproar in the Temple courts, was camping there with his friends.

All afternoon, Nicodemus had been in heated discussions with other members of the Sanhedrin. Some wondered if this man could possibly be the Messiah. Others wondered how they could eliminate, or at the very least, control him. Nicodemus wondered why his own heart had burned as he listened to the man teach. Then in the back of his mind, he remembered a Galilean boy, just emerging into manhood, who had taught so powerfully many years before—could they be the same person?

Walking around the numerous campsites that dotted the rolling mountain, Nicodemus entered the grove of olive trees.

Cautiously avoiding twisted roots and low hanging branches, he wandered from campfire to campfire until he came across a group of men. They were coarse working men who spoke with a Galilean inflection.

"Jesus? Jesus the carpenter from Nazareth?" Nicodemus said the name he had heard at the Temple.

All the men stopped their conversations and looked up at him. One man stood. "I am Jesus. Do you wish to speak with me?"

"In private?" Nicodemus responded. "Could we step away from the fire?"

Jesus followed Nicodemus into the shadows while his companions followed the unusual encounter with their eyes. Within the shadows of the spirit realm, another cloaked being followed the two teachers. Satan leaned in to listen to their conversation.

Lowering his voice, Nicodemus said, "This morning, your authority in the Temple amazed me. I had already objected to allowing the market to expand into the area of instruction. I was ridiculed, and I am convinced if my disciples and I had taken the action that you took, we would have been expelled from the Temple permanently. How do you act with such authority and remain untouched?

Jesus smiled. "First, I am not concerned with protecting my position, my property, even my reputation. All that, I leave in the hands of my Father.

"Your father?" Nicodemus asked.

"He's your Father too," Jesus responded. "If you listen, he will direct every word and every action. Today, I heard the Spirit of God shouting, 'Clean these robbers out of my house. Remove both the men and their demons.'"

Nicodemus changed the subject. "In the afternoon, my disciples and I listened to you teach. We saw you touch people and speak words that gave them new life. *Rabbi,* we understand you are from Galilee and that you have not studied under any of the Jerusalem rabbis. Still, *we know you are a teacher who has come from God. For no one could perform the miraculous signs you are doing if God were not with him.*[1] How can this be?"

"So you were impressed with the miraculous signs?" Jesus incredulously asked. "You should have realized that those miracles were merely the banners of the Kingdom of God. You should have been more impressed with the Spirit of justice and righteousness that prevailed over Greed and Injustice when the Temple market closed for the day."

Satan cringed as he recalled how his most powerful demons had fled when confronted with pure righteousness.

Jesus continued, "Many get excited over miracles, but only a few see past the miracles into the conflict that rages between the Kingdom of God and the kingdom of Satan."

For a long silent moment, the well-known rabbi studied the face of Jesus. "Tell me, are you a prophet?"

"A prophet?" Jesus echoed. "A prophet is just a man or woman who hears the voice of God and then obeys."

"Could you be the Promised One?" Nicodemus quickly withdrew his question by adding, "No, you are from Galilee."

"I was born in Bethlehem, the city of David," Jesus countered.

"Impossible! Impossible!" Satan shouted into the ponderings of the old rabbi.

"Your heritage?" Nicodemus continued to question.

"I belong to the tribe of Judah," Jesus answered. My mother and the man she married are both direct descendants of King David."

Nicodemus looked sharply at Jesus. "The man she married? That is an unusual way to describe your father."

"I already told you. My Father is the God of Abraham."

"How can God unite with a woman to have a son?" Nicodemus incredulously pressed.

"It is the fulfillment of the prophecy the Creator spoke to Adam and Eve, the seed of the woman." Jesus calmly stated.

Nicodemus began to get excited. "I have lived to see the Promised One! When will you gather an army? When will you remove the Romans and reestablish the royal line of King David?"

Slowly shaking his head, Jesus said, "You are a great teacher in Jerusalem. You have studied the prophecies concerning the Messiah, yet you have the same distorted interpretation as every man on the street." Then Jesus, speaking more to himself than to Nicodemus, said, "I should not be surprised. *I tell you the truth, no one can see the kingdom of God unless* he *is born again.*[2] You need to become a man who has experienced this rebirth."

Satan whispered to Nicodemus, "This talk of rebirth is nonsense, and this story about Jesus being the offspring of God uniting with a woman is equal nonsense."

A look of confusion crossed the rabbi's face. "First you tell me you were born from the union of God and woman. Then you tell me I must experience birth again. *How can* a *man be born when he is old?" Nicodemus asked. "Surely he cannot enter a second time into his mother's womb to be born!"*[3]

Jesus was aware that Satan himself was trying to bring confusion into the mind of the teacher, so he looked the master teacher directly in the eyes and focused on communicating clearly. He knew the rabbi's questions were genuine.

Jesus answered, "You have been to the fresh-water springs on the other side of the Jordan where the prophet John is teaching. He invites the people to dip beneath the water and to come out of the water with a changed mind and a changed heart so they can live new lives that are directed by God. When they begin this new life, they are like newborns and part of a fledgling community, the Kingdom of God. *I tell you the truth, no one can enter the kingdom of God unless he is born of water and the Spirit. Flesh gives birth to flesh, but the Spirit gives birth to spirit. You should not be surprised at my saying, 'You must be born again.'*[4] This phrase is used by all our great teachers to describe the spiritual change that takes place when a person who was not born into Judaism embraces our beliefs and our way of life. They are immersed in water. Men are circumcised. Then we say they have been "born again" as sons and daughters of Abraham."

"Yes, yes," Nicodemus agreed. "I have used that phrase to describe those who have converted, but I did not convert. I was born a Jew."

"Again let me say that I am not talking about the travail of women that produces a child. I am talking about a work of God through his Spirit. I am talking about an internal change in your thoughts and your emotions. It is a change that connects you with the heart of God. This change is demonstrated by righteous words and just deeds. *The wind blows wherever it pleases. You hear its sound, but you cannot tell where it comes from or where it is going. So it is with everyone born of the Spirit.*[5] They naturally live by the law of God. Everyone who has experienced this internal change is a citizen of the Kingdom of God."

"Your words puzzle me." Nicodemus thoughtfully paused. "I went to the river near Jericho and heard the prophet who is immersing the people. He said the kingdom of heaven was near. Now you speak of that same kingdom as if it has arrived. Tell me about this kingdom. Who is its king? Does it levy taxes? What about an army and borders?"

"You are Israel's teacher," said Jesus, "and do you not understand these things? I tell you the truth, we speak of what we know, and we testify to what we have seen, but still you people do not accept our testimony.[6] John, the prophet at the river, and I have both experienced the Kingdom of God. We live in that kingdom by staying in constant connection with God through his Holy Spirit. We do not respond to men or to demons. We only do and say the things we hear from heaven. Everyone who enters the Kingdom of God is part of the army of God. They fight evil by offering undeserved goodness to everyone. Land and physical property are unimportant. The wealth of the kingdom is love, joy, peace, faithfulness, long suffering, goodness, and patience."

As Jesus clarified kingdom living, Satan clinched his fists and ground his teeth. He swore by his own beauty and wisdom, "Yeshua, you are on Earth as a man. I will not give you a moment's peace until you have responded to me instead of heaven. I will rip the wealth of the kingdom from your heart!"

Jesus ignored the Evil One who was trying to insert himself into the conversation. He continued putting his entire attention on the teacher. "Nicodemus, *I have spoken to you of earthly things and you do not believe; how then will you believe if I speak of heavenly things?*[7] What if I told you the things I have seen in my Father's house? The sapphire throne sits atop heavenly Mt. Zion. An emerald bow arches over it and angelic choirs sing above it. In front of the throne room is a massive expanse of crystal, like a sea of fine glass. Food is abundant, growing on every tree, year round. Gold is the dirt of heaven. It has been compressed to build roads. There is a city with magnificent walls embedded with gemstones." Jesus looked directly at Nicodemus and stated, "*No one has ever gone into heaven except the one who came from heaven—the Son* from the union *of Man* and God."[8]

"You are talking about yourself?" Nicodemus waited for clarification.

With a knowing look in his eye, Jesus nodded. "Hasn't all Israel been waiting for the seed of the woman? I have heard you teach. 'The seed of God will be united with the seed of an ordinary woman to produce a man that is the image of God just as the first man, Adam, was the image of God.' This son of Adam is the only one who can take back what Adam lost." Jesus searched the rabbi's eyes for understanding. Then he nodded with satisfaction as he could see that the old man remembered and understood.

"How?" Nicodemus asked. "How will this son of Adam restore us to the paradise that was the home of Adam and Eve?"

Satan did not want Nicodemus to hear the answer. With a thought, the Evil One summoned demons and fallen angels from the city. He ordered them to cloak the light of the moon, to send a chill wind, and to distract Jesus and Nicodemus from further conversation.

The wind came and the moonlight disappeared behind a black cloud, but Jesus did not seem to notice. He continued explaining, "First, the Anointed One will satisfy the law. He will live in perfect obedience, honoring God with every aspect of his life. Then *just as Moses lifted up the snake in the desert, so the Son of Man must be lifted up, that everyone who believes in him may have eternal life*."[9]

"The cross?" Nicodemus interrupted.

Jesus nodded affirmatively. "Death will not be the end of my life. After three days, I will come out of the tomb, alive."

"What about all the others who sleep in the Place of the Dead?" Nicodemus jumped into an often debated subject.

"There will be another resurrection of the dead when the Messiah makes his victorious return. The Pharisees teach that correctly. But first, the Promised One must suffer and die. He must break the power of Death. After that, he will return to his heavenly home while his kingdom on Earth expands. Citizenship in my kingdom is voluntary. All of humanity must be offered a choice. Every citizen of the kingdom must believe that *God so loved the world that he gave his one and only Son, that whoever believes in him shall not perish but have eternal life*."[10]

"Why?" Nicodemus asked. "Why must they believe?"

Jesus replied, "You are a master teacher of the law, so you know the law condemns every person who tries to keep it. No matter how observant a man tries to be, at some point, he fails and the law condemns him. One man must keep God's law perfectly. He must then die, taking the punishment for all those who failed and deserved the penalty of eternal death."

Nicodemus leaned forward contemplating each word.

A remembering look came across the face of Jesus. "I told you about heaven. Now I must tell you about my Father, God. His heart is full of mercy for all who love his law and attempt to live by it. *For God did not send his Son into the world to condemn the world, but to save the world through him.*[11]

"Belief is what is important, not belief in man's interpretation of the law or in a particular school of theology. You must believe in the divine Son of God who is also a descendant of Adam. You must believe that he will accept the penalty for the disobedience of Adam and Eve as well as the penalty for every man's disobedience. After the Anointed One goes to the grave, he will come out alive. The power of the law of God to convict and inflict eternal death will be broken.

"Then, *whoever believes in him is not condemned, but whoever does not believe stands condemned already because he has not believed in the name of God's one and only Son.*"[12]

Jesus looked past Nicodemus, who was contemplating all he had heard. He looked directly at his ancient evil enemy. Then he pointed to the cloud-covered moon and said, *"This is the verdict: Light has come into the world!"*[13]

Immediately, the demons and fallen angels that had been cloaking the moon fled. Satan slunk further into the shadows, and glorious white light bathed the area where the two men sat.

Jesus returned to instructing the great rabbi, "Since the sin of Adam and Eve, men have *loved darkness instead of light because their deeds were evil. Everyone who does evil hates the light, and will not come into the light for fear that his deeds will be exposed. But whoever lives by the truth comes into the light, so that it may be seen plainly that what he has done has been done through God.*[14] You see me. I am sitting in the light. Everything I have done has been done through God, the Eternal One. I represent his kingdom. The time has come! Now, I am calling all men to live in the Kingdom of God."

Index of Characters

Biblical Characters

Abraham	The father of the Jewish race (Genesis 11–50)
Abel	The second son of Adam and Eve; he was killed by his brother Cain. (Genesis 4:1–12)
Adam	The first man. He was created by God and placed in the Garden of Eden. (Genesis 2–4)
Ahab	A wicked king of Israel (1 Kings 16–22)
Andrew	Brother of Peter, son of Jona, fisherman, one of the twelve disciples of Jesus, later an apostle (John 1:42)
Annas	High priest during the life of Jesus (Luke 3:1–3)
Barabbas	The criminal that Pilate freed at Passover when Jesus was crucified (Matthew 27:15–26, Mark 15:6–15, Luke 23:13–25, John 18:39–40)

Beggar at the Beautiful Gate	Fictionalized as Ichabod the crippled son of Asa, the Temple perfumer (Acts 3)
Boaz	The kinsman redeemer for Ruth; ancestor of King David and Jesus (Ruth 1–4)
Caiaphas	High priest during the life of Jesus (Luke 3:1–3)
Cain	The firstborn son of Adam and Eve, he became the first murderer (Genesis 4:1–18)
Cuza	Officer in the court of Herod, manager of Herod's household, husband to Joanna, fictionalized as father of Casper (Luke 8:3)
Cyrus	King of Persia who enabled the Jews to return to Jerusalem and rebuild (2 Chronicles 36:22–23)
Daniel	A prophet during the Babylonian captivity (Daniel 1–12)
David	A king of Israel and ancestor of Jesus (1 Samuel 16–2 Samuel 24, 1 Chronicles 11–29
Elimelech	Husband of Naomi, father-in-law of Ruth (Ruth 1–4)

Elijah	Old Testament prophet in Israel who challenged King Ahab and Queen Jezebel (1 Kings 7—2 Kings 2)
Elisha	Old Testament prophet who succeeded Elijah and had a double portion of Elijah's anointing (1 Kings 19—2 Kings 13)
Enoch	Prophet, son of Jared, great-great-great-grandson of Adam (Genesis 5:18, Jude 1:14)
Enosh	Son of Seth, grandson of Adam (Genesis 5:6)
Eve	The first woman; she was created by God from Adam's rib. She was Adam's wife and was the first to fall into sin. (Genesis 2–4)
Ezra	One of the leaders of Israel who brought the Jews back to Jerusalem to rebuild the city and the Temple (Ezra 7–10, Nehemiah 8–12)
Gabriel	An angel who brings messages to Earth (Daniel 8:16, 9:21; Luke 1:10, 26)
Gamaliel	Important member of Sanhedrin, grandson of Hillel (Acts 5:34, 22:3)

Goliath	The Philistine giant that was killed by David (1 Samuel 17)
Heli	Grandfather of Jesus (Luke 3:23) (One theory is that the genealogy in Luke is actually the genealogy of Mary.)
Herod Antipas	The Son of Herod the Great and ruler of Galilee (Matthew 14:1–11, Luke 23:6–12)
Herod the Great	The King Herod who killed the babies in Bethlehem, hoping to kill Jesus (Matthew 2:1–9)
Herod Philip	One of the sons of Herod the Great, he was a half brother to Herod Antipas, and married to Herodias. (Luke 3:1–3)
Herodias	The second wife of Herod Antipas, formerly the wife of his half-brother, Phillip (Matthew 14:1–12, Mark 6:14–29, Luke 3:19–20)
Holy Spirit	Third person of the Godhead
Isaiah	An Old Testament prophet (2 Kings 19–20, 2 Chronicles 26–32, Isaiah)

Jacob	The son of Isaac who was tricked into marrying the wrong woman (Genesis 29:23–25)
Jairus	A leader of the synagogue in Capernaum; Jesus raised his daughter from the dead (Mark 5 and Luke 8)
Jared	Son of Mahalalel, great-great-grandson of Adam (Genesis 5:15)
James son of Joseph and Mary	The brother of Jesus, later a leader in the early church and writer of the book of James (Matthew 13:55)
James son of Zebedee	Possibly a cousin of Jesus, one of the twelve disciples, the brother of the disciple John whom Jesus loved, a fisherman, later an apostle (Mark 1:19–20, Mark 9:2–8, Mark 10:35–45, Mark 14:33)
Jeremiah	Old Testament prophet (Jeremiah 1–51)
Jesse	The grandson of Boaz and the father of King David, an ancestor of Jesus (Matthew 1:6)
Jesus	Son of God and Son of Mary (Gospels of Matthew, Mark, Luke, and John)

Jezebel	The wicked wife of King Ahab (1 Kings 16–2 Kings 9)
Joanna	Wife of Cuza, supporter of Jesus, associated with the court of Herod Antipas (Luke 8:3)
Job	A man who was tested by Satan (Job 1–2)
John son of Zebedee	Possibly a cousin of Jesus, one of the twelve disciples, the brother of the disciple James, a fisherman, later an apostle, writer of the books of John and Revelation (Mark 1:19–20, Mark 9:2–8, Mark 14, 32–42)
John son of Zechariah	John the Baptist, a cousin of Jesus (Mark 1:1–11, Luke 1:36–80, Luke 7:18–23, Mark 6:14–29)
Jona	Father of Simon Peter and Andrew, fishing partner with Zebedee (John 1:42 KJV)
Jose	Brother of Jesus, son of Joseph and Mary (Matthew 13:55 KJV)
Joseph	Carpenter of Nazareth, husband of Mary, earthly father of Jesus (Matthew 1:18–24)

Joseph of Arimathea	A wealthy man, member of the Sanhedrin who was able to approach Pilate (Mark 15:43)
Jude	A brother of Jesus, a son of Mary and Joseph, his name is sometimes spelled Juda or Judas. Probably the author of the book of Jude (Jude 1:1, Matthew 13:55, Mark 6:3)
Kenan	Son of Enosh, grandson of Adam (Genesis 5:9)
Kilion	One of the sons of Naomi (Ruth 1)
Lamech	Father of Noah, son of Methuselah, great-great-great-great-great-grandson of Adam (Genesis 5:25–29)
Lazarus	Friend of Jesus who lived in Bethany, fictionalized as the elder brother in the parable of the prodigal son (John 11)
Mahalalel	Son of Kenan, great grandson of Adam (Genesis 5:12)
Mahlon	One of the sons of Naomi (Ruth 1)
Manaen	Childhood companion to Herod Antipas, his mother was most likely the wet nurse for Antipas, later an important member of the early Christian community. (Acts 13:1)

Martha	The sister of Mary and Lazarus of Bethany (John 11)
Mary	The mother of Jesus, wife of Joseph (Matthew 1–2, Luke 1–2)
Mary	The sister of Lazarus who lives in Bethany (John 11)
Matthew	The tax collector at Capernaum, later one of the twelve disciples, author of the Gospel of Matthew (Matthew 9:9)
Methuselah	Had the longest recorded life, son of Enoch, great-great-great-great-grandson of Adam (Genesis 5:21–25)
Michael	A prince of angels who fought the forces of evil to bring a message from God to Daniel (Daniel 10:13)
Moses	A deliverer chosen by God to lead Israel out of Egypt (Exodus, Numbers, Deuteronomy)
Naboth	A man that was murdered so Ahab could have his vineyard (1 Kings 21, 2 Kings 9)
Naomi	Ruth's mother-in-law (Ruth 1–4)

Nathanael	One of the twelve disciples (John 1:43–49)
Nebuchadnezzar	King of Babylon who laid siege to Jerusalem and destroyed Solomon's Temple (2 Kings 24–25, 1 Chronicles 6–36)
Nicodemus	A rabbi in Jerusalem (John 3)
Noah	An ancestor of Jesus, builder of the ark (Genesis 6–9)
Orpah	Naomi's daughter-in-law who returned to her home in Moab (Ruth 1)
Peter	Simon Peter, son of Jona, brother of Andrew, fisherman, one of the twelve disciples of Jesus, later an apostle, writer of First and Second Peter (John 1:42)
Philip	One of the twelve disciples, later an apostle (John 1:43–49)
Pontius Pilate	Governor of Judea, probably appointed by Sejanus (Luke 3:1–3)
Ruth	Widowed daughter-in-law of Naomi who becomes an ancestor of King David and Jesus (Ruth 1–4)

Salome	The sister of Mary and the wife of Zebedee (Mark 15:40, Matthew 27:55–56) This relationship is theorized by comparing the two scriptural passages about the women who were with Mary at the cross.
Salome	Daughter of Herodias and her first husband Philip. Her name is recorded in the writings of Josephus. She later married her uncle who was another son of Herod the Great, Philip the Tetrarch. (Matthew 14:6, Mark 6:22)
Samuel	The last judge of Israel, a prophet, he anointed the first kings of Israel. (1 Samuel)
Saul	The first king of Israel (1 Samuel 9–31)
Seth	Son of Adam (Genesis 5:3)
Shem	A son of Noah, ancestor of Jesus (Genesis 6–9)
Simon the Zealot	One of the twelve disciples of Jesus (Acts 1:12–14) (Fictionalized as a childhood friend of Jesus who moved to Cana)

Simon the Leper	Fictionalized as the older brother of Jonathan who married Mary the sister of Lazarus (Matthew 26:6–7, Mark 14:3)
Simon (Brother of Jesus)	Son of Mary and Joseph (Matthew 13:55)
Solomon	A king of Israel, and the wisest man who ever lived (1 Kings 2:12)
Susanna	A wealthy supporter of the ministry of Jesus (Luke 8:3)
Yeshua the Creator	Yeshua is the Hebrew name for Jesus. In this story, it is used as the heavenly person of Jesus.
Zebedee	A fisherman married to Salome, his sons are James and John, possibly the uncle of Jesus (Matthew 4:21–22.)

Fictional Characters

Ahaz	The son of Moshe the tanner of Nazareth, childhood friend of Jesus
Alon	The father of Deborah the shepherdess who is the bride of Jose
Asa	The father of Ichabod, perfumer for the Temple

Baruch	Shepherd of Nazareth, grandfather of Deborah, deceased
Casper	The young son of Cuza and Joanna
Chebar	President of the synagogue of Nazareth
Deborah	Shepherdess, granddaughter of Baruch, wife of Jose
Elesheva	Jabek's widow, wife of Toma
Enos	Son of James the brother of Jesus, Jesus's nephew
Geber	An Essene teacher, friend of John the Baptist
Gerizem	Samaritan fisherman
Harim	The son of Moshe the tanner, boyhood friend of Jesus
Ichabod	The beggar by the beautiful gate, later healed by Peter and John
Jessie	Husband to Martha, sister of Lazarus of Bethany
Kheti	Egyptian owner of a trading caravan, Toma is his partner.

Lemuel	Teacher (rabbi) of the synagogue school in Nazareth
Moshe	A tanner in Nazareth, friend of Joseph
Nodab	The fictional name for the prodigal son and fictional brother of Lazarus of Bethany, works the trading caravan with Toma and Kheti
Salmon	The owner of an olive grove in Nazareth
Seth	The adopted son of Toma
Toma	Joseph's cousin, co-owner of a trading caravan, lives in Bethlehem, his first family was killed when the infants were slaughtered. He remarried Elishava.

Historical Characters

Antiochus Epiphanes	A Syrian King who tried to force the Greek culture on the Jewish nation about 175 BC
Aretas IV	Nabataean king 9 BC–AD 40, Herod Antipas married his daughter and opened trade relations with his nation.
Judah Maccabee	The hero of Hanukkah who defeated Antiochus Epiphanes

Phasaelis	Wife of Herod Antipas, daughter of Nabataean king, Aretas IV
Procila	Wife of Pilate (slightly altered spelling to make pronunciation easier)
Sejanus	Roman ruler under Tiberius. He became too powerful, and he was killed by Tiberius. Then many of those Sejanus appointed to government positions were in danger.
Simon	Son of Hillel, head of Sanhedrin about AD 30
Tiberius	Emperor of Rome

Traditional Characters

Longinus	Centurion at the crucifixion, commander of the Fortress of Antonia under Pilate

Biblical References

Introduction

1. Luke 2:51

Prologue

1. Romans 6:23
2. Genesis 3:19
3. Job 12:13,16
4. Job 13:1
5. Job 16:16
6. Job 16:19–21
7. Job 17:1
8. Job 14:1
9. Job 14:8–9
10. Jude 1:14–15
11. Revelation 21:3–4

Chapter 1

1. Isaiah 50:10
2. Isaiah 57:1–2
3. Psalms 116:15
4. Psalms 4:3
5. Job 36:2
6. Job 36:5
7. Job 36:7
8. Job 14:1–2
9. Isaiah 25:7–9
10. Psalms 30:5
11. Romans 5:12
12. Job 1:7
13. Job 1:7–10
14. Job 1:11–12

Chapter 2
1. Deuteronomy 18:18–19
2. Isaiah 46:9–11
3. Isaiah 46:12–13
4. Luke 1:76–77

Chapter 3
1. Deuteronomy 21:23
2. Leviticus 15:31
3. Malachi 4:1
4. Malachi 4:4

Chapter 4
1. Malachi 2:10
2. Isaiah 53:7
3. Exodus 6:7
4. Jude 14

Chapter 5
1. Exodus 20:3–5
2. Exodus 20:4

Chapter 6
1. Isaiah 40:1–2
2. Isaiah 54:5
3. Isaiah 54:8
4. Isaiah 62:5
5. 1 Corinthians 13:7

Chapter 7
1. Leviticus 20:21
2. Leviticus 20:22
3. Galatians 6:7–8

4. Ephesians 4:26
5. Deuteronomy 30:19

Chapter 8

1. Exodus 20:2
2. Exodus 20:3
3. Exodus 20:4
4. Exodus 20:5–6
5. Ecclesiastes 10:8
6. Deuteronomy 30:19
7. 1 Samuel 16:7
8. Exodus 20:12–17
9. Deuteronomy 32:35
10. Judges 17:6
11. Ruth 1:8–13
12. Ruth 1:14–17
13. Ruth 1:22
14. Ruth 2:3
15. Ruth 2:23
16. Ruth 3:9
17. Ruth 4:13
18. Micah 5:2

Chapter 9

1. Leviticus 19:18
2. Deuteronomy 15:10–11
3. Genesis 1:10
4. Ezra 10:1–4
5. Deuteronomy 17:14–20
6. Leviticus 18:1–3
7. Leviticus 20:21
8. Proverbs 15:3
9. Leviticus 20:22–23
10. Luke 3:15–16

11. Luke 3:16–17
12. John 1:26–27

Chapter 10

1. 1 Kings 21:20 -22
2. 1 Kings 21:27 -28

Chapter 11

1. Isaiah 5:1–3
2. Isaiah 5:7
3. Mark 12:1–8
4. Isaiah 63:8–10
5. Isaiah 63:3–5
6. Psalms 19:1
7. Isaiah 14:12–15

Chapter 12

1. Isaiah 48:15
2. John 1:33
3. Deuteronomy 8:2–3
4. Joel 1:2–3
5. Joel 1:2–6
6. Joel 2:13–14
7. Malachi 2:2
8. Malachi 2:14–16
9. Deuteronomy 30:2–3
10. Deuteronomy 30:6
11. Psalms 53:2–3
12. Matthew 3:17
13. John 1:32–33

Chapter 13

1. Ezekiel 28:11–14
2. Ezekiel 28:15–16

3. Ezekiel 28:17
4. Isaiah 14:13–14
5. Psalms 145:1–5
6. Psalms 145:9–13
7. Psalms 145:14–19
8. Job 37:23
9. Job 37:23–24
10. Lamentations 3:24–26
11. Genesis 2:8–9
12. Genesis 2:15–17
13. Genesis 3:1
14. Genesis 3:14
15. Lamentations 3:28
16. Psalms 27:4
17. Psalms 27:5
18. Psalms 5:2–4
19. Job 13:15
20. Joel 2:1
21. Joel 2:11
22. Psalms 119:97
23. Deuteronomy 10:12–13
24. Isaiah 58:1
25. Psalms 27:7–8
26. Romans 8:22
27. Psalms 22:9–10
28. 1 Samuel 15:22
29. Psalms 18:30–33
30. Matthew 4:3
31. Matthew 3:17
32. Matthew 4:4
33. Matthew 4:6
34. Exodus 3:14
35. Matthew 4:7
36. Matthew 4:9
37. Matthew 4:10

Chapter 14

1. John 1:29–31
2. John 1:36–39
3. John 1:41–42
4. John 1:43–51

Chapter 15

1. Isaiah 9:1
2. Proverbs 30:4
3. Isaiah 66:5
4. Exodus 31:16–17
5. Isaiah 58:13–14
6. Psalms 127:1–2
7. Isaiah 2:3
8. Exodus 13:1–2
9. Exodus 13:9
10. Psalms 119:97
11. Psalms 119:165
12. Hosea 2:16–17
13. Hosea 2:21–22
14. Deuteronomy 6:8
15. 1 Kings 8:27
16. 1 Kings 8:7
17. 1 Kings 8:10–11
18. 2 Kings 25:1
19. 2 Kings 25:3–4
20. 2 Kings 25:7
21. 2 Kings 25:9–11
22. 2 Chronicles 36:22–23
23. Nehemiah 1:8–9
24. Jeremiah 7:3–4
25. Jeremiah 7:9–11
26. Jeremiah 7:20

Chapter 16

1. Jeremiah 33:10–11
2. Psalms 136:2–4
3. Genesis 1:1
4. John 2:9–10
5. John 2:11–12

Chapter 17

1. Deuteronomy 30:6
2. Isaiah 29:18–19
3. Isaiah 2:3

Chapter 18

1. John 2:13
2. Psalms 45:6–7
3. Malachi 4:2
4. 1 Samuel 15:22
5. Malachi 3:9
6. 2 Chronicles 7:14–16
7. Proverbs 20:8–9
8. Psalms 50:1
9. Psalms 50:5–6
10. Psalms 50:16–17

Chapter 19

1. John 3:2
2. John 3:3
3. John 3:4
4. John 3:5–7
5. John 3:8
6. John 3:10–11
7. John 3:12
8. John 3:13
9. John 3:14–15

10. John 3:16
11. John 3:17
12. John 3:18
13. John 3:19
14. John 3:19–20